Gardeners' World

PERFECT PLANTS
FOR PROBLEM PLACES

Gardeners' World

PERFECT PLANTS
FOR PROBLEM PLACES

Gay Search

BCA

LONDON   NEW YORK   SYDNEY   TORONTO

This edition published 1994
by BCA by arrangement with BBC Books
a division of BBC Enterprises Limited
Woodlands, 80 Wood Lane
London W12 0TT

First published 1994
© Gay Search 1994
CN 5054

Illustrations by Judith Robertson
Set in Horley Old Style by Selwood Systems,
Midsomer Norton
Printed and bound in Great Britain by
Butler & Tanner Ltd, Frome and London
Cover printed by Clays Ltd, St Ives Plc

Picture credits

BBC Books would like to thank the following for providing photographs and for permission to reproduce copyright material. While every effort has been made to trace and acknowledge all copyright holders, we would like to apologise should there have been any errors or omissions.

BBC Gardeners' World Magazine back cover (Neil Campbell-Sharp); Liz Eddison pages 80 and 93; Garden Picture Library pages 13 (Ron Sutherland), 16 (Steven Wooster), 28–9 (John Miller), 72 (John Glover), 85 (John Glover) and 116 (Lamontagne); John Glover pages 97, 100, 105, 109, 113, 128, 133, 144 and 149; Jerry Harpur pages 5, 112 and 137; Andrew Lawson pages 20 (bottom), 21, 24 (top), 49 (top), 69 (right) and 88 (top); W. Anthony Lord page 1; S. & O. Matthews front cover; Tania Midgley pages 96, 121, 125, 129, 145 and 156; Clive Nichols pages 8, 9, 36, 40–1, 45, 53, 56, 60–1, 64, 101, 124, 132, 136 and 153; Harry Smith Collection pages 33, 37, 84, 108, 117 and 141; Trip pages 77 (W. Halliday) and 104 (Eye Ubiquitous/J. B. Pickering).

Front cover photograph: Trillium grandiflorum, Hyacinthoides hispanicus, Rodgersia aesculifolia
Back cover photograph: Gay Search in the shady 'tunnelback' garden
Half title page: A cottage border in early summer with foxgloves, delphiniums, roses, poppies and stocks
Contents page: Lavender edging the path leads the eye through the rose-framed arch

Acknowledgements

Many thanks to Martin Cracknell of Pershore College of Horticulture and Clive Daws of King's College, London for botanical advice. Any errors, however, are entirely my own. I would also like to thank the following people and companies for their generous help in transforming our problem places:

For accessories

Joan and Stuart Mungall of Patio Pots, 155, Battersea Park Road, London SW8 4BU Mike Carr of Carr's Organic Fertilizers, The Ley, Weobley, Hereford HR4 8QR Forest Fencing, Stanford Bridge, nr Worcester WR6 6SR: Greenacres Horticulture, PO Box 1228 Iver, Bucks SL0 0EH: Monsanto Garden Care, Thomas Tower, Burleys Way, Leicester LE1 3TP Plantex Weed Control, TDP Ltd., The Pump House, Duffield, Derby DE56 4AA: Sadolin Wood Stains, Meadow Lane, St Ives, Cambs. PE17 4UY Silverland Stone, Holloway Hill, Chertsey, Surrey KT6 0AE Sunshine of Africa, Afton Manor, Freshwater, Isle of Wight PO40 9TW Traditional Garden Supply Co., Unit 12, Hewitt's Industrial Estate, Elmbridge Road, Cranleigh, Surrey GU6 8LW Zeneca Garden Products, (formerly ICI) Fernhurst, Haslemere, Surrey GU27 3JE.

For plants

David Sutton of Abbotsbury Plants, Abbotsbury Sub-Tropical Gardens, nr Weymouth, Dorset DT3 4LA, Anthony Archer-Wills of Anthony Archer-Wills Ltd, Broadford Bridge Rd, West Chillington, W. Sussex RH20 2HF, Chris Blom of Walter Blom and Son, Coombelands Nursery, Milton Earnest, Bedford MK44 1RQ, Tim Jeffries of Country Gardens, (Head Office) Turnpike Road, Thatcham, Berks. RG13 3AN, David Crampton of Drysdales, Bowerwood Road, Fordingbridge, Hants. SP6 1BN, Harkness Roses, Cambridge Road, Letchworth, Herts. Hilliers Nurseries, Ampfield House, nr Romsey, Hants. SO51 9PA Kelways, Langport, Somerset, TA10 9SL, John Powys of The Romantic Garden Nursery, The Street, Swannington, Norwich, Norfolk NR9 5NW, Ashley Wallis of Scotts Nurseries (Merriot), Merriot, Somerset TA16 5PL, Steve Morgan of Wyevale Garden Centres (Head Office) Kings Acre Road, Hereford HR4 0SE.

CONTENTS

INTRODUCTION · 6

SHADY PLACES · 12

HOT, DRY PLACES · 44

BOGGY PLACES · 65

WINDY PLACES · 82

COLD PLACES · 95

SEASIDE PLACES · 108

CLAY SOIL · 119

ACID SOIL · 131

ALKALINE SOIL · 140

INDEX · 156

INTRODUCTION

It's a fair assumption to make that the only people ever to have gardened in 100 per cent perfect conditions were Adam and Eve, pre-Fall. The rest of us, in the real world, have to cope with situations that range from the almost perfect, down to the almost total disaster. Even those of us lucky enough to garden on moderately good soil in a sunny, sheltered position have one or two problem areas where things don't grow quite as well as they should, while for some of the really unlucky gardeners it's the other way round, with one or two places where things will grow, and the rest a whole range of problems! And of course there is every possible combination between those two extremes.

But gardening is the art of the possible, and one of its many joys is the discovery that, with very few exceptions, you can solve, or at the very least alleviate, most problems by learning to work with nature instead of fighting against it, and choosing plants that are adapted to the conditions you're offering. When you think about the vast range of different conditions in which plants grow in the wild – on snow-covered mountains, in deserts, in icy tundra, on sandy beaches, on sunbaked rocks, in shady valleys, in marshes and even deep water – you realise there is bound to be something that will grow happily in even the most unpromising corner of your garden.

And while not wishing to sound too Pollyanna-ish about it, it is also true that in some cases what may appear as a problem is in fact an opportunity. Without any shade in your garden, for instance, you

couldn't grow beautiful shade-loving plants like hostas, foxgloves, Japanese rhododendrons, maples (assuming that the soil beneath the shade is also acid), ferns, and so on. Without boggy soil, you couldn't grow exquisite candelabra primulas or irises, lush foliage plants like rodgersias or lysichitons and so forth.

But of course in some cases you can have too much of an opportunity. Hardly any shade-loving plants, for instance, do better in dense shade than they do in light or dappled or part shade, so if dense shade is the problem, then it will pay dividends to look at ways of alleviating it to some extent. While there are certainly some wonderful plants that will grow in very thin, dry, sunbaked soil – think of Mediterranean plants like thymes, rosemary, silvery artemisias – there are many more plants that will thrive in slightly less thin, less dry soil, so by modifying the conditions a bit you increase the choice available considerably.

What I aim to do in *Perfect Plants for Problem Places* is look at a number of very common problems that many of us face in our gardens, examine a whole variety of ways of improving them to some extent, and, most important, suggest plants that are likely to thrive in the situation you're offering. In other words, if you can give plants conditions as close as possible to those in which they, or rather their wild relatives, grow in their native habitats, you are far more likely to succeed. We all need success, but it's particularly important for new gardeners to avoid the extremely dispiriting experience of seeing the plants they've enthusiastically chosen and planted gradually sicken and die.

We have tackled a number of these problem places in real gardens in a series of items for BBC's *Gardeners' World*; with the help of top designer Robin Williams we showed how to make them an asset rather than a liability by choosing the perfect plants. There just wasn't time to deal with everything on screen, so I've included more problem places in this book.

While there will be plant lists at the end of each chapter, what I also aim to do whenever possible is give you a few rules of thumb to help you look at any plant you come across and make an educated guess as to whether it will thrive in the spot you have in mind for it in your garden. Any plant with finely divided silvery leaves, for example, like the artemisias, will almost certainly thrive in thin, poor, dry soil in a very sunny spot because they are adapted for drought. If a plant has large thin leaves, on the other hand, then chances are it will give of its best in shade since leaves like that would be likely to shrivel in hot sun, and, what's more, they are adapted to make the most of what light is available to manufacture the food the plant needs. While it's not necessary to have a GCSE in botany to garden pleasurably and successfully, knowing just a few basics about how plants grow and what are the particular needs of plants that thrive in different situations can only help you to choose the right plants in the first place and to grow them well.

All plants have the same basic needs – oxygen, carbon and hydrogen, which they get from sunlight, air and water, and a range of nutrients which they get from the soil. But they need them in varying quantities, though, and, just to make matters even more complicated, the amount of each that they need often depends on how much – or how little – of another of these essentials is available to them. Take, for example, moisture and light. Some plants, like astilbes, will grow happily in dappled shade, in moist soil. But they will also grow well in an open, sunny position, *provided* you can give them very moist, even wet soil – in a bog garden by a pool perhaps.

Light is essential. Chlorophyll (the substance contained in leaves that gives them their green colour – and even plants with red, silver or gold leaves contain some chlorophyll) captures the energy in light waves from the sun, and then, by combining water from the soil and carbon dioxide from the air, the plant manufactures sugars and other nutrients which it then uses to grow. All green plants need light. Even mosses which will grow in very shady places where nothing else will – look under basement steps, or under trees in midsummer in a beech wood – won't grow in total darkness. (And before you say 'What about mushrooms?' let me add quickly that they are not green plants, but fungi.) Some plants need maximum sunlight to do their best. Certain plants that originate in hot and sunny climates like the trumpet vine (*Campsis grandiflora*) and the cup-and-saucer vine (*Cobaea scandens*) won't produce flowers in a dull cool summer in this country. Others can do with hardly any direct sunlight as long as they get plenty of *indirect* light – think, for example, of the lovely climbing hydrangea (*H. petiolaris*) flowering prolifically on a north wall. Others still can cope with varying degrees of shade of different kinds (see Chapter 2).

All plants need moisture. Their leaves and stems consist of 90 per cent water, after all.

Even those that will grow without soil – air plants, for example, alpines growing in tufa (rock), or those grown hydroponically – must have moisture. But again, the needs of different plants vary enormously. Some will die if they have too much water – many choice alpines, for example, which grow in very free-draining conditions in the wild, will rot if the soil is too damp or if their leaves get wet for any length of time, while others, like many irises, primulas, hostas and indeed all bog plants, will die if they have too little.

Above: Geranium psilostemon *carries these startlingly vivid magenta flowers in mid summer. It forms a large clump of attractively divided bright green leaves which colour attractively in the autumn.*

Right: *This damp, shady spot isn't a problem, it's an opportunity for some lush planting of contrasting leaf shapes – finely divided fronds of the fern, solid shapes of hostas like 'Gold Standard', the hellebores; hand-shaped leaves, and the heart-shaped leaves of the ligularias, all set off to perfection by the smooth, round shape of the pot.*

Obviously, the nature of your soil is a key factor in how much moisture is available to the plants. Heavy clay soils will retain moisture, but they can be too wet for many plants since water fills all the spaces in, and between, particles of soil, excluding essential air – and without that, some plants' roots will rot. In hot weather, clay soils can become baked hard as concrete on the surface, though the soil a few inches down will retain moisture in all but long periods of drought. Gravelly or sandy soils are almost too free-draining for many plants although, if they're shallow over a solid layer of rock, or chalk, they can be very wet because rainwater can't drain away very easily but also very dry when it finally does.

The ideal soil is somewhere in the middle – rich, moisture-retentive but well drained – with the right balance of loam, organic matter and air. Few of us are lucky enough to inherit soil like this, but it is possible to improve any soil type – to make clay soils better drained by digging in gravel and organic matter, which opens up the soil and creates minute air pockets, and to make the free-draining types more moisture-retentive by working into them bulky organic matter which holds water.

Again, the amount of moisture in the soil affects the other requirements of certain plants. As I've already said, the more moisture there is in the soil, the more sunlight some plants can tolerate. Equally, some plants like artemisias or Mediterranean herbs like rosemary or sage, which would succumb to frost in a wet, heavy soil, are more likely to survive the winter in a free-draining soil because their roots are less likely to be encased in a solid block of ice.

But plants don't take moisture only from the soil. They also take it from the air. If you want to see how important moist air is to many plants, you only have to look indoors where the dry air of central heating is death – literally – to many thousands of houseplants every year. We British gardeners don't have to worry too much about dry air long-term, though, but of course any moving air – wind, in other words – has a drying effect on plants, taking the moisture out of the leaves. Plants that will survive quite happily in an average-to-moist soil in a very sheltered garden may need a moister soil in a windier garden, or even in a windier spot in a sheltered garden. Evergreen shrubs like many conifers, particularly in the first year or so after they're planted, are especially vulnerable because the wind dries out their fine foliage very easily and the root system isn't well enough established to replace from the soil the moisture lost through the leaves. The result is that the foliage shrivels and turns brown, and while many broadleafed evergreens will regrow from old wood if you cut them back, there are very few conifers that will, so a wind-damaged conifer is in most cases a permanently damaged one. That's why, if you plant conifers in an exposed position – and ironically they do make excellent wind-breaks *eventually* – it's a very good idea to erect some kind of temporary windbreak to give them some protection, just until they get established and can look after themselves.

All plants need food, nutrients that they produce themselves and also extract from the soil. Plants need nitrogen for leaf growth, phosphate for root growth and potassium or potash for fruit and flowers. They also need magnesium, calcium and sulphur as well as 'trace elements' – minute quantities of substances like iron, zinc, copper, manganese, boron and molybdenum. If you take a mineral and vitamin supplement yourself, you will recognize many of those names from the label – so that's something we have in common with our plants!

All these nutrients are present in more or less the right balance in rich, fertile soil, which has quantities of bulky organic matter added to it on a regular basis. A thin, free-draining soil is very likely to be deficient in many of them because they simply drain away along with moisture before the plants are able to take them up. So digging lots of organic matter into such a soil has a doubly beneficial effect – it not only increases the moisture-retaining and therefore nutrient-retaining quality, it also increases the amount of nutrients present in the first place.

The degree to which your soil is acid or alkaline (see pages 131 to 156) or neutral also affects the nutrients available to plants, so it's essential to know which it is before you plant anything.

Where the soil is poor, and you don't have all the bulky organic matter necessary to increase the nutrients to the proper levels, or don't want to wait the several years necessary to achieve the desired levels of fertility, you may need to add fertilizers. If the soil is poor and thin and has clearly been neglected, a general organic fertilizer, like seaweed meal, will add most of the nutrients needed, though specific deficiencies, like nitrogen or potash, need specific treatment. If the plants are clearly not growing well, or the leaves are yellowing, then it's well worth getting a soil-testing kit (available from all garden centres) and testing soil from various parts of the garden to find out what the deficiencies are. While these kits will give you some idea, if there is clearly a serious problem with the soil it would be worth getting a sample of it professionally tested to find out exactly what the deficiency is – because many of them have similar symptoms.

Once you have done as much as you can to alleviate the problem, then it's a question of choosing the plants that will thrive in the conditions you're offering. In almost every case, I have chosen plants that will do well in particular situations, not those that will just about tolerate them. Given that there are almost always enough of the former to choose from, it seems a bit pointless to bother with the latter. But in a few particularly tough situations where not many plants will truly thrive, I've listed plants that will give some sort of show, even though they don't grow as large or as lush or flower as freely as they would in more favourable conditions.

Some plants crop up again and again – tough old warhorses like euonymus, dogwood, cotoneaster, mountain ash, viburnum – and I make no apology for that because they do seem to thrive in a whole range of problem places, *and*, most important, they are plants well worth having in any garden on their merits. And since I assume that you will look at the sections that apply to the particular problem places you have in your own garden, you'll want to see all the suitable plants listed there, even if the detailed descriptions are in another section.

One final thought. It seems to me that most people can make a garden that is a source of great pleasure in near-perfect conditions, but there is very real satisfaction to be found in tackling a range of problems, turning them to your advantage and ending up with a lovely garden.

SHADY PLACES

To many new gardeners, a shady area often seems a real problem. In fact, in most cases, it is an opportunity to grow some of the loveliest, admittedly more subtle, less showy, plants around – once you discover how beautiful many of them are, you will never be without shade in a garden again, even if you have to plant trees to create it! To be fair, though, there is shade and shade. Light, dappled shade under a young, slender silver birch or small rowan where you can grow a vast range of lovely shrubs and perennials is one thing. Dense shade under a huge, mature copper beech tree or under the steps in a basement area is quite another. And between the two extremes is a wide range of variations. The descriptions of shade that you come across in most gardening books are often less than helpful because they are so imprecise. What exactly is 'partial shade'? Is it an area always in dappled shade that never gets full sun on it? Or is it one that gets a couple of hours' full sun a day in midsummer and none in winter?

'Half shade' can be equally confusing. Does it mean that a plant described as 'suitable for half shade' does best in roughly equal amounts of sun and shade all day long – 50/50 dappled shade in other words? Or does it need to be half the day in shade, half in full sun? It's very important to know because very different kinds of plants thrive in each of those situations. Camellias, for example, would do well in 50/50 dappled shade, though they wouldn't thrive in an east-facing spot that gets full sun in the morning but is in shade all afternoon, since the early morning sun thaws their frosted buds and flowers too quickly and kills them. Equally, if the border faces west and gets no sun in the morning but bakes all afternoon, it will be too hot for most shade-loving plants. In fact you'll find that almost all plants described as needing full sun will do pretty well in that situation.

Once you know just how much shade a particular part of your garden gets, and what kind of shade it is, then dappled shade and partial shade really don't present much of a problem. If you have an acid soil, for example, there is the vast array of rhododendrons (which now embrace azaleas under their botanical umbrella) to choose from, as well as exotic-looking but in fact quite tough camellias and the wonderful pieris family, with its bunches of lily-of-the-valley-like flowers in spring, along with the most spectacular new scarlet foliage. There are the exquisite Japanese maples, with their coloured, often finely divided foliage, that must have dappled shade to protect those delicate leaves from scorching in overhead sun, and a whole range of golden foliage plants like the dramatic golden cut-leafed elder (*Sambucus racemosa* 'Plumosa Aurea' or 'Sutherland') which need a delicate balance of sun to bring out the brightest golden colour and shade to prevent it from scorching.

The real problem places are full shade and, toughest of all, dense shade. Full shade is what you get beneath a north-facing wall,

Campanula poscharskyana *will produce its trails of starry blue flowers even in deep, dry shade.*

or in an area surrounded by tall buildings where the sun never shines – a 'tunnelback', for instance, that narrow strip between the kitchen extension and the garden wall which many Victorian terraced houses have – especially if there are big trees or tall buildings nearby to block out what little sunlight it might otherwise have got. The one consolation is that if the area is open to the sky then you will get a fair amount of light and air, which will increase the number of plants you can grow.

Dense shade, on the other hand, is what you get under a mature tree with a heavy canopy, like a copper beech for example or, worse still, a holm oak or conifers which are evergreen and so cast equally heavy shade all year round, or under a balcony on a north-facing wall, or beneath basement steps where no sun and very little light at all can penetrate. And such places tend to be dank and airless as well. The lack of light is a major problem with full and dense shade, but if that wasn't enough, it's often compounded by other factors too. Most important is lack of moisture. Soil tends to be dry at the foot of a wall, especially if it is under the eaves of a house or in the lee of the winds that usually bring rain. That's why you should always plant climbers a good 30cm or more away from any wall. By doing so, they will stand a much better chance of getting the moisture they need.

Under trees, you will often find you're faced with a tangle of roots on or just below the surface and soil that's as dry as dust. That's because the dense canopy of leaves keeps most of the rain off the soil directly beneath it – the drops run from leaf to leaf and drip off the outer edges, exactly as they do off an umbrella – and of course the tree's extensive and greedy roots suck up what little moisture there is left in the soil.

The balance between light and moisture is key. As I have said, plants can cope with more sunlight (and more breeze, since that also takes moisture out of the leaves) the more moisture there is in the soil. While there are a very few plants that will just about survive in dense shade and very dry soil, the number that will grow where there is a bit more light and a bit more moisture is so much greater that it's well worth looking at all the aspects of this particular problem and seeing what can be done about each of them.

Take the dryness of the soil. While you're never going to change its character entirely, you can improve its moisture-retaining qualities enough to make a significant difference. What holds water in the soil is bulky organic matter and that comes in a whole range of different forms. Well-rotted garden compost, for example, or leaf mould are both excellent, although if you're just starting work on your garden you're unlikely to have a plentiful supply of either. Farmyard manure is also very good, as long as it's well-rotted, and though its obviously easier to get in country districts it's surprising how many riding stables or city farms there are in urban areas nowadays. Spent mushroom compost – which starts life as horse manure then has chalk and various chemicals added – is another good bulky soil conditioner, though you need to make sure it has been stored for a season to allow all the chemicals to leach out of it, and since chalk is alkaline you shouldn't use it if you're planning to grow acid-loving, lime-hating plants like rhododendrons. If you live near the sea, don't forget seaweed which is full of nutrients. You can either compost it – it rots down very quickly – or you can dig it straight into the soil. If none of these is a realistic option, you can buy products like composted straw, composted bark, and products based on farmyard manure, cleanly packed and ready to use in most garden centres now, though they are expensive. In this instance, what you don't want is a *concentrated* manure product, since it's the bulk as much as the nutrients that you're after.

The ideal soil for nearly all shade-loving plants, which are in most cases woodland plants by origin, is rich but light, moisture-retentive, but well drained. The American guru on the subject of shade gardening, George Schenk, describes it as 'fluffy, woodsy soil out of which you can steal a fern with a stick as a digging tool'. So if your basic soil underneath that powdery layer is sticky clay – like plasticine in winter and concrete in summer – then you'll also need to open it up with grit or sharp sand (*not* builder's sand since that will only compound the pudding-like quality of the soil) as well as organic matter. You'll need roughly a bucketful of grit per square metre and twice that amount of organic matter.

If your dry shady area is a border in the lee of a wall, then work it in to the soil as you dig. Dig a trench widthwise across the border at one end and pile the soil you've removed at the far end. Then, working backwards along the border, spread gravel and organic matter in the bottom and along the far side of the trench. That way, you make sure the organic matter and grit are incorporated at several different levels. Then throw the soil from the next trench you dig forward on to the first one, and carry on like that along the border. When you reach the end, use the soil you dug out

of the very first trench to fill in the last. Since you are adding so much matter to the soil, you'll wind up with a border slightly higher than before. If the border is deep enough you can make it slope gently up from front to back, but if it's too narrow to do that, you could hold the soil in place by a row of edging tiles – the reproduction Victorian rope twist ones are very attractive and not too expensive – or, if you have room, old railway sleepers. If you are dealing with only a very small area and very poor soil, you could dig out all the soil to a spade's depth and discard about a third of it (or bulk it up with organic matter and use it elsewhere in the garden), then mix up two shovelfuls of organic matter with one of soil and one of grit or sharp sand, and refill the border with that.

If your border is under the lee of a wall and gets hardly any rain, then you could make life much easier for yourself by installing a porous hose along the length of the border, weaving it around the plants that you've put in, and burying it in the soil. These hoses slowly leak water along their entire length, so it's a very efficient way of watering – one turn of the tap and the job is done. It's also very economical with water, too, since it goes straight to the plants' roots where it's needed and none of it soaks the path or evaporates in the air as it does with sprays or sprinklers.

Improving the moisture-retentive quality of the soil under trees is slightly more difficult. For one thing, digging it over is a nightmare because you will probably find a veritable Clapham Junction of roots just under the surface of the soil, and even if you were strong enough to do it, hacking your way through them won't do the tree any good at all.

What you might be able to do is find spaces between the largest, thickest roots and create planting pockets, by digging out the poor thin soil and replacing it with the two parts organic matter, one part grit, one part soil mixture mentioned earlier and growing plants in that. If you really do have Clapham Junction under your tree, then you could try spreading rich soil mixture over the area – a depth of 15–20cm would be enough to grow a large number of plants. What you mustn't do, though, is spread the new soil right up to the trunk, as it could rot the bark and so kill the tree.

Another approach would be to create a raised bed around the tree – again making quite sure that you don't pile the soil right up against the trunk. Depending on the style of your garden, you could use stone or brick, or, perhaps most suitable in a woodland setting, split logs or logroll (split logs already wired together in lengths). To protect the trunk, you could use the same material to make an inner circle with a clearance of 15–20cm. The height of such a raised bed depends on the size of the tree and the area you want to cover – it has to be in scale to look right – but you could get away with something 30cm high or even less, since many shade-loving perennials will grow quite happily in 20cm of good woodland soil.

Whether you simply spread some soil beneath the tree or create a raised bed, you will need to water regularly and thoroughly for the first season. Too little too seldom will simply bring the tree's roots up to the surface to find it, and make the problem

In Beth Chatto's woodland garden, tall stems of pink and white Turk's cap lilies (L. martagon) rise up above the leaves of astrantias, the blue hosta 'Halcyon' and Heuchera 'Palace Purple'.

worse. Mulching every spring with whatever bulky organic matter you can find will help enormously and, as it breaks down in the soil, will provide some valuable nutrients too. (If you use cocoa shells as a mulch they will make the soil slightly acid, which most woodland plants like, and they have the added benefit of being rather too crisp and crunchy for the average slug to fancy crawling over.) You'll need to feed regularly as well, though, with an organic fertilizer like blood, fish and bone, or pelletted chicken manure, or non-organic rose fertilizer each spring. Although the tree will take a lot of it, there will still be some left over for the plants.

Having done something about the lack of moisture in the soil, the next problem to tackle is the lack of light. In the full shade cast by buildings, one relatively easy way to make the area seem lighter is to paint the walls a pale colour – white ideally, but a very pale cream, pink, grey or beige would do almost as well if white appears too stark – to reflect any available light. A cleverly positioned mirror could have an equally beneficial effect, and also make a poky corner appear much bigger. And don't forget the floor – very pale paving slabs, cream-coloured Cotswold chippings or gravel will also reflect light much better than dark slabs or brick or tarmac. Gravel as a mulch under a tree will also reflect what little light there is there, but in dense shade under trees usually the only option is to prune the tree to allow more light to penetrate. Maybe thinning the canopy by taking out a few large branches will be the answer, or raising it by removing some of the lower branches to allow more light in from the sides. Pruning mature trees is not merely a dangerous job if undertaken by unskilled amateurs, done properly it is also an art – an experienced tree surgeon can do the job to allow in a lot more light but at the same time preserve the tree's shape and beauty. A cowboy with a chainsaw can simply butcher it, leaving it a permanent eyesore if not killing it off altogether. Don't try to do it yourself, and make sure you get in a properly qualified and, just as important, properly insured tree surgeon to do it for you – don't succumb to the cowboy who turns up on your doorstep, looking for work. The Arboricultural Association (Ampfield House, Romsey, Hampshire SO51 9PA) publishes a list of its members all over the country, and will send it to you free of charge in return for a stamped addressed envelope. Before you allow anyone to touch a tree, do check with the local planning department whether it is covered by any sort of preservation order. It could have an individual tree preservation order on it, or, if you happen to live in some sort of conservation area, you'll find that every tree above a certain size is protected even if it is of no particular merit or beauty. Most councils are not unreasonable, though, and will allow a certain amount of judicious pruning if you seek permission. It really isn't worth going ahead and hoping no one will notice. You may well get away with it, but if you don't you'll wind up paying a hefty fine!

PERFECT PLANTS

In order to understand what kinds of plants will do well in these situations, you need to look at those that thrive in similar conditions in the wild – in this instance, in woodland. But again, there's woodland and woodland. While a lot of plants thrive in the dappled, seasonal shade of deciduous woodland, particularly on the fringes, not a lot will grow at the heart of a beech wood, for instance, or under a plantation of evergreen conifers, apart from moss.

Many of the plants that thrive under deciduous trees are autumn-, winter- and particularly spring-flowering. They give their display when there are no leaves on the trees and they can get the light (and the moisture) they need to produce flowers and make the necessary growth for the year. Think of bulbs like the cyclamen (*C. hederifolium*) which flowers from September onwards, winter aconites (*Eranthis hyemalis*), which start flowering in January, and in spring wood anemones (*Anemone nemorosa*), various relatives of the exquisite dog's-tooth violet (*Erythronium dens-canis, E. revolutum*) and of course bluebells (*Endymion* or *Hyacinthoides non-scriptus*). Although, sadly, you have to hunt around for one these days, there is nothing quite like the sight of that rich hazy blue carpet of a bluebell wood in spring.

Most of these will have flowered and their leaves, having completed the food manufacturing process ready for next year's flowers, will have died away completely before the trees are fully in leaf. Think, too, of lovely woodland perennials like primroses, Solomon's seal (Polygonatum) with its pearl-white lockets dangling singly along the undersides of its fresh green arching stems, Siberian bugloss (*Brunnera macrophylla*) with its vibrant blue flowers and bleeding heart (*Dicentra spectabilis*) – they too flower in spring and the bleeding heart's foliage dies before midsummer, to reappear again the following spring.

Another clue to a plant's ability to cope with shade is the size of its leaves. Shade-lovers tend to have broad, thin leaves – broad to make the most of any available light to manufacture food, and thin because there is no point in having layer upon layer of chlorophyll (the substance that converts sunlight into food, and which gives leaves their green colour), since the little light available is unlikely to penetrate beyond the first layer and stimulate a second. If you were to look at the leaves of nettles or brambles growing on the edge of a woodland, and compare them to those from plants growing further in, you'd see that the former were quite noticeably smaller and thicker than the latter.

Shade-lovers that fall into this category include hostas, lady's mantle (*Alchemilla mollis*), foamflower (*Tiarella cordifolia*), and the piggy-back plant (*Tolmiea menziesii*). Other first-class shade-loving plants that spring to mind here are the false castor oil plant (*Fatsia japonica*), with its large hand-shaped leaves, and elephant's ears (*Bergenia*) with their paddle-shaped leaves, but they have other qualities as well that enable them to cope admirably with shade. For one thing they are evergreen, so that under deciduous trees they can make the most of the available light in spring and autumn for food production, and for another they have glossy leaves which can reflect what little light there is on to each other. Strangely enough, busy lizzie (*Impatiens*), one of the few bedding plants that really thrive in shade, falls into this category. In its native habitat, where it is much warmer than it is here, it's an evergreen perennial, and so its broad, thin, glossy evergreen leaves make the most of the available light all year round.

The fact that the leaves of plants like these and of ivy are very tough as well

as glossy also means that they don't lose moisture that easily, which makes them very good candidates for dry shade. In fact, ivy is probably the plant of last resort where practically nothing else will grow. In Cambridge University's Botanic Gardens, for example, they have some huge and handsome evergreen holm oaks, which cast a stygian gloom even on a sunny day, but underneath them is a rich green carpet of Irish ivy (*Hedera helix* 'Hibernica'). If you can plant it in the moistest soil possible – at the edge of your dry shady area perhaps – and direct the growth into the gloom, it should do very well.

One reason ivy is such a good plant for dense shade is that it is adapted for it in several different ways. Apart from its evergreen qualities, it climbs (or spreads across the ground until it reaches something to climb) to seek the light. Light under trees is deficient in certain red wavelengths, and that fact has a very marked effect on ivy. Without those red wavelengths, the plant will not flower and will keep climbing. When it is exposed to them, it doesn't just flower – its whole character changes. The growth becomes stiff and woody, it stops climbing and producing the aerial roots by which it clings and its leaves are a different size and shape. A similar thing happens with a shady wall. The ivy keeps on clinging and climbing until it reaches the light at the top, then undergoes a metamorphosis.

Another group of plants superbly adapted for shade is ferns. Their growth rate is quite slow, and they can put all their energies into producing fronds since they don't have to waste any on producing flowers, seeds or fruit. The fact that the leaves are so finely divided means that they cover a wide area and so can pick up more of the available light, but without having to provide a solid mass of leaf with water and nutrients.

OUR PROBLEM PLACES

We chose to tackle two different, but very common, shady problem places. The first was a 'tunnelback' - that long narrow strip that so many houses have between the kitchen extension and the garden wall. In

Right: *This north-facing 'tunnelback' was a real problem place. Hardly anything grew there and the view from the kitchen sink was bleak. Two months later, the view from the kitchen window* (**below**) *is rather formal with 'off-the-peg' green trellis, ivy and two half-standard box balls, while from the garden* (**far right**) *the effect is lush and jungly, with shade-lovers like* Fatsia japonica, *hostas,* Aucuba japonica, *and white busy lizzies.*

Shady Tunnelback

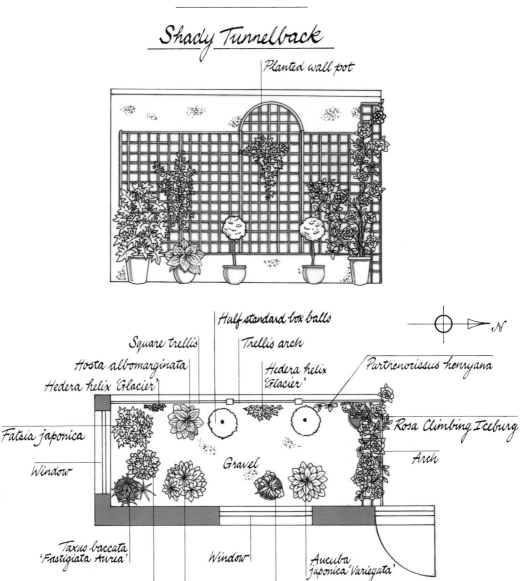

Planted wall pot

Half standard box balls

Square trellis

Trellis arch

Hosta albomarginata

Hedera helix 'Glacier'

Hedera helix 'Glacier'

Parthenocissus henryana

Fatsia japonica

Rosa Climbing Iceburg

Window

Gravel

Arch

Taxus baccata 'Fastigiata Aurea'

Window

Aucuba japonica 'Variegata'

Impatiens (White Busy Lizzies)

Fargesia nitida

Lilium longiflorum underplanted with Hedera helix 'Anne Marie'

the one we chose to tackle, behind a small Victorian railwayman's cottage, there were two additional factors to make things even more difficult: first, it faced due north, and second, in place of the original garden wall there was the side wall of the neighbour's bathroom extension – a 4m long × 3m high oblong of pebbledash. It meant that not only was the view from the kitchen windows bleak, to say the least, but that the rear living room, the window of which looked out onto the tunnelback, got even less light than before – to such an extent that very few houseplants thrived and the odd one that did was right next to the window. The owners, both pensioners and keen gardeners, had tried a number of solutions, but having found that little else would grow except ivy and busy lizzies in the summer, had simply put some gravel down and used the area to store equipment.

One option would have been to grow a self-clinging climber like a bright variegated ivy, for example *H.h.* 'Goldheart', or a Virginia creeper over the blank wall, but while that would have been fine on a brick or rendered wall, it's not advisable on pebbledash, as it can pull the stones off.

We certainly needed to do something to brighten the view from the kitchen sink, and so our designer Robin Williams suggested fixing ordinary off-the-peg square trellis panels and a round-topped panel (which come ready-painted dark green or white) on the extension directly opposite the kitchen window, and fixing a terracotta wall pot in the centre, filled with a tumbling plant like a delicate, small-leafed ivy or campanula.

The one 'plus' about this problem place was that the back door was at the garden end of the extension, not at the house end, so the only access needed to the area was for maintaining the plants. That meant we could pack the area with plants in containers to create a lovely jungly effect from the rear living room's window. We decided to use terracotta pots to match the lovely warm red of the bricks, simple shapes in a variety of sizes. We opted for French terracotta which is much paler than Italian or Spanish or our own because the area is so dark that we needed whatever lightness we could get. At the garden end, where the neighbour's extension ends and there is more light, we made a very simple arch from trellis panels, and planted a climbing rose, the lovely scented, creamy-white flowered 'Climbing Iceberg'. It is moderately vigorous and very

free-flowering and should cover the arch relatively quickly, but since it's growing in a large pot, it shouldn't get over-ambitious.

As for the main planting, we chose shrubs that would brighten the area as much as possible for as long as possible, and that meant shade-tolerant evergreens with variegated leaves – cream and green hostas, gold-speckled ancubas, a splash of gold in the golden Irish yew – and, to add to the jungly effect around the living room window, the glossy-leafed, dramatic *Fatsia japonica*. But our tunnelback was seen from two viewpoints, so from the kitchen window we played up the formal look of the trellis with two half-standard clipped box, one each side of the arch. The only flowering plants we used were white lilies and busy lizzies, ideal annuals for shade as they flower profusely, and a pale colour like white, pale pink or peach is ideal as it gleams in the shadows.

Since almost all the planting is permanent, we used a compost based on worm-digested manure, which is not quite as heavy as ordinary soil but heavier than a soilless compost, full of nutrients, and with slow-release fertilizers to take over later on. We added a special water-retaining gel to prevent the pots drying out too quickly, although watering in this instance didn't present any problems as there was an outside tap fitted below the kitchen window.

Just two months on, we were well on the way to creating the jungly effect we set out to achieve. The fatsia was already producing new leaves, the bamboo beginning to spread, and the ivies, climbing up the trellis. Although the 'Climbing Iceberg' rose hadn't done much climbing, it was smothered in flowers, as were the busy lizzies. The whole area was transformed.

The second problem place was a border, running along inside the low boundary wall in a vicarage garden, and about as shady as could be since the trees in question included a purple-leafed cherry, *Prunus pissardii*, as well as laburnum and a very bushy haw-thorn, blocking light from the sides as well as from above. The soil in the area is inclined to be sandy and this was par-ticularly poor and thin because of the trees, though it was supporting a fair crop of weeds and some rather spindly, self-seeded *Kerria japonica*. Although on the garden side the wall was about 45cm deep, on the pavement side it was only about 15cm, so some rather flimsy metal hoops, usually used for edging borders, had been attached to give at least the idea of a barrier between the pavement and the garden.

The few plusses were that all the trees were deciduous, apart from one large conifer

Dry shade under trees can be a real problem place. But having thinned the trees to let in more light and made the soil more moisture-retentive, we had a wider range of plants to choose from. Two months later, they are growing well and starting to cover the ground while the blue Liriope muscari *and the pink* Anemone *'September Charm' are flowering freely.*

to the west, so the area got more light and moisture from autumn to spring, and it faced south so that the front would get some sunlight during that part of the year when the sun is lower in the sky.

The first job was to clear the ground as far as possible, to tidy up the trees a little, thin out some of the lower branches to allow a bit more light to enter, and to improve the soil. Digging wasn't as difficult as we'd expected because there was a good few inches of soil, albeit very dusty soil, above the tree roots in most places. So we dug in plenty of fine composted bark to improve the moisture-retaining properties and so increase the range of plants we could grow.

The soil was just slightly alkaline, so using composted bark which is slightly acidic helped reduce the alkalinity of the soil a little, which would suit some of the woodland plants we were going to grow. In addition, once we'd finished, we mulched with cocoa shells, which are also acid, to keep the moisture in and the weeds at bay. This is a first-class mulch because, once it gets wet, it releases a resinous gum which helps the small, fine flakes stick together and stops them being blown about the garden too easily.

At the back of the border we debated what to do with the wire fence on top of the low brick wall. It didn't look very attractive, and we toyed with the idea of putting up something like a picket fence or even some woven hurdles, which would provide a natural-looking backdrop for the plants and, since they were only 1m high,

Dry, Shady Border

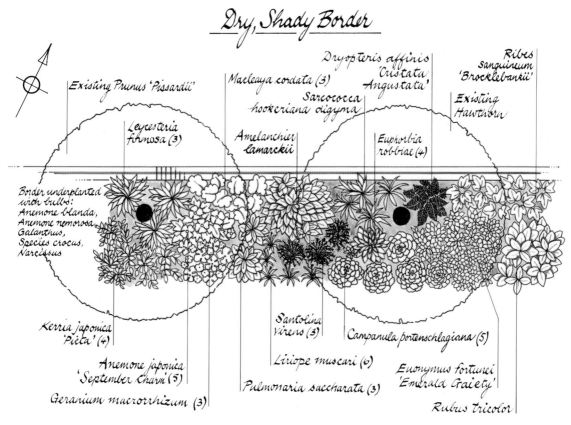

Existing Prunus 'Pissardii'

Leycesteria formosa (3)

Macleaya cordata (3)

Dryopteris affinis 'Cristata Angustata'

Sarcococca hookeriana digyna

Amelanchier lamarckii

Euphorbia robbiae (4)

Ribes sanguineum 'Brocklebankii'

Existing Hawthorn

Border underplanted with bulbs: Anemone blanda, Anemone nemorosa, Galanthus, Species crocus, Narcissus

Kerria japonica 'Picta' (4)

Anemone japonica 'September Charm' (5)

Geranium macrorrhizum (3)

Santolina virens (3)

Liriope muscari (6)

Pulmonaria saccharata (3)

Campanula portenschlagiana (5)

Euonymus fortunei 'Emerald Gaiety'

Rubus tricolor

wouldn't prevent passers-by from seeing into the garden. But in the end we decided that as the border received valuable light from that direction – north light admittedly, but still better than nothing – it wasn't a good idea to fill it in, so we relied on the taller plants at the back to do that for us.

As for the planting, we chose to major on two types of plant. First there were the spring-flowering plants to make the most of the extra light and moisture available before the trees came into leaf – bulbs like aconites, snowdrops, species crocus and narcissi (the daffodils that Wordsworth would have seen fluttering and dancing in the breeze), erythroniums (dog's-tooth violets) and herbaceous plants like pulmonaria, which have attractive ground-covering leaves when the flowering period is over, or *Dicentra spectabilis alba* – even lovelier than the pink form – whose foliage dies away in midsummer. For autumn and winter, we also planted the beautiful hardy cyclamen *C. hederifolium*, with pink flowers, miniature versions of their houseplant relations', from October on, and lovely round marbled silver leaves all winter, dying away in spring.

For the most difficult time, in summer when the trees are in full leaf, we went for a framework of some of the really tough evergreen shrubs that will give a splash of brightness in these rather murky conditions – the Christmas box (*Sarcococca humilis*) with its glossy leaves and lovely scented flowers in winter (a bonus for passers-by), *Euonymus fortunei* 'Emerald Gaiety', with cream and green variegated leaves that take on a pinkish tinge in winter, especially if it's very cold, and really tough deciduous shrubs like the attractive variegated Bachelor's Buttons (*Kerria japonica*

'Picta') whose green and white leaves add some welcome lightness, and the golden-leafed flowering currant (*Ribes sanguineum* 'Brocklebankii'). Its foliage won't be as golden as it would be in part shade or dappled shade, but it will be a light, yellowish green which will cheer up the border no end. We also chose the flowering nutmeg (*Leycesteria formosa*) which will also cope with shade under trees, since it's often recommended to gamekeepers for planting as game coverts! Although its silver relative must have a sunny spot, there is probably just enough sunlight at the front of the border for *Santolina virens*, with its bright apple-green foliage and lemon-yellow bobble flowers in late spring/early summer, to grow well enough.

At the back of the border where there is more light coming from the road, we planted the tall plume poppy (*Macleyea cordata*) with its superb large lobed green leaves with silvery undersides and sprays of tiny white flowers in mid to late summer. Although it's tall it's very open, so that while it will help distract the eye from the fence, it won't block the view of the border from the pavement.

As for the other herbaceous plants, the spurge (*Euphorbia robbiae*) with its tough-as-old-boots, dark green foliage and brighter lime-green bracts in spring is hard to beat for a very dry, very shady spot. It can get a bit tired and straggly but if you cut it back hard after flowering, it will reward you with healthy, fresh new growth. The almost evergreen cranesbill, *Geranium macrorrhizum*, is also an invaluable plant here. I've grown it in my garden under an ash tree for ten years and have never known it lose its soft, aromatic leaves, even in a very hard winter, though some do turn an attractive shade of red in autumn. The one I grow is *G.m.* 'Album' which has lovely blush-white flowers, supposedly in late spring, but I've known it flower as early as February, along with the early spring-flowering *Iris reticulata*. Others including the deeper pink 'Ingwersen's Variety' and the more magenta 'Bevan's Variety' are also first-class. Another smashing plant for this particular problem place is the turf lily (*Liriope muscari*) which has grass-like evergreen leaves and spikes of blue flowers, not unlike a grape hyacinth's, from late summer through into early winter. It is such a useful plant that whenever we have planted it on television, we are always inundated with calls from people wanting to know where to find it. *The Plant Finder* (the invaluable book that lists thousands of plant varieties and where to get them says it's 'widely available' and so no suppliers are listed, but Blooms of Bressingham (Tel: 0379 88 464) will supply it mail order as will PW Plants (0953 888212) or Beth Chatto (0206 822007).) While it will cheerfully cope with dry shade, it's not keen on too limy soils, but the combination of composted bark or cocoa shells dug into the soil and spread on top should create the right conditions.

Ferns are a must in this situation, and we chose one that can cope with drier conditions than many – a relative of the common male fern, *Dryopteris* 'Cristata Angustata', with lovely, slender, finely divided fronds. For ground cover at the lowest level we planted some lungwort (*Pulmonaria saccharata*) with its silver-spotted leaves and the lovely *Lamium maculatum* 'White Nancy' two of the very few silver-leafed plants to grow happily in shade. This particular lamium has creamy-white flowers, which are very good in shade.

Its foliage begins to look decidedly tatty after flowering, so it's best to cut it back with shears, and it will produce bright silver fresh new growth in a few weeks. Although *Campanula portenschlagiana* is a bit of a thug in more favourable conditions, the poor soil and low light levels reduce its ambitions considerably, and we can be grateful for its freely produced blue flowers all summer long. Another excellent ground-cover plant for dry shade is the ornamental bramble *Rubus tricolor*, especially if you plant it at the edge of the shady area and allow its trailing stems, which root as they go, to creep in towards the denser shade.

In late August, with everything growing well and the Japanese anemones and *Liriope* flowering profusely, we planted a large number of spring-flowering bulbs in natural-looking drifts in among the shrubs and herbaceous plants – species crocuses – white and blue – *Anemone nemorosa*, bluebells (*Hyacinthoides non-scriptus*), small, wild daffodils (*N. lobularis*), dog's-tooth violets (*Erythroniums dens-canis*), star of Bethlehem (*Ornithogalum nutans*).

PLANTS

The plants listed below can cope with almost no sun at all, while the comparatively few that will survive in dense shade are marked **D**. The main list is of plants for a reasonably moist soil – those that are like that naturally or have been improved as recommended earlier in this chapter. Those that can cope with dry soil are listed separately at the end.

Conifers

Yew (*Taxus baccata*) See page 146.

Canada hemlock (*Tsuga canadensis*) This is one of the few conifers that will grow happily in deep shade, provided the soil is moist enough and isn't

limy. There is a lovely golden form, *T.c.* 'Aurea', which forms an open, feathery, conical bush, a fraction of the size of its plain green relative, but needs more sun to bring out the lovely golden colour.
▷ *Approx. height and spread after 20 years: 5-15 × 3-8m (16-50 × 10-25ft).*

Climbers

Clematis All clematis need their roots in the shade, even those that flower best in sun, but there are a few which will flower well enough in full shade, mainly in the spring. Good small-flowered varieties include the rampant *Clematis montana* (*C. m. rubens*, with bronzy foliage and smoky-pink flowers, is more manageable than most), as well as varieties of the much less vigorous *C. alpina* which have nodding blue, white or pale pink flowers, and *C. macropetala*, which has similar flowers in the same range of colours as *C. alpina*, and flowers slightly later. None of these types need pruning unless they outgrow their allotted space.

Most varieties do best in a slightly limy soil, though they will grow well enough in a neutral or slightly acid soil. Adding a few handfuls of calcified seaweed to the soil when you plant helps.
▷ *Height after 10 years 3-9m (10-30ft).*

Ivy (Hedera) D Probably the best evergreen climber – and ground-cover plant – for shade in any kind of soil. One of the variegated kinds, like the small-leafed, bright gold and green 'Goldheart', or the much larger-leafed *H. colchica* 'Paddy's Pride', really would brighten up a dark wall or fence. A small-leafed ivy could also be allowed to scramble up a tree trunk, but the larger, more vigorous kinds might be a bit much for their hosts. If you want a plain green – as a background for variegated shrubs, perhaps, or under trees – then the Irish ivy (*H.* 'Hibernica') with large, glossy dark green leaves is ideal. Ivies are self-clinging, but only the new aerial roots, not the

Previous page: *In this paved town garden, the planting of shade-lovers like* Fatsia japonica *and ivies creates an oasis of green with just a few splashes of colour from the lilies and the clematis.*

old ones, will cling, so if the plant comes trained up a bamboo cane, leave the cane in place and push the tip against the wall, so that as the new growth is produced the roots can take hold.
▷ *Approx. height after 10 years: 5m (16ft).*

Climbing hydrangea (Hydrangea petiolaris) A marvellous self-clinging climber for all soils and for shade. It has large flat heads of white flowers in early summer, which turn brown in autumn and remain, attractively, on the bare stems in winter but it's worth growing just for the masses of bright, fresh green leaves it produces each spring. Good on walls or up big mature tree trunks.
▷ *Approx. height and spread after 10 years: 3 × 4m + (10 × 13ft +)*

Honeysuckles (Lonicera) A few varieties will cope in shade. *L. americana* has very sweetly scented flowers which open white and slowly fade to yellow, flushed with pink. The gold-netted Japanese honeysuckle, *L. japonica* 'Aureo-reticulata', isn't as vigorous as *L. americana*, but has attractive semi-evergreen foliage, as well as sweetly scented small yellow flowers in summer.
▷ *Approx. height after 10 years: 3.5-8m (12-26ft).*

Virginia creeper (Parthenocissus) Well worth growing for its superb autumn colour and, if you make a point of seeking out *P. henryana*, you will get the benefit of its beautiful, dark, velvety green leaves deeply veined with silver and pink in spring and summer, too. It's not as vigorous as some of the other Virginia creepers, but quite vigorous enough to cover a garden wall or fence in a couple of years. Like all its relatives, it's a self-clinger. Get new plants started as you would ivies.
▷ *Approx height and spread after 10 years: 5 × 3m (16 × 10ft).*

Shrubs

Spotted laurel (Aucuba japonica) D One of the most accommodating of all evergreen shrubs, it will grow happily in practically any type of soil, including a limy soil, and will also tolerate deep shade. Female forms will produce clusters of bright red berries in autumn and keep them

throughout the winter, but only if there is a male form nearby. Look for *A.j.* 'Crotonifolia' (male) which has large leaves speckled with gold, and *A.j.* 'Variegata' (female) whose smaller leaves are splashed with gold and yellow over about half their area. It grows quite large, though you can cut it back, so it's a good choice for the back of a border or particularly for a very shady corner.
▷ *Approx. height and spread after 10 years: 1.8 × 1.8m (5ft 6in × 5ft 6in).*

Dogwood (*Cornus*) See page 73.

Daphne *Daphne pontica* is a small, slow-growing evergreen with shiny leaves and yellow flowers in spring which are sweetly perfumed at night. It will stand full shade. *Daphne odora* 'Aureomarginata', with attractive evergreen variegated leaves, and sweetly scented pink flowers in spring, needs a little more light.
▷ *Approx. height and spread after 10 years: 80 × 90cm (2ft 6in × 3ft).*

Elaeagnus The most widely grown elaeagnus is probably the green and gold variegated *E. pungens* 'Maculata', and although it will grow in shade without losing its golden colour, it will be leggier than it would be with a bit more light. Other good varieties that will cope in these conditions are *E. × ebbingei* 'Gilt Edge' and *E. × e.* 'Limelight' with a green edge and gold centre. The main drawback is that it has long, slender, vicious thorns close to the leaf so you often feel them before you see them!
▷ *Approx. height and spread after 10 years: 2 × 2m (6ft 6in × 6ft 6in).*

Spindle (*Euonymus fortunei*) Excellent, low-growing evergreens that will lighten a shady spot. Try the gold and green variegated *E.f.* 'Emerald 'n' Gold', or 'Sunspot' whose dark green leaves have a central golden splash, or the cooler cream and green *E.f.* 'Emerald Gaiety'. Given the opportunity, they will also climb walls, or even trees.
▷ *Approx. height and spread after 10 years: 60cm × 2m (2 × 6ft).*

False castor oil plant (*Fatsia japonica*) D Often thought of as a houseplant, it is extremely hardy and thrives in deep to medium shade. It is what's known as an architectural shrub for the bold dramatic shape of its large, handsome, glossy, evergreen leaves. In spring, it produces spikes of creamy-white flowers rather like golf balls, which eventually turn into clusters of black berries. Removing these will encourage the plant to produce larger leaves. There is a very attractive variegated version, with splashes of cream on the leaves but it is nothing like as hardy as its plain green cousin.
▷ *Approx. height and spread after 10 years: 3 × 3m (10 × 10ft).*

Garryea elliptica Grown mainly for its long pale grey-green catkins in winter; some people feel the rather dull green foliage the rest of the year is too high a price to pay. If you want one, make sure it's *G.e.* 'James Roof', the catkins of which are twice as long.
▷ *Approx. height and spread after 10 years: 3.5 × 2.5m (12 × 8ft).*

Hydrangeas (*Hydrangea macrophylla*) The best-known 'mop-head' and 'lacecap' varieties, the former with large round heads of flowers and the latter with flatter heads of flowers, do best in sun or medium shade. But well worth considering for full shade is the oak-leafed hydrangea (*H. quercifolia*) which has heads of white flowers from midsummer through till autumn and excellent orange-red autumn foliage colour, and will tolerate dry soils. Where there's a bit more light and space, try the stately *H. villosa* with soft felty green leaves and flattened blue-purple flowerheads in late summer.
▷ *Approx. height and spread after 10 years: 1.8-3m × 1.8-3m (6-10ft × 6-10ft).*

Ilex (Holly) This will cope well with deep shade, and the variegated forms will brighten up a dark corner. Both *I.* 'Silver Queen', with white markings, and *I.* 'Golden King', with gold variegations, are good varieties. To confuse matters 'Silver Queen' is a male form (no berries) while 'Golden King' is female (berries provided there is a male somewhere in the area!). Of the plain green hollies, 'J.C. van Tol' has a lot to offer - almost

spineless, glossy green leaves and regular crops of red berries.
▷ *Approx. height and spread after 10 years: 4 × 2.5m (13 × 8ft).*

Bachelor's Buttons (*Kerria japonica*) D You will often find this tough, extremely accommodating shrub growing in parts of the garden where little else will, and its invasive nature which can be a problem in better conditions is kept in check. Its tall stems carry single or double dandelion flowers in spring. The double-flowered *K.j.* 'Flore Pleno' is one of the best, and even more useful in a small garden is *K.j.* 'Picta' (or 'Variegata') which has single buttercup flowers in spring, and bright green and cream variegated foliage. It doesn't reach more than 1m (3ft) in height or spread, and isn't invasive.
▷ *Approx. height and spread after 10 years: 3 × 2.5m (10 × 8ft).*

Flowering nutmeg (*Leycesteria formosa*) This useful shrub does well in medium shade, but will tolerate dense shade if it's not bone dry. It has long tassels of wine-red bracts above small white flowers from midsummer to autumn, and purple-black berries. Once the leaves fall, it reveals its vivid sea-green stems. It responds well to cutting hard back in early spring, to produce strong new growth and keep it reasonably small.
▷ *Approx. height and spread after ten years: 2.5 × 3.5m (8 × 12ft).*

Oregon grape (*Mahonia aquifolium*) D This is a valuable shrub for moist and dry shade. It has jagged, architectural, evergreen leaves, sprays of scented yellow flowers in early spring and, in autumn, the leaves turn a purply-red. It can get a bit straggly, particularly in deep shade, but if you cut back the old woody growth to ground level every three or four years it will produce new growth very quickly. The taller *M. japonica* has foliage that is deep green on acid soil, and is tinged with red on a limy soil. It also has very fragrant yellow flowers which sometimes appear before Christmas. Look out for the hybrid 'Charity' too which is one of the best.
▷ *Approx. height and spread after 10 years: 1 × 2m (3 × 6ft). M. japonica: 2.5 × 2.8m (8 × 9ft).*

Pachysandra terminalis D Happiest on a neutral or acid soil, it forms a carpet of serrated, diamond-shaped light green leaves and spikes of small white flowers in mid spring. It will thrive in deep shade, provided there is enough moisture.
▷ *Approx. height and spread after 10 years: 30 cm × 1.5m (1 × 5ft).*

Pyracantha (Firethorn) An ideal shrub for training against a shady wall, it has glossy evergreen leaves, white flowers in early summer, and clusters of yellow, orange or red berries in autumn. Good varieties include *P.* 'Mojave', with orange-red berries, *P.* 'Orange Glow', with very dark foliage and lots of orange berries, and *P.* 'Soleil d'Or', with mid-green leaves and deep yellow berries.
▷ *Approx. height and spread after 10 years: 3.5 × 2m (12 × 6ft).*

Flowering currant (*Ribes sanguineum*) An accommodating plant in a shady spot and in most soil types. It doesn't like boggy soil, nor does it like extremely dry, but if you add organic matter to a dry soil it should cope well enough then. 'Pulborough Scarlet' is a good variety and so is the golden-leafed *R.s.* 'Brocklebankii'. It needs some shade to prevent its leaves from scorching, and though in deep shade it will be more of a greenish-yellow than a true gold, it still adds some welcome brightness in an otherwise dark spot.
▷ *Approx. height and spread after 10 years: 2 × 2m (6 × 6ft).*

Flowering bramble (*Rubus*) The ground-covering varieties like *R. calycinoides* and especially *R. tricolor* are useful in deep shade. If possible plant them at the edge of the tree cover, so that they get the maximum available light when they are getting established. Once they are growing well, direct the growth towards the shadiest areas.
▷ *Approx. height and spread after 10 years: 50cm × 2.5m (1ft 8in × 8ft).*

Christmas box (*Sarcococca humilis*) A dwarf evergreen, thicket-forming shrub with narrow pointed glossy green leaves and unspectacular-looking but very sweet vanilla-scented small white flowers as early as February. It needs a rich soil but will tolerate some lime, and will grow in deep

Kerria japonica *'Picta'*.

shade, though not quite as well as it does with a little more light.
▷ *Approx. height and spread after 10 years:*
50 × 60cm (1ft 8in × 2ft).

Skimmia As invaluable small evergreen shrub for shade, provided it gets the right soil conditions. It won't tolerate any lime, and dislikes extremes of waterlogging and drought. It has shiny aromatic leaves, scented white flowers in late spring, and clusters of shiny red or white berries in autumn. To be sure of berries you need to plant at least one male with any number of females. Good varieties include *Skimmia japonica* 'Nymans' or 'Foremanii' (both female) and *S.j.* 'Rubella', a male form which has fat short pokers of deep red buds which open eventually to blush-white, sweetly scented flowers, but no berries.
▷ *Approx. height and spread after 10 years:*
60 × 60cm (2 × 2ft).

Snowberry (*Symphoricarpos*) See page 74.

Viburnum There are lots of good varieties for shady corners. *Viburnum davidii*, which forms an attractive, low, spreading, evergreen shrub, has large, leathery, dark green, glossy leaves, and white flowers in June followed by striking turquoise fruits, provided there is a male plant around to pollinate the female. It's not easy to sex a viburnum but, if you have room, plant at least three and increase the odds of getting both genders! For some reason these look tatty when you see them in the garden centre, but they improve enormously once they're planted in the garden.
▷ *Approx. height and spread after 10 years:*
1.2 × 1.2m (4 × 4ft).

The guelder rose (*Viburnum opulus*) is even more accommodating – it will grow in waterlogged

soil and in dry soil and is tolerant of acidity and lime. *Viburnum opulus* 'Sterile', the snowball shrub, produces as its common name suggests white snowball-like flowerheads in May or June. As its botanical name suggests, it doesn't produce any berries, whereas *V.o.* 'Notcutt's Variety' produces both white lacecap flowers, not unlike the hydrangea, and large clusters of translucent red berries in autumn. Where space really is at a premium, try *V.o.* 'Compactum', which also has white lacecap flowers, red fruits and a very pleasing rounded shape but reaches only half the size of the other two.
▷ *Approx. height and spread after 10 years: 3 × 3m (10 × 10ft).*

A viburnum that divides opinion sharply is *V. rhytidophyllum*, which makes a large shrub with huge, leathery, deeply veined leaves that have grey-brown, felty undersides that droop in cold weather. It has heads of buff white flowers, then red berries which eventually turn black, some people think it's dull, others consider it to be a striking architectural shrub – an acquired taste, perhaps, but excellent in a very shady corner.
▷ *Approx. height and spread after 10 years: 3 × 3m + (10 × 10ft +).*

Lesser periwinkle (*Vinca minor*) This trailing, ground-covering evergreen shrub will tolerate deep shade and dry soil. It's more attractive, and better suited to small gardens, than the ordinary periwinkle (*Vinca major*). It flowers from April to June, and among the best varieties are *V.m.* 'Bowles' Variety' which has larger than average light blue flowers, *V.* 'Gertrude Jekyll', which has small, pure white flowers, and *V.m.* 'Variegata' which also has white flowers and cream and green variegated foliage.
▷ *Approx. height and spread after 10 years: 15 × 60cm (6in × 2ft).*

Herbaceous plants

Monkshood (*Aconitum*) Its tall spikes of hooded dark blue flowers in summer and glossy deeply divided leaves make this a good choice for the back of a partially shaded border, though as it is poisonous in all its parts it is best avoided if you have small children. Good varieties include: *A.*

napellus 'Bressingham Spire' or *A. carmichaelii* 'Arendsii' (both deep blue) or the shorter-growing, creamy-yellow flowered *A. orientale*.
▷ *Height and spread: 1m × 40cm (3ft × 1in).*

Lady's mantle (*Alchemilla mollis*) A star among herbaceous plants. Its fresh green leaves look like carefully folded fans as they open, and it carries sprays of tiny yellow-green flowers for months on end in summer. It will grow practically anywhere - sun or shade, damp or dry soil, acid or lime. It seeds itself with abandon in the crevices of paving, walls or steps, but usually looks so good that you just leave it there. Cut back the flowers as they fade and you'll be sure to get a new crop of beautiful leaves.
▷ *Height and spread: 50 × 30cm (18 × 12in).*

Japanese anemones (*Anemone japonica or × hybrida*) Excellent for late summer/early autumn colour with their masses of tall pink or white flowering stems. Good varieties to look out for include *A.j.* 'Queen Charlotte', which has semi-double rich pink flowers with gold stamens, and *A.j.* 'Alba' or the tall *A.j.* 'Honorine Joubert', both with large white flowers.
▷ *Height and spread: 50cm-1m × 35cm (18in-3ft × 15in).*

Elephant's Ears (*Bergenia*) These most accommodating plants have very attractive, large, rounded, evergreen leaves, some of which take on a bronze or red tint in winter, and spikes of white pink or red flowers in spring and summer. Good varieties include *B. cordifolia* 'Purpurea' which has large wavy round leaves, turning a purplish-red in winter, and magenta flowers on and off throughout the summer; *B.* 'Abendglut' with neat crinkle-edged leaves, good autumn colour and vivid rose-red flowers; and *B.* 'Ballawley', the largest of all, with good autumn colour and rose-red flowers in spring and, occasionally, a few in autumn.
▷ *Height and spread: 30-60cm × 30-60cm (15in-2ft × 15in-2ft).*

Bleeding heart (*Dicentra spectabilis*) A beautiful late spring/early summer flowering plant, with graceful arching stems of small flowers like deep pink hearts with a white teardrop underneath. It

also has attractive ferny foliage which dies down in midsummer, so don't panic and think you've somehow managed to kill it off! There is also a beautiful white version, *D.s.*'Alba'.
▷ *Height and spread: 60 × 50cm (2ft × 18in).*

Christmas rose (*Helleborus niger*) and Lenten rose (*Helleborus orientalis*) The Christmas rose (more usually in flower in January than at Christmas, in fact) has leathery evergreen leaves and large, waxy white flowers with gold stamens, which last for weeks. The Lenten rose, which flowers in late winter, has similar shaped flowers but in a whole range of colours from white and green through mauvy-pinks to purple. It's a slightly larger plant than the Christmas rose and both of them are happy in limy soil.
▷ *Height and spread: 30 × 40cm (12 × 15in). Lenten rose: 50 × 50cm (18 × 18in).*

Coral flower (*Heuchera sanguinea*) In dappled shade and rich soil, this makes good weed-suppressing clumps of scalloped evergreen leaves with tall, thin stems of tiny red or pink flowers from April to June. Good varieties include *H.* 'Palace Purple' with mounds of wine-coloured foliage and sprays of tiny white flowers, *H.* 'Snow Storm', the leaves of which are speckled white, and the new *H.* 'Pewter Moon', which has leaves that are purple underneath and marbled pewter on top.
▷ *Height and spread: 60 × 50cm (2ft × 18in).*

Plantain lilies (*Hosta*) These are outstanding foliage plants in moist soil and a reason all on their own for having a shady bit of garden. There are many different ones to choose from, some with very small leaves, like *H.* 'Ginko Craig', some with huge leaves like *H. sieboldiana* 'Elegans', the blue-green, deeply ribbed leaves of which are almost 30cm (1ft) wide. There are gold-leafed varieties, like *H. fortunei* 'Aurea', many shades of green, as well as blue, and variegated leaves too, like *H.* 'Thomas Hogg' whose elegant pointed leaves have creamy margins. They also produce spikes of either mauve or white flowers in midsummer and have good autumn colour before the leaves finally rot away. The only snag with hostas is that slugs and snails love them almost as much as discerning gardeners do, and can reduce a large

leaf to a skeleton overnight. Some form of anti-slug precaution is essential – a cocoa shell mulch or a circle of cinders or baked, broken-up eggshells is a more eco-friendly alternative to slug pellets. In pots, try smearing Vaseline around the rim.
▷ *Height and spread (of foliage): 30-60cm × 30cm-1m (1-2 × 1-3ft).*

Dead-nettle (*Lamium maculatum*) Marvellous ground cover for shade, spreading quickly and covering a large area with attractive variegated foliage, creating areas of brightness among the shade. *L.m.* 'Beacon Silver', *L.m.* 'White Nancy' and *L.m.* 'Shell-Pink' all have silver variegated leaves and produce respectively clear pink, ivory-white and shell-pink flowers from May to July. After the flowers have faded, it's worth trimming the plant with shears to remove the dead flower heads and any upward growing leafy shoots to encourage it to produce new foliage and keep it close to the ground.
▷ *Height and spread: 20 × 50cm (8 × 18in).*

Knotweed (*Persicaria*, formerly known as *Polygonum*) These are useful plants, flowering throughout the summer, though make sure you go for the better behaved varieties like *P. affinis* 'Superba' or 'Dimity' whose pink flowers darken to a rusty-red with age and whose fresh green foliage turns russet-brown in winter, staying on the plant until new growth appears in spring. They make good, weed-suppressing clumps, and if they do get over-ambitious, simply chop them back with a spade.
▷ *Height and spread: 25 × 50cm (10 × 18in).*

Solomon's seal (*Polygonatum × hybridum*) A woodland plant with a quiet beauty, it has elegant arching stems with slender, fresh green leaves all the way along, from which dangle small white flowers, rather like miniature white pears with a green base, in early summer. There is a variegated form, with leaves boldly striped in creamy white. As with hostas, slugs also find its young foliage irresistible, so protect it in the same way especially when the young shoots are emerging.
▷ *Height and spread: 75 × 40cm (2ft 6in × 15in).*

Primulas (*Primula*) See page 78.

Left: *A blue and white carpet of* Anemone blanda *in spring before the trees are in leaf.*

Above: *Gold and silver –* Hosta fortunei *'Aurea' and* Lamium *'Beacon Silver' one of the few shade-loving silver plants.*

Lungwort (*Pulmonaria*) An excellent ground-cover plant for shade where it's not too dry, with sprays of small, long-lasting, pink, white or blue flowers in spring, and clumps of weed-smothering, attractive leaves spotted or frosted with silver. Good varieties to look out for include *P. officinalis* 'Cambridge Blue' which has heart-shaped, spotted leaves, and masses of blue flowers opening from pink buds, giving it a bi-colour effect; *P. saccharata* 'Sissinghurst White' which has much larger leaves, marbled with silver, and white flowers; and *P.s.* 'Highdown' which has rich blue flowers.
▷ *Height and spread: 25-30 × 25cm (10-12 × 10in).*

Smilacina racemosa For an acid soil. See page 139.

Comfrey (*Symphytum*) Some of this family are real garden thugs and will smother everything in

sight, but well worth having is the milder-mannered variegated kind, *S. × uplandicum* 'Variegatum', with handsome cream and green leaves as well as pretty blue flowers in late spring/early summer. Pick off any plain green shoots as soon as you see them, otherwise the plant can revert.
▷ *Height and spread: 1m × 60cm (3ft 3in × 2ft).*

Tiarella cordifolia D A good ground-cover plant in deep shade. During winter its almost evergreen heart-shaped leaves become tinged with bronze, spreading out from the veins, and it has spikes of small white flowers in late spring/early summer. It doesn't produce such a dense carpet where the soil is dry.
▷ *Height and spread: 25 × 30cm (10 × 12in).*

Wake-robin (*Trillium grandiflorum*)
See page 139.

Viola labradorica A superb ground-cover plant for virtually any type of soil, which seeds itself so freely when it's established that it could almost be a nuisance if it weren't so attractive! It has small round green leaves, flushed with purple, while its flowers, produced in spring, are small mauve violets which tone perfectly with the leaves.
▷ *Height and spread: 10-15 × 30cm (4-6 × 12in).*

Ferns

Ferns are making a much-deserved comeback after many years out of fashion, and while you will find an increasing number of varieties in garden centres, you may have to buy anything out of the ordinary by mail order from a fern specialist like J. and D. Marston in Driffield, East Yorkshire (0377 44487) or Fibrex in Stratford-upon-Avon (0789 720788).

Hardy maidenhair fern (*Adiantum*) These small, semi-evergreen ferns are ideal in a partly shaded spot in acid soil where it's not too dry. Look for *A. pedatum*, the smaller *A.p.* 'Minor' and the carpeting *A. venustum*. If you can find them, the maidenhair and black spleenworts (*A. trichomanes* and *A. adiantum-niger*) will add instant age to a wall or steps.
▷ *Height and spread: 15-20 × 30cm (6-8 × 12in).*

Lady fern (*Athyrium filix-femina*) This native fern is no less attractive for being common. The smaller *A. f-f.* 'Minutum' is as its name suggests a miniature version, reaching only about 12cm (5in), good for the front of a shady border or between the stones of a wall.
▷ *Height and spread: 60cm-1.2m × 30cm-1m (2-4ft × 1-3ft).*

Japanese painted fern (*Athyrium nipponicum pictum*) A real stunner, with wine-red stems and silver-grey foliage which gleams in a shady spot. It could be killed by frost, so plant it in a sheltered place, or protect the crown with its own dead foliage or bracken in really cold weather.
▷ *Height and spread: 30 × 30cm (1 × 1ft).*

Hard fern (*Blechnum spicant*) With its tough slender fronds, this evergreen fern can cope in very shady places and in drier soil than many others, though it grows larger and lusher where there is more moisture. *B. tabulare* has broader, longer fronds, which have a copper tint when they first unfurl. It's only semi-evergreen in colder areas. Both benefit from the regular removal of older faded fronds.
▷ *Height and spread: 75-90 × 30-45cm (2-3ft × 1ft-1ft 6in).*

Male fern (*Dryopteris filix-mas*) Another excellent and easy fern for deep shade. In mild areas it can keep its fronds through the winter, through which the new bright green ones unfurl in spring.
▷ *Height: 1 × 1m (3 × 3ft).*

Shuttlecock or Ostrich plume fern (*Matteuccia struthiopteris*) See page 81.

Hart's-tongue fern (*Phyllitis*, sometimes *Asplenium*, *scolopendrium* 'Crispum') A good choice for limy soils, this has bright green, long, slender frilled fronds, rather like crepe paper Christmas decorations.
▷ *Height and spread: 30 × 4cm (1ft × 1ft 6in).*

***Polypodium vulgare* 'Cornubiense'** A small, lacy evergreen fern which will put up with slightly drier soil than most other ferns.
▷ *Height: 30 × 30cm (1 × 1ft).*

Soft shield fern (*Polystichum setiferum*) Perhaps the most finely divided of all ferns, this evergreen or semi-evergreen fern will also tolerate slightly drier soil, though it is lusher and greener where the soil is moist. There are a number of varieties available, divided into two main groups: the 'Acutilobum' whose leaves are tough and sharp in outline, and 'Divisilobum', with softer leaves, fuzzier in outline.
▷ *Height and spread: 60 × 45cm (2ft × 1ft 6in).*

Annuals

While the vast majority of annuals really need a sunny position, there are a few that will do well in shade, and they are such excellent plants that their quality compensates for the limited choice!

Busy lizzies (*Impatiens*) A superb choice for a shady border because they will go on flowering prolifically from June until the first frosts. They come in a whole range of colours, from pure white through many shades of pink and salmon to orange, red and even violet, though in deep shade the paler colours – white, very pale pink or mauve – gleam while brighter ones lose their impact. For maximum effect, plant a group of the same colour.
▷ *Height and spread: 20-30 × 20cm (8-12 × 8in).*

Monkey flower (*Mimulus*) See page 81.

Baby blue eyes (*Nemophila insignis*) A very pretty, front-of-the-border plant which has sky-blue cup-shaped flowers with white centres, carried on slightly trailing, ferny foliage throughout the summer. It's a hardy annual so it can be sown straight into the ground where you want it to flower. Also worth trying is *N. maculata* 'Five Spot', which has white petals, each with a purple spot at the tip. Slugs consider the young foliage a real treat, so protect the young plants.
▷ *Height and spread: 15 × 15cm (6 × 6in).*

Bulbs

Many flowering bulbs thrive in woodland conditions during spring and autumn when the trees under which they grow are bare and allow a reasonable amount of light and moisture through.

Allium Try *A. triquetrum* (see page 155).

Wood anemone (*Anemone nemorosa*) This lovely woodland plant (a tuber technically) has a mass of starry white (or very pale pinky-mauve flowers in the case of *A.n.* 'Robinsoniana') in early spring over a dense carpet of attractive ferny leaves, which die away by midsummer. The only drawback is that some unscrupulous firms are taking tubers from the wild to sell, so do make sure you buy from a reputable source. Also try *Anemone blanda* which has white, blue or pink flowers.
▷ *Height and spread: 15 × 30cm (6 × 12in).*

Arum italicum 'Pictum' An exotic-looking plant which produces heads like drumsticks of poisonous, bright orange berries in late summer, followed by the leaves which are spear-shaped, glossy dark green, strikingly marked with grey and cream, and which keep appearing until the spring. It does flower, but not so as you'd notice.
▷ *Height and spread: 30-45 × 30cm (12-18 × 12in).*

Cyclamen (*Cyclamen hederifolium*) The deep mauve-pink or white flowers are thumbnail-sized versions of the pot plants we all buy, but they would be worth growing just for the beautiful ivy-shaped leaves, marbled with silver, which appear at the same time as, or just follow, the flowers. A soil just either side of neutral suits them best, but they will tolerate some degree of alkalinity provided the soil is rich and moist.
▷ *Height and spread: 10 × 15cm (4 × 6in).*

Winter aconite (*Eranthis hyemalis*) With its bright yellow, buttercup-like flowers set on a ruff of dark green leaves, this is one of the first bulbs to appear after Christmas. It's happy in moist soils – acid or alkaline – and in shade.
▷ *Height and spread: 5-10 × 10cm (2-4 × 4in).*

Dog's-tooth violet (*Erythronium dens-canis*) This has delicate, nodding flowers in shades of white, pink, lilac and carmine in spring and attractive mottled leaves. Good varieties to look for include *E.d-c.* 'White Splendour', 'Rose Beauty' and 'Lilac Wonder'. The tubers dislike

drying out, so buy in pots or by mail order from a reputable supplier and plant them as soon as possible after they arrive.
▷ *Height and spread: 10-15×10-12cm (4-6×4-5in).*

Snowdrops (*Galanthus nivalis*) Their pure white flowers show up very well in shade. They tolerate most types of soil, though in a sandy soil you need to dig in plenty of moisture-retaining organic matter before planting. See page 81.

Grape hyacinths (*Muscari armeniacum*) This particular variety is taller and has paler blue flowers than the most commonly grown variety, *M. botryoides*, and most important it will tolerate a greater degree of shade.
▷ *Height and spread: 10-20×8-10cm (4-8×3-4in).*

Dry Shade

All the plants listed here will also grow in moist shade, but they will give almost as good an account of themselves in dry shade as well, though in most cases they won't grow as large or flower as prolifically as they would in better conditions.

Climbers

Ivy (*Hedera helix* or *H. colchica*) See page 30.
Climbing hydrangea (*H. petiolaris*) See page 30.
Virginia creeper (*Parthenocissus*) See page 30.

Shrubs

Aucuba japonica See page 30.

Barberry (*Berberis*) A family of tough, accommodating shrubs, some of which will put on a reasonable show in dry shade. They include the evergreens *B. darwinii*, which has small, jagged,

One of the later-flowering snowdrops with green-blotched inner petals growing through a carpet of Pulmonaria saccarata *whose flowers really are 'sky-blue-pink' – pink in bud but turning sky blue when they open.*

evergreen leaves, and clusters of bright orange flowers in spring, and *B. stenophylla*, with long thin leaves, olive on top and silver underneath, and double yellow flowers in spring.
▷ *Approx. height and spread after 10 years: 2.2 × 2m (7 × 6ft).*

Box (*Buxus sempervirens*) A very useful evergreen for a formal setting since it can be clipped to make a hedge or used as topiary either in a border or in containers. In fact gravel and box topiary in tubs is an elegant, simple solution to a dry, shady strip. For a dwarf hedge you need *B.s.* 'Suffruticosa' which has much smaller, brighter leaves and reaches only a fraction of the height. There are variegated forms, like the gold and green *B.s.* 'Aureovariegata' and cream and green *B.s.* 'Elegantissima', but the variegation is nothing like as vivid in shade as it is in a sunnier spot.
▷ *Approx. height and spread after 10 years: 2 × 2m (6ft 6in × 6ft 6in).*

Cotoneaster This is another large family with members of all shapes and sizes, deciduous and evergreen, some of which will cope with sun and shade, moist or dry soil. Some of the very low-growing, small-leafed evergreens are very accommodating in this particular situation. Look for *C. dammeri* or the very similar *C. × suecicus* 'Skogholm' and 'Coral Beauty' which are particularly good forms, both with white flowers in summer followed by sealing-wax-red berries, and forming a completely flat carpet. The slow-growing *C. microphyllus*, which forms a low mound rather than growing flat, is good for covering a bank or for growing over a wall, with masses of tiny grey-green leaves and dark red fruits in autumn.
▷ *Approx. height and spread after 10 years: 30-60cm × 2m (1-2 × 6ft).*

Gaultheria shallon See page 00.

Golden privet (*Ligustrum ovalifolium* 'Aureum') Although this would not be top of the list in moister soils where other more interesting shrubs will grow, it serves very well in these unpromising conditions, providing a splash of brightness. It will make a serviceable hedge, but is more attractive as a free-standing shrub. Its leaves, which would be variegated green and gold in sun, are a uniform green-gold in shade. While you can trim it to keep it tidy, don't cut it back hard – the poor conditions don't make it vigorous enough to withstand that kind of treatment.
▷ *Approx. height and spread after 10 years: 4 × 4m (14 × 14ft).*

Oregon grape (*Mahonia aquifolium*) See page 32.
Cherry laurel (*Prunus laurocerasus* 'Otto Luyken') See page 127.
Flowering currant (*Ribes sanguineum* 'Pulborough Scarlet') See page 32.
***Rubus calcycinoides* (Ornamental bramble)** See page 32.
Guelder rose (*Viburnum opulus*) See page 34.
Lesser periwinkle (*Vinca minor*) See page 34.

Herbaceous plants

Bugle (*Ajuga reptans*) A good carpeter, with short spikes on intense blue flowers in early summer, for this difficult situation. There are some lovely variegated kinds, though the green and pale buff 'Variegata' does better in deep shade than the dark metallic purple 'Atropurpurea' and the mottled wine-red 'Burgundy Glow'. They don't form such a dense, weed-proof carpet as they do in moist soil, but still do well.
▷ *Height and spread: 15cm × 1m (6in × 3ft).*

Lady's mantle (*Alchemilla mollis*) See page 34.
Elephant's Ears (*Bergenia*) See page 34.

Eastern bleeding heart (*Dicentra eximia*) This is a much bushier plant with more feathery foliage than its native cousin, though its pink flowers, borne intermittently throughout the summer are more tubular than heart-shaped. 'Bleeding Heart' (*D. spectabilis*) will tolerate dry shade to a degree, but *D. eximia* tolerates it better.
▷ *Height and spread: 30 × 50cm (12 × 20in).*

Foxgloves (*Digitalis*) These are really tough customers and will do well here. Our native foxglove, *D. purpurea*, which flowers in summer, is strictly speaking a biennial (growing one year, flowering the next, then dying) but they may survive a year or two longer. They usually seed themselves very freely anyway, so it's not a problem. There are

perennial foxgloves, like *D. grandiflora* which has pale yellow flowers, *D. ferruginea* which has very unusual coppery-yellow flowers veined with brown, and *D. × mertonensis* which has flowers the colour of strawberry sorbet.
▷ *Height and spread: 90 × 30cm (3 × 1ft).*

Spurge (*Euphorbia*) Of this large and useful family, the best plant for dry shade is *E. robbiae*, which has tall rosettes of leathery dark green leaves, topped with yellow-green flowers all summer long which take on bronze tints in autumn. Cut it back after flowering to encourage bushy new growth.
▷ *Height and spread: 60 × 60cm + (2 × 2ft +).*

Cranesbills (*Geranium macrorrhizum*) These particular varieties do sterling work in dry shade, with their lovely aromatic semi-evergreen leaves which sometimes turn red in autumn, and sprays of flowers in white or pink in late spring/early summer. Look for *G.m.* 'Album' whose flowers are blush-white rather than pure white, *G.m.* 'Ingwersen's Variety', with soft, mauvy-pink flowers, and *G.m.* 'Bevan's Variety' with taller stems of vivid magenta-pink flowers.
▷ *Height and spread: 40 × 40cm (16 × 16in).*

Stinking hellebore (*Helleborus foetidus*) Ignore the name – this is a stunning plant for dry shade. It makes neat clumps of deep green, sharply divided fan-shaped leaves, with clusters of pale green bell-shaped flowers in winter and early spring.
▷ *Height and spread: 60 × 40cm (2ft × 16in).*

Stinking iris (*Iris foetidissima*) Another one whose name doesn't do it justice since this is a lovely iris, which thrives in dry shade. It has long strap-like leaves, unremarkable mauve and yellowish-green flowers in early summer, and spectacularly large pods of bright orange seeds in winter. There is a variegated version, *I.f.* 'Variegata', which is grown for its foliage, since it almost never flowers.
▷ *Height and spread: 45-60 × 45cm (18in-2ft × 18in).*

Dead-nettle (*Lamium maculatum*) See page 35.

Lily-turf (*Liriope muscari*) This is a superb plant which should be more widely grown. It has narrow, strap-like evergreen leaves and, in autumn spikes of violet-blue flowers that look like grape hyacinths.
▷ *Height and spread: 40 × 40cm (16 × 16in).*

Bowles' golden grass (*Milium effusum* 'Aureum') See page 00.
Lungwort (*Pulmonaria*) See page 37.

Piggy-back (*Tolmiea menziesii* 'Variegata') This gets its common name from the fact that it produces small plantlets on top of its leaves, which will root if carefully removed and pressed into the ground. It has very attractive, round, yellow-speckled leaves, and though it's often sold as a houseplant, it's perfectly hardy. The flowers are insignificant.
▷ *Height and spread: 30 × 30cm (1 × 1ft).*

Viola labradorica See page 38.

Waldsteinia ternata A lovely evergreen carpeter with glossy dark green three-lobed leaves, not unlike a strawberry's, which sometimes take on a bronze tint in winter, and sprays of golden-yellow flowers, also rather like a strawberry's, in spring.
▷ *Height and spread: 8-10cm × 1m (3-4in × 3ft).*

Annuals

No annuals will really thrive in dry shade, though if you have a few busy lizzies to spare it would be worth planting them out and taking a chance.

Bulbs

Wood anemone (*Anemone nemorosa*) See page 39.

***Arum italicum* 'Pictum'** This will grow well enough in dry shade beneath a wall, provided there is some moisture below the surface and the bulbs are planted quite deep. See page 39.

Meadow saffron (*Colchicum speciosum*) See page 155.

Cyclamen hederifolium See page 38.

HOT, DRY PLACES

 If you had any choice in the matter of which problem you were going to have in your garden, this would be one of the better ones to choose. For one thing it's not that difficult to improve the situation enough to make a big difference, and for another, there are some absolutely beautiful plants that will grow happily in these conditions. Think of the lovely aromatic herbs, silvery, blue-flowered teucrium, cistus, yucca, Californian poppy (*Eschscholzia*), mesembryanthemums, and so on.

You might find the soil is thin and gravelly because that's the nature of the area, or because you've had building work done and some of the topsoil's been removed or buried, or because it's on a bank and most of the top soil has washed away over the years.

Long exposure to hot sun causes water in the plant's leaves and in the soil to evaporate, and where the soil is thin and poor these problems are compounded by the fact that the soil is too free-draining, losing not only moisture but essential nutrients with it. In these conditions, plants that thrive in average-to-moist soils will simply grow feeble and die. One way round this problem is to water and feed frequently and copiously, but not only is that very time-consuming – and not one of the more pleasurable jobs in the garden – but in the long dry summers we've had in recent years, with the resulting hosepipe bans, it's no longer an option anyway.

On the plus side, though, the right plants will thrive and some tender species, like the cabbage palm (cordyline), some of the most beautiful but less hardy cistus varieties, the variegated hebes, or the tender pittosporums that would succumb to frost even in a less sunny, less free-draining spot elsewhere in your own garden, stand a greater chance of surviving the winter, because it's the combination of cold and wet that is most likely to kill this type of plant. In a hot dry spot, the stems of these plants become ripened or hardened by the sun, which makes them more woody and less susceptible to damage by the frost than plants with greener, softer stems. That's even more true if you have a wall at the back of the border, because that acts as a storage heater, absorbing what warmth there is and slowly releasing it, to keep the ambient temperature just that bit higher.

To see plants that thrive in these conditions in the wild you need to travel abroad – the Mediterranean, Mexico, the southern states of the USA, southern Africa, even Australia. The south of France – off the beaten track, anyway – smells wonderfully in early summer of wild thyme that grows on hillsides and even dusty verges. In Malta, the wonderfully scented but tender *Pittosporum tobira* grows perfectly well in a few inches of scrubby soil on top of rock, and, walking down a dusty track to the beach in Lindos on Rhodes one summer, I was astonished to see silvery *Helichrysum petiolatum* tumbling down dry stone walls. Admittedly it was a bit limp (in hanging baskets and containers here, it indicates it needs water by the fact that the tips of the shoots curl over), but

to be fair, it was July and about 100 degrees!

But even drought-loving plants need *some* water – after all, water makes up 90 per cent of the leaves and stems of all plants – so to grow this type of plant successfully, you must add some bulky organic matter to the soil, which will not only increase its ability to hold water and therefore nutrients,

A lovely hot dry border at Glazeley Old Rectory, with silvery Stachys lanata *'Silver Carpet', spiky metallic blue eryngiums, yellow achilleas and the vivid magenta flowers of* Lychnis coronaria *in the background.*

but it will also boost its fertility a bit. It's worth remembering, though, that most drought-lovers thrive on poor soil, and they won't thank you for over-generous feeding. The resulting growth tends to be a bit soft and sappy and that makes the plant more vulnerable to pests and also to frost.

Since organic matter breaks down very quickly in soils like this, after you've prepared the area initially by digging some into the soil the best way to add it is to spread it on the surface each spring, and let the worms and the weather gradually draw it down. At the same time it acts as a mulch, helping to keep the moisture in, and saves you work by inhibiting the growth of annual weeds.

Not suprisingly, plants that come from hot climates will usually do well in this situation, but of course you can't always tell just by looking at them what their origins are. So, a few visual clues are very useful. For a start, almost all grey- and silver-leafed plants – lavender, artemisias, lamb's lugs (*Stachys lanata*), *Brachyglottis* (which used to be called, much more mellifluously, *Senecio* until the botanists mugged it!), *Convolvulus cneorum* – will thrive in these conditions. There are a number of reasons why these plants cope with hot dry conditions so well. For one thing, the silvery, whitish colour reflects heat away from the plant. For another, the silvery colour comes from a covering of very fine hairs which traps moist air between itself and the leaf's surface and creates a moist microclimate which not only prevents the leaf scorching or shrivelling up but also means the plant needs less via its roots from the soil. Given that the very fine hairs on roots actually *increase* dramatically the surface area they cover, and enable the plant to take up much more moisture from the soil, you might think that these hairs on the leaves would increase

their surface area considerably, and therefore increase the amount of water *lost* by an equally dramatic amount. If the hairs were alive, they would do precisely that, but they are dead and hollow (hence their very pale colour) so don't.

Few drought-lovers have leaves with a large surface area. They have either no real leaves, like some brooms, or gorse, very small ones like lavender and cotton lavender (*Santolina chamaecyparissus*) or rue, or very narrow ones, like pinks (dianthus) or very delicate, finely divided ones, like the artemisias, or large, but very jagged ones like the globe thistle (*Echinops ritro*), so they cover the maximum amount of space and absorb as much light as possible, without having a large surface area through which to lose moisture.

A number of these Mediterranean plants – rosemary, lemon verbena (*Lippia citriodora*), lavender, sage, thyme – also have aromatic oils in their leaves, which on hot days float like a miasma just above the surface of the leaf and deflect heat. That's why the herb garden is the perfect place to be on a warm summer's evening. It's these aromatic oils that are released into the air when the leaves are crushed, or even just brushed against, which makes them good plants to place at the front of a border or on the corner of a busy thoroughfare, where you are most likely to brush against them.

The aromatics have other ways of protecting themselves against heat. They also tend to have very highly concentrated sap, which has a greater capacity for drawing available moisture out of the soil and for storing it – a bit like the gel you can buy for hanging baskets and containers to prevent them drying out so quickly. Since the sap is so concentrated, it is also very strongly flavoured. Compare the taste of, say, sage, with lettuce, which has a very mild flavour – it has such weak sap and therefore poor resistance to drought. Mediterranean herbs like rosemary and lavender also protect themselves from heat and drought by the arrangement of their very fine needle-like leaves. They're arranged in such a way that they shade each other and only a percentage of them is exposed to the sun at the same time. That is also true of desert cacti which have very deep grooves, casting shadows, so that at any one time only a small proportion of the plants' surface area is exposed to the sun. Other drought-loving plants, like stonecrops (sedums), houseleeks (sempervivums), Livingstone daisies (mesembryanthemums) and crassulas (which although usually grown as houseplants will grow outside in a very sunny spot in the summer), protect themselves against drought by being able to store water in their thick fleshy leaves. Others like bergenias and many evergreen shrubs have leaves which aren't particularly thick, but are as tough as leather and so in no danger of shrivelling up, while others, like the sun-loving spurges (euphorbias), have a waxy coating to protect their surface, and the slight whitish bloom it gives the leaves also help deflect the heat.

Anyone who's gone away on holiday and come back to find their hanging baskets completely dead except for the pelargoniums can testify to the drought-resisting properties of that species! Though their leaves are quite large and thin, they *are* covered with hairs, which helps, and in some cases the leaves contain wonderfully sweet aromatic oils, but more important in this case is the structure of the plants. The gaps between leaf joints (the internodes) on the stems are comparatively short, and the nodes act as braces, almost, supporting the stem. Add to that the fact that the tissue of the stems is also comparatively hard, with plenty of structural tissue, you can see that a lack of water is much less likely to cause pelargoniums to collapse than, say, primulas, which bear their flowers on much thinner stems that don't have leaves.

I've said very little about flowers because although they are essential if plants are to reproduce themselves, they are not vital for perennial plants to survive from year to year. In fact, you can often identify drought-lovers by their spectacular flowers with brightly coloured petals to attract the insects they need for pollination; some close in dull or wet weather because their customers – insects – aren't flying, so it's a waste of time opening. Their flowers are often very short-lived, sometimes lasting only a day – like cistus – but produced in profusion. This is because in the wild, when there is enough rain to start the plant's flowering cycle, it has to flower, be pollinated by insects, set seed and then scatter it, all while there is still some moisture around, if it is to germinate and so reproduce successfully. By dead-heading plants like this and not allowing them to set seed, you encourage them to flower for longer.

Ironically, there is another group of plants that are ideal for free-draining soil in an open spot that thrive in totally different conditions in the wild – alpines (see page 106–107). They are adapted for growing in very shallow soils – or indeed in practically no soil at all – on top of sloping rocks or in rocky crevices. You could be forgiven for thinking that if your thin poor soil is due to the fact that it's just a shallow layer on top of a layer of solid rock, alpines are the answer to your prayers. They could well be if the area slopes, because the key factor here about alpines in the wild is that they grow on mountainsides, and in crevices, so although they get an ample supply of moisture it passes over their roots very quickly, and they are never sitting in water. If your patch is level, and in wet weather water takes a long time to drain away, you'll find that many of the choicer alpines will just rot. They are adapted to cope quite happily with water in its solid state – they'll survive the winter very well under a blanket of snow – but not in its liquid form! Too much water at their roots as well as too much on their leaves will cause them to rot.

Alpines can also be excellent plants for walls, dry-stone walls particularly, since they have ready-made planting pockets and,

of course, very free drainage. One problem with planting vertically is keeping the soil in the hole. To solve that one, take some small pieces of turf, one for each plant, lay them face down until the grass has died off, then wrap the rootball of each plant in a piece of dead turf with the grass outside, and then push the whole thing carefully into the hole. That way you're giving each plant its own bit of soil, held together by the roots of the dead grass so it can't fall out, and the layer of dead grass itself also provides a handy source of organic matter.

OUR PROBLEM PLACE

Our problem place was, at first sight, a real challenge. It's a steep slope, about 2.4m wide and almost 3m long, with a drop of

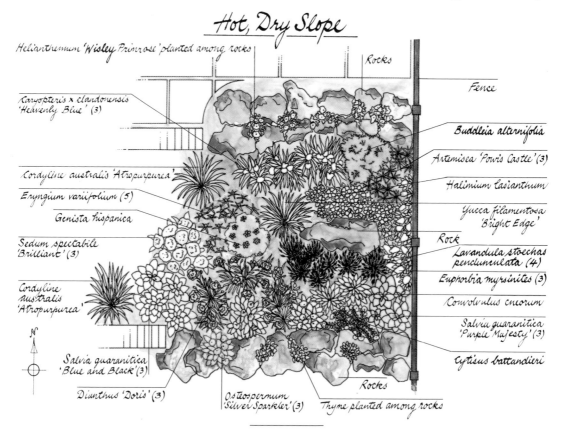

Hot, Dry Slope

Helianthemum 'Wisley Primrose' planted among rocks

Rocks

Fence

Caryopteris x clandonensis 'Heavenly Blue' (3)

Buddleia alternifolia

Artemisea 'Powis Castle' (3)

Halimium lasianthum

Cordyline australis 'Atropurpurea'

Eryngium variifolium (5)

Yucca filamentosa 'Bright Edge'

Genista hispanica

Rock

Sedum spectabile 'Brilliant' (3)

Lavandula stoechas pendunculata (4)

Euphorbia myrsinites (3)

Cordyline australis 'Atropurpurea'

Convolvulus cneorum

Salvia guaranitica 'Purple Majesty' (3)

Cytisus battandieri

Salvia guaranitica 'Blue and Black' (3)

Dianthus 'Doris' (3)

Ostuospermum 'Silver Sparkler' (3)

Rocks

Thyme planted among rocks

Our hot, dry bank was a major problem place when
we first saw it in June – covered in bindweed
and lumps of stone, with the soil baked rock
hard. By September, the sun-loving plants we chose
were thriving – the blue caryopteris, the pink
Dianthus 'Doris' and the osteospermums had
been flowering for weeks, and the flat, carmine heads
of the Sedum spectabile 'Brilliant' were just opening.
The slatey blue crushed limestone sets of the
mainly blue-grey foliage colours to perfection.

about 2m from the patio at the top to the lawn at the bottom. It faces due south and the soil, which is very thin, very free-draining and alkaline, was baked hard by the sun. We knew it would sustain plant growth, though, because it was supporting a fine crop of bindweed. At some stage previous owners must have attempted some kind of rockery because there are a number of large rocks scattered about the slope, often hidden under the bindweed.

The first thing to do was to clear the site. We sprayed the whole area with a weedkiller containing glyphosate to kill off the bindweed. Because glyphosate is a systemic weedkiller which is taken down through the leaves and will kill off the roots rather than just the top growth, it is by far the best bet here. Even so, bindweed is such a tough customer, growing from even the smallest piece of root left in the soil, that even this won't get rid of it completely in one go, so over the summer we had to keep on top of it, painting new growth with glyphosate as it appeared, and eventually it will die off. Many organic gardeners find glyphosate acceptable because it becomes inactive the moment it hits the soil, and so does no harm to any soil organisms, but if you are determined to use no chemicals at all in your garden, the only way to get rid of something as pernicious as bindweed is to cover the area completely with black polythene, or even an old carpet, weight it down to exclude all light so that effectively the plant starves, and leave it for a year.

The next step was to dig over the soil – easier said than done given it was baked hard – and work in bulky organic matter, in this instance a product based on composted cow manure, to increase its ability to hold moisture and nutrients. We recycled the large pieces of rock, using a double row, with pockets of soil for rock plants, at the top to bridge the gap from the patio to the bank, and the rest at the bottom to retain the soil.

As for the plants we chose a wide range of drought-lovers. The colours are mainly blue, gold, white and pink, but planted in such a way that we placed only blue, white and gold together, or blue, white and pink together, either because they were grouped in separate areas, or because they flowered at different times. Foliage colour was also important, and since many drought-lovers have silver or grey-green foliage, that was the predominant colour, with enough plain green to prevent it looking, as Beth Chatto once said, like an 'ash heap'!

On the west-facing fence, we planted a pineapple broom (*Cytisus battandieri*), both for its spikes of bright yellow, pineapple-scented flowers in late spring/early summer, and for its silky silvery leaves. Since we want to grow it as a wall shrub, we tied the side shoots on to the existing wires and trimmed any forward-growing shoots. It will easily spread to 3m across and so will cover the fence completely.

In among the rocks at the top, we planted a lovely pale yellow rock rose – *Helianthemum* 'Wisley Primrose', which will trail down and form an evergreen carpet of silvery grey foliage, attractive even when the very long flowering period is over.

Below the rocks, in the south-west facing corner, we planted a buddleia – not the usual *davidii* but *B. alternifolia*, an elegant arching shrub with long slender grey-green leaves and neat clusters of scented mauve flowers in early summer. Next to it, we planted caryopteris, a good late-summer flowering shrub with aromatic grey-green leaves and masses of small, vivid blue flowers. We actually chose C. 'Heavenly Blue', which has darker blue flowers and smaller and neater growth. On the far side, next to the wall by the steps, as a contrast to the grey foliage of the caryopteris, we put the wine-red cabbage palm, *Cordyline australis* 'Atropurpurea', with its strong, architectural sword-like leaves. Their bold, clean shape is a good contrast, too, to the very jagged, almost skeletal cream and green marbled leaves of *Eryngium variifolium* which we planted around it. It's a marvellous plant for this situation, with these intriguing evergreen leaves and vivid blue thistle-like flowers in mid to late summer. In the centre, we chose another very strong architectural plant – *Yucca filamentosa* 'Bright Edge'. Its leaves are edged not only with gold, but with small white curly threads. Although the one we planted was a young plant, it was already in flower. Next to that, and behind a low rock placed half-way down the slope to help anchor the soil we planted a shrub that isn't completely hardy and so must have a warm, protected site with very free-draining soil – *Halimium lasianthum*. It's a relative of the cistus and has similar flowers, except they are yellow, with small dark brown blotches at the base. Although its main flowering time is spring and early summer, it sometimes flowers again in autumn. Its evergreen leaves are a sagey-green and, since it forms a low mound, it will tumble over the rock.

Between it and the fence we planted *Artemisia* 'Lambrook Silver' and some salvias – *S. patens* in this instance, with its vivid blue flowers in late summer. Below the rock we planted a blue, pink and white group, with the fashionable French lavender *L. stoechas* 'Pendunculata', *Convolvulus*

cneorum, the long-flowering pink 'Doris', with bright rose-pink flowers borne for months, and, to spill over the rocks, the stunning variegated osteospermum, 'Silver Sparkler', with bright white daisy flowers, the reverse of which is a pearly blue-grey, which have vivid metallic blue centres. To spill over the rocks on the far side, we planted the low-growing *Euphorbia myrsinites*, which sends out snaking growths of fleshy, evergreen blue-green leaves. It has greeny-yellow flowers in spring, before the lavender or the pinks are in flower.

On the other side we planted Spanish broom, *Genista hispanica*, with fine bright green spines rather than proper leaves, and masses of vivid yellow pea-flowers in spring; the ice plant, *Sedum spectabile* 'Brilliant', .which has fleshy pale green leaves and flat heads of deep pink flowers in late summer, long after the broom's flowers have gone, and salvia, *S. guaranitica*, with deep purple flowers in late summer.

Once we'd finished planting, we gave all the plants a thorough watering. Although they will all cope splendidly with hot dry conditions once they're established, it makes sense to get them off to the best possible start by giving them as much help as possible. We wanted to cover the soil with a mulch, partly to help retain what moisture there is in the soil, partly to make life more difficult for the bindweed and partly because it would set the plants off beautifully. Since we had used the rocks top and bottom, some sort of hard material, rather than something soft like bark, seemed an obvious choice, but something like pea gravel, which is round and smooth, wouldn't be practical since it would simply keep rolling down the slope. In the end we settled for coarse limestone chippings –

limestone because that's what the rocks are, and so it would all blend in, and chippings because they are irregular, rough shapes, which would lock together and not roll down the slope as gravel would. When we went back two months later the area was looking very soft and pretty, with the blue caryopteris in full flower, and the osteospermums and dianthus still flowering vigorously. Although it was the very end of August, the *Sedum* and the *Salvia guaranitica* were still to bloom, so the area would have a very long season of interest.

PLANTS

Trees

Mount Etna broom (*Genista aetnensis*) A native of Sicily - hence its name - and very happy in these conditions, this is either a large spindly shrub or a small graceful tree depending on your point of view. It is a mass of bright golden pea-flowers in early summer, but its foliage is very sparse. It hates being pruned, so if you plant it, allow it the space it needs.
▷ *Approx. height and spread after 5 years: 2.5 × 2.5m (8 × 8ft). After 10 years + : 4.5m × 4.5m (14ft 6in × 14ft 6in).*

Climbers

Pineapple broom (*Cytisus battandieri*)
See page 50.

Passionflower (*Passiflora*) Given a warm, sheltered wall or fence, this will produce a succession of its large, intriguing flowers that are meant to symbolize the Crucifixion, and which give the plant its common name. The individual flowers are not long-lived, but so many of them are produced between June and September that it doesn't matter. In mild areas it is almost evergreen but a really hard frost will cut the growth to the ground. If it gets out of hand, or straggly, you

can hack it back to the ground in early spring, and it will produce fresh new growth. In colder areas, protecting the roots in winter with straw or bracken should ensure its survival.
▷ *Approx. height and spread (in mild areas): 4 × 3m (13 × 10ft).*

Shrubs

Barberry (*Berberis thunbergii*) The purple-, red- and pink-leafed forms need full sun to give of their best. Apart from striking foliage, they also have flowers in spring, berries in autumn and, in most cases, lovely autumn colour. There are several different shapes to choose from. One of the best stiff, upright varieties is *B.t.* 'Helmond Pillar' with deep purple leaves, while for something tall but with gracefully arching branches look for the brilliant wine-red *B.t.* 'Red Chief'. For a low, semi-spreading shrub, *B.t.* 'Dart's Red Lady', with its deep purple leaves that turn a vivid fiery red in autumn, is hard to beat, while the little bun-shaped *B.t.* 'Bagatelle' which reaches no more than 30cm (1ft) in height, is ideal in a group for the front of a border.
▷ *Approx. height and spread after 5 years: 1m × 60cm (3 × 2ft). After 10 years: 1.8 × 1.5m (5ft 6in × 5ft).*

***Brachyglottis* (formerly *Senecio*) 'Sunshine'** An attractive grey-leaved foliage shrub which has acid-yellow daisy flowers in midsummer. If the colour is not to your taste, snip off the flower buds when they appear. The plant can be cut back hard in spring to prevent it becoming woody and sprawling.
▷ *Approx. height and spread after 5 years: 80 × 80cm (2ft 6in × 2ft 6in) After 10 years: 1 × 1m (3 × 3ft).*

Butterfly bush (*Buddleia davidii*) A shrub that grows wild on derelict sites or out of the cracks of walls can clearly cope with very thin, poor, soil, though it will be more vigorous in richer, moister soil. There are many excellent named varieties of this shrub, which acts like a magnet for butterflies, with flowers in a range of colours from white to almost black (*B.d.* 'Black Knight') but where space is limited, smaller growing varieties like *B.d.*

'Nanho Alba' and 'Nanho Purple' are a good choice. Two lovely varieties well worth considering are *B. fallowiana* 'Alba', which has sweetly scented pure white flowers with an orange eye, and foliage that's silver-white when young, fading to very pale grey, and *B.x.* 'Lochinch', with lavender-blue flowers, again with an orange eye, and similar silvery-grey foliage. All these buddleias benefit from being cut back hard every year or two, otherwise they become straggly and produce smaller flowers. It also keeps them small. *Buddleia alternifolia* is another excellent shrub for these conditions, with a graceful arching habit and slender clusters of scented mauve flowers in early summer. One-third of the old wood should be cut out after flowering

A hot colour for a hot place. This helianthemum is appropriately named 'Fire Dragon', but this excellent plant for these conditions also comes in many other colours.

each year. It can be trained as a small weeping tree.
▷ *Approx. height and spread after 10 years (if unpruned): 2-3.5 × 2-3.5m (6-12ft).*

Blue spiraea (*Caryopteris incana*, still sometimes sold as *C. × clandonensis*) This low-growing shrub has green-grey foliage and clusters of pale violet-blue flowers in late summer/early autumn. All its shoots should be cut back to near ground level in mid-spring, and for that reason it

never grows too large. Good varieties to look out for are *C.i.* 'Heavenly Blue' with bright blue flowers and *C.* 'Kew Blue' with darker flowers.
▷ *Approx. height and spread after 10 years: 70 × 80cm (2ft 4in × 2ft 8in).*

Hardy plumbago (*Ceratostigma willmottianum*) A very useful small shrub, producing masses of deep blue, saucer-shaped flowers from August to the first autumn frosts, followed by rusty-red seed heads. If the stems aren't cut back to the ground by a hard frost then you should prune them back in spring to stop the shrub becoming leggy and to encourage flowering.
▷ *Approx. height and spread after 10 years: 1 × 1m (3 × 3ft).*

Rock roses (*Cistus*) The single, open, paper-thin flowers - in a range of colours from white, and white attractively blotched with crimson or purple, through various shades of pink to crimson – last only a day but they are borne in such profusion throughout the summer that it doesn't matter. Many have attractive grey foliage. Only a few varieties are reliably hardy, but in these conditions, where the wood is most likely to be ripened, they stand the best chance of surviving the winter. Look out for the small, mound-forming *C. × corbariensis*, which has small pure white flowers with bright gold stamens opening from buds tinted crimson; 'Silver Pink' with, not surprisingly, silver-pink flowers born in clusters; the tall *C × cyprius*, with large white flowers blotched with crimson; and the equally tall *C. laurifolius*, which has leathery, dark bluey-green leaves and white flowers with yellow centres. They like any dry soil, including lime.
▷ *Approx. height and spread after 10 years: 80cm-2m × 80cm-2m (2ft 6in-6ft × 2ft 6in-6ft).*

Convolvulus cneorum A superb plant that has fine silver leaves with a faint silky sheen, and a succession of ivory trumpets emerging from long, tightly rolled rose-pink buds. In these conditions it is pretty hardy but, as belt and braces, it's probably worth giving it some winter protection during its first year.
▷ *Approx. height and spread after 10 years: 50 × 80cm (1ft 8in × 2ft 8in).*

Cabbage palm (*Cordyline australis*) This shrub, which actually comes from New Zealand, gives a garden a sub-tropical, Mediterranean feel, with its spiky sword-like leaves. It's good for containers, though more vulnerable to frost there than it would be planted in the soil. In very mild areas, it can eventually become a small tree.
▷ *Approx. height and spread after 10 years: 2 × 2m (6ft 6in × 6ft 6in).*

Broom (*Cytisus*) Although most people think of them as having yellow flowers, in fact these free-flowering shrubs come in a range of colours from cream through pink and mauve to rich red and maroon. Among the excellent low-growing varieties, look for *C. kewensis*, with masses of cream flowers in May, *C. × beanii*, with rich yellow flowers at the same time, and *C. purpureus*, with lovely soft mauve-pink flowers. Among the taller varieties, look for *C. scoparius* 'Lena', which has superb ruby-red and pale yellow flowers, and the much taller *C. praecox* 'Allgold', which is a blaze of golden-yellow flowers in spring. They are not particularly long-lived, so make good shrubs for filling-in a newly planted garden while the permanent shrubs get established.
▷ *Approx. height and spread after 10 years (low-growing: 50cm × 1.2m (1ft 8in × 4ft). Taller-growing 1.2 × 2m (4 × 6ft).*

Spanish gorse (*Genista hispanica*) This makes a small, very prickly, rounded bush, with light yellow flowers in spring, while *G. lydia*, with golden yellow flowers, has a more spreading habit, which makes it ideal for a dry bank or for tumbling over a wall.
▷ *Approx. height and spread after 10 years (G. hispanica): 60cm × 1m (2 × 3ft 3in). G. lydia: 60cm × 2m (2 × 6ft 6in).*

Halimium This low, spreading, evergreen shrub has grey-green leaves and small yellow flowers, sometimes with a central red blotch, in early summer. It needs some shelter in cold areas.
▷ *Approx. height and spread after 10 years: 50cm × 1m (1ft 8in × 3ft 3in).*

Hebe These natives of New Zealand stand their best chance of survival in these conditions. Some of the smaller hebes are worth growing for their foliage alone – the ground-covering, blue-grey *H. pinguifolia* 'Pagei', for example, the very striking *H. pimeleoides* 'Quicksilver' with pale silver leaves

and almost black stems, and the mound-forming *H. albicans* 'Red Edge', with densely packed, small, elliptical grey-green leaves with – you guessed – a red edge. They all have stubby spikes of white flowers from early summer onwards, won't reach much more than 50cm × 1m (1ft 8in × 3ft) in 10 years, and are the hardiest of their family. Of the larger hebes, 'Midsummer Beauty', *H. franciscana* 'Blue Gem' and 'Autumn Glory', which all have mauve or lavender-blue flowers at various times throughout the summer, and the pink-flowered 'Great Orme', are not totally hardy but all so good that it's worth taking the risk.
▷ *Approx. height and spread after 10 years: 1.5 × 1.5m (5 × 5ft).*

Rock roses (*Helianthemum*) Although they are related to the much taller growing cistuses, these are ground-hugging plants, many with grey foliage, which have white, pink, red, orange or yellow flowers throughout the summer. Trimming them with shears after flowering stops them becoming straggly. There are many good varieties and new ones becoming available all the time, but of the old reliables try the tawny orange-gold 'Ben Nevis', the double red 'Mrs Earle' (aka 'Fireball'), the red and white 'Raspberry Ripple' and the 'Wisleys'-Pink, Primrose and White.
▷ *Approx. height and spread after 10 years: 20cm × 1m (8in × 3ft 3in).*

Lavender (*Lavandula*) An ideal shrub for this situation, with its narrow silvery foliage and spikes of strongly scented lavender-blue flowers all summer long. It's versatile, too - it can be clipped to make a low informal hedge or edging to a border, or allowed to grow into a rounded bush. Good varieties include *L. spica*, the highly fragrant Old English lavender, the dark lavender-blue 'Munstead Dwarf', and the even smaller 'Hidcote' with the most silvery foliage and the most intense blue flowers. You can also plant white- or pink-flowered lavenders – *L. angustifolia alba* or the dwarf 'Nana Alba' or 'Lodden Pink'. Fashionable now is French lavender, *L. stoechas* 'Pendunculus' or 'Papillon', which has several wavy petals like helicopter rotors on top of the densely packed lavender flowerhead. There is also a white version.
▷ *Approx. height and spread after 10 years: 30-80cm × 30-80cm (1-2ft 7in × 1-2ft 7in).*

Russian sage (*Perovskia*) This plant will grow into a tall spire of very thin stems which are so silvery they are almost white, and which are covered in spikes of lavender-blue flowers in late summer. The best form is one called 'Blue Spire'. It should be cut back hard each spring (if the frost doesn't do it for you because it isn't reliably hardy everywhere) to encourage really silvery new stems, so it never outgrows the space allowed for it.
▷ *Approx. height and spread (in one season): 90 × 60cm (3 × 2ft).*

Jerusalem sage (*Phlomis fruticosa*) It's a very striking, architectural plant with long, slightly wavy leaves not unlike sage in texture and colour, and whorls of pale yellow flowers in midsummer. The young foliage is the most attractive, so it needs to be pruned back in spring. Less easy to find and slightly less hardy, but certainly worth the effort and the risk, is *P. italica*, which has pale, pinky-mauve flowers.
▷ *Approx. height and spread after 10 years: 1 × 1.2m (3 × 4ft).*

New Zealand flax (*Phormium tenax*) A dramatic, spiky, architectural foliage shrub with a number of particularly attractive forms. Hybrids of *P. cookianum*, like 'Cream Delight' which has olive-green leaves with a central cream band, are hardier than most of the *P. tenax* hybrids, but if you're going to get away with them anywhere, these are the best possible conditions. *P.t.* 'Yellow Wave' has a central yellow band, 'Maori Sunrise' and 'Dazzler' both have red-purple leaves with rose-pink and bronze veining, and 'Purpureum' has stiff, broad, bronze-purple leaves. Some varieties do produce flower spikes, but not for some years. They will eventually form surprisingly substantial plants so allow plenty of room. In hard winters, it's worth protecting the centre of the plant from frost with bracken or straw, or by tying the leaves together and covering them with sacking.
▷ *Approx. height and spread after 10 years: 1.2 × 1.5m (4 × 5ft).*

Rosemary (*Rosmarinus officinalis*) With its spiky dark green leaves, and blue flowers in late spring, it makes a good background shrub for the middle of a dry border. Good varieties include

This predominantly silver, yellow and purple border shows clearly how effective it can be to restrict yourself to just a few colours. Planted in among sun-loving ornamental plants like Stachys byzantina, Anaphalis triplinervis, violas, Santolina incana, *there are lots of Mediterranean herbs as well – carpets of thyme, purple sage, feathery fennel and tarragon, helping to make it a fragrant border as well.*

the more compact and hardier 'Jessup's Upright', the smaller 'Beneden Blue' and the even smaller 'Severn Sea', which has brilliant blue flowers and reaches about one-third the average height and spread. It will survive all but the hardest winters, when temperatures stay below freezing for weeks, but it is so easy to grow from cuttings that it's worth taking a few in midsummer, just in case.
▷ *Approx. height and spread after 10 years: 1.2 × 1.5m (4 × 5ft).*

Cotton lavender (Santolina chamaecyparissus)
This is grown for its lovely delicate silvery foliage, and you can ensure plenty for new growth by pruning hard in spring, and snipping off the flower

buds when they appear. The flowers are a brassy yellow, and since they also spoil the shrub's attractive neat bun shape, they are no great loss. *S. neapolitana* 'Sulphurea' has grey-green leaves and deep cream flowers. There is also a green variety, *S. virens*, which has bright green thread-like foliage - very valuable in providing a contrast to the greys in a dry garden.
▷ *Approx. height and spread after 10 years: 50cm × 1m (1ft 6in × 3ft).*

Spanish broom (Spartium) Like other brooms, this one thrives in dry conditions and produces masses of bright yellow pea-flowers in mid-summer. Its way of coping with drought is to

dispense with leaves altogether and have lots of very fine bright green spines instead. It dislikes being pruned back into old wood so, if you need to keep its size in check, start pruning it early in its life and prune only the current season's growth.
▷ *Approx. height and spread after 10 years: 3 × 2m (10 × 6ft).*

Germander (*Teucrium fruticans*) In a hot dry, sheltered spot, this is a very attractive shrub, with its arching branches of small oval silver leaves, and clusters of small powder-blue flowers throughout the summer. It really doesn't like the cold and wet, so you may lose it in a really bad winter, but it's such a lovely shrub that I think it's well worth the gamble. Cut the stems back by about two-thirds each spring to get fresh new silver foliage.
▷ *Approx. height and spread after 10 years: 1.5 × 1.5m (5 × 5ft).*

Yucca These come originally from Mexico and certainly look as if they belong growing next to cacti in a sun-baked desert, though in fact they'll grow happily in British gardens, gives full sun and a dry soil. They are slow-growing, and usually quite slow to produce flowers, but they are well worth waiting for since they are spikes up to 2m (6ft) high of huge creamy bells, like lily-of-the-valley. Good varieties include *Y. filamentosa* and its variegated forms and *Y. gloriosa*, though its leaves are so spiky that it's best not planted where children are likely to run around.
▷ *Approx. height and spread after 10 years: 2 × 2m (6ft 6in × 6ft 6in).*

Herbaceous plants

Bear's breeches (*Acanthus mollis*) A tall, striking plant, with spires of curious purple-hooded, white-rimmed flowers all summer and very jagged foliage. *A. spinosus* has similar flowers and even more finely cut, positively prickly leaves, while *A. spinosissimus* has leaves so finely cut that they are positively skeletal.
▷ *Height and spread: 1.2m × 70cm (4ft × 2ft 3in).*

Yarrow (*Achillea*) Many members of this family, both small and large, are ideal for these conditions. Among the dwarf varieties, 'King Edward' with ferny green-grey foliage and primrose-yellow flowers is lovely. Among the tall varieties, both *A.* 'Moonbeam' and *A. filipendulina* 'Gold Plate', with greyish foliage and flat heads of pale yellow and bright yellow flowers respectively, are good, as is *A. millefolium* 'Cerise Queen' with flat heads of intense cerise pink. Quite different is *A. ptarmica* 'The Pearl' which has pure white double, button flowers. All flower in midsummer.
▷ *Height and spread: 10-75 × 40-50cm (4in-2ft 6in × 16-18in).*

African lily (*Agapanthus*) A dramatic plant with rounded heads of blue or white flowers on long bare stems from midsummer to autumn, rising above clumps of strap-like leaves. Good varieties include *A. campanulatus* 'Albus', *A.c.* 'Isis', the darkest blue, and 'Headbourne Hybrids' in various shades of blue. Good in pots.
▷ *Height and spread: 1m × 70cm (3ft × 2ft 3in).*

Alyssum saxatile This is the acid-yellow flowering plant you often see sprawling over a sunny wall in late spring/early summer, battling with bright purple aubrieta. It has some subtler relatives with grey-green foliage, like 'Citrinum' which has cool lemon flowers and 'Dudley Neville' with soft, apricot-yellow flowers. There's also a variegated form of 'Dudley Neville'.
▷ *Height and spread: 25 × 25cm (9 × 9in).*

Ox-eye chamomile (*Anthemis tinctoria*) The variety 'E. C. Buxton', with its ferny green leaves, and masses of creamy-yellow daisies carried throughout the summer, always attracts attention wherever it's planted, and deservedly because it is a superb plant for these conditions. The taller 'Wargrave Variety' with cool lemon yellow flowers is also first-class.
▷ *Height and spread: 50 × 30cm (1ft 6in × 1ft).*

Artemisia These are superb silver foliage plants for this situation. One of the tallest and hardiest is 'Lambrook Silver' with very fine, thread-like foliage and small bobbly grey flowers, while 'Powis Castle' is slightly smaller with the same fine silver foliage and no flowers worthy of the name. They keep their leaves all year, but look pretty scruffy by the spring, so it's a good idea to prune them

hard then to encourage fresh new growth. *A. ludoviciana* 'Silver Queen' has larger, deeply divided, silvery-white leaves. The smallest of all, *A. schmidtiana*, makes low mounds of silver thread-like foliage. There is a new form that's caused a bit of a stir, provisionally called *A. lactiflora* 'Guizho', which has dark, smoky green, finely cut leaves and creamy-white flowers. Call me old-fashioned, but a dark green artemisia belongs with red delphiniums and blue roses!
▷ *Height and spread: 10-90cm × 30-60cm (4in-3ft × 1-2ft).*

Ballota pseudodictamnus This plant produces mauve flowers in midsummer, but some people think they spoil the effect of the long curving stems of felty, silver-white round leaves and so cut them off. It will die back naturally in all but the mildest winters, and if it doesn't, prune it back in spring to prevent it becoming straggly and encourage it to produce the most silvery new leaves.
▷ *Height and spread: 50 × 60cm (1ft 8in × 2ft).*

Coreopsis This drought-lover has very finely divided ferny green foliage, and masses of yellow daisy flowers from midsummer to autumn. *C. verticillata* 'Grandiflora' has rich gold daisies, while the newer *C.v.* 'Moonbeam' with pale creamy yellow flowers is a real 'must have' – people see it and want it.
▷ *Height and spread: 40 × 30cm (1ft 4in × 1ft).*

Crocosmia These add a blaze of colour from midsummer onwards and there are new hybrids appearing now in a range of shades from pale yellow to fiery red. Among the best of old and new are the flame-red 'Lucifer', the deep, burnt-orange 'Emberglow' and, for something altogether softer and more subtle, the pale apricot-yellow 'Solfatare', with its bronze-green leaves.
▷ *Height and spread: 70 × 40cm (2ft 3in × 1ft 4in).*

Pinks (*Dianthus*) There are many different forms – Chinese pinks, Cheddar pinks, maiden pinks, border pinks or carnations – but they all love hot, dry, alkaline soils. Of the dwarf varieties, look for the mat-forming *D. deltoides* 'Flashing Light' (salmon-red flowers), 'Samos' (carmine) and 'Brighteyes' (red with a white eye), and

hybrids like 'Little Jock', 'Nyewoods Cream' and 'Pike's Pink'. Of the taller varieties, look for longer-flowering, modern hybrids – the *allwoodii* pinks like the rose-pink 'Doris' for example, or the Devon pinks – 'Devon Glow', 'Devon Blush' and 'Devon Cream', – which flower right through the summer.
▷ *Height and spread: 10-30cm × 25-75cm (4in-1ft × 9in-2ft 6in).*

Globe thistle (*Echinops ritro*) A striking plant for the back of a border, with prickly silver-green foliage, and steel-blue, round, thistle-flowers in late summer. *E. humilis* 'Taplow Blue' is similar but has paler blue thistle-flowers.
▷ *Height and spread: 1.2m × 70cm (4ft × 2ft 3in).*

Sea holly (*Eryngium*) Another plant that looks like a thistle. *E. variifolium* has dramatic, almost skeletal, spiky leaves, marbled with white and blue thistle-head flowers, but some varieties aren't all prickly to touch. *E. oliverianum* has deeply cut green leaves, but its stems and flower heads are all deep blue, while the taller *E. tripartitum* has stems and flowers of the most vivid metallic blue. 'Miss Willmott's Ghost' (*E. giganteum*) - named after the redoubtable Victorian gardener who was said to scatter its seed secretly whenever she visited other people's gardens – has silvery-green flowers surrounded by metallic silver bracts, like ruffles. It is in fact biennial, but seeds itself so freely that once you've got it, you are likely to be haunted by it for ever. It flowers in midsummer.
▷ *Height and spread: 70 × 40cm (2ft 3in × 1ft 4in).*

Spurge (*Euphorbia*) An invaluable family with members suitable for many problem places. For these conditions, look for the prostrate *E. myrsinites* with its low-growing, spreading stems, covered in waxy-blue leaves, at the end of which are large heads of yellow-green flowers. The larger *E. polychroma* has heads of sulphur-yellow flowers in early summer, while the most spectacular is *E. wulfenii*, which is a large, dramatic, clump-forming plant with tall stems of blue-grey evergreen leaves topped by large heads of sulphur-yellow flowers in late spring/early summer.
▷ *Height and spread: 15cm-1.1m × 30-70cm (6in-4ft × 1ft-2ft 3in).*

Baby's breath (*Gypsophila*) 'Gyp' as flower-sellers call it, produces sprays of tiny white flowers which add a soft misty effect to a bouquet and, indeed, to a border. Its botanical name means 'chalk lover' so it will obviously thrive on chalky soil. The best white form is 'Bristol White' and there's a very pretty pink one, called 'Rosy Veil'. The dwarf gypsophilas, like *G. repens* 'Dorothy Teacher', will stand very dry conditions, like the crevices of walls. They flower from midsummer to early autumn.
▷ *Height and spread: 90 × 70cm (3ft × 2ft 3in).*

Candytuft (*Iberis saxatilis*) This is invaluable in the dry sunny border not only for its chalk-white flowers in spring, but for its spreading mats of evergreen dark green foliage, a very useful contrast to silver plants.
▷ *Height and spread: 8 × 60cm (3in × 2ft).*

Algerian iris (*Iris unguicularis* or *I. stylosa*) A rare iris in that it flowers in winter, this has lovely lavender-blue flowers which are also scented – they smell rather of honeysuckle – which is a bonus at this time of year. It grows well in poor stony soil, perhaps at the foot of a sunbaked wall. 'Mary Barnard' has richer purple flowers while 'Walter Butt' has the palest ice-blue flowers. They look lovely grown together.
▷ *Height and spread: 30 × 20cm (1ft × 8in).*

Rose campion (*Lychnis coronaria*) The downy grey leaves are a perfect foil for branching heads of small intense magenta-pink flowers all summer long. There is also a much cooler, more elegant white form. They seed themselves freely unless they are regularly dead-headed.
▷ *Height and spread 60 × 40cm (2ft × 1ft 4in).*

Catmint (*Nepeta mussinii* or × *faassenii*) This plant, which gets its common name from the fact that cats love rolling in it, makes good weed-suppressing clumps of grey-green foliage, with lavender-blue flowers from late spring through to the autumn. *N.m.* 'Six Hills Giant' is almost twice the size, likely to be hardier in colder areas, and will tolerate a bit more moisture in the soil.
▷ *Height and spread: 30-60 × 30-60cm (1-2 × 1-2ft).*

Evening primrose (*Oenothera missouriensis*) A good choice for the front of a border, producing-mats of narrow pointed leaves, above which are carried masses of large trumpet-shaped, lemon flowers from midsummer onwards. They are supposed to open only in the evenings, but they certainly do sometimes open in the daytime.
▷ *Height and spread: 25 × 45cm (9 × 18in).*

Osteospermum These have become increasingly popular in the last few years with many excellent hybrids now available although it has to be said most are not hardy, so be prepared to offer them winter protection or take cuttings as an insurance policy. Look for the sprawling *O. ecklonii prostrata* with white flowers and a vivid blue eye (one of the hardiest, incidentally); 'Whirlygig', which has white waisted petals and a brilliant electric-blue eye, and its pink relation 'Pink Whirls'; 'Silver Sparkler' with the same coloured flowers as 'Whirlygig' but green and white variegated leaves; and 'Buttermilk' with lovely soft yellow flowers. There are two very recent introductions, 'Sunny Girl' with pink flowers and 'Sunny Boy' with white flowers with a blue tinge – which are both said to be hardy, but it's too soon to say for certain. You may find that the flowers close in the later part of the afternoon whether the sun is shining or not. That's because their flowering time is controlled by day length.
▷ *Approx. height and spread: 30-60 × 30-60cm (1-2 × 1-2ft).*

Penstemon Also enjoying an upswing in popularity because of their long flowering season, and there are many excellent varieties of these available. Their spikes of foxglove-like flowers come in a range of sizes – as a rule, the smaller the flowers the hardier they are – and colours from white through a whole range of pinks and mauves to bright and deep red. Some varieties are hardy and the neat clumps of foliage will usually survive the winter in these conditions, but in colder areas or when severe frost is forecast, it's worth covering them with a mulch.
▷ *Height and spread: 60-75 × 60cm (2-2ft 6in × 2ft).*

Sage (*Salvia officinalis*) Another herb that's invaluable for this situation. Apart from the ordinary culinary form with its sage-green leaves, and purple-blue flowers in midsummer, there's a variegated cream-and gold-leafed form, *S.o.* 'Icterina', the purple-leafed form, 'Purpurascans', and the smaller 'Tricolor', variegated in white, pink and purple. The latter two need some winter protection in colder areas. Most of the non-culinary perennial sages, all of which flower in mid to late summer, will do well here, too. Among the best are *S. patens*, with vivid mid-blue flowers. *S. x superba* (also known as *S. nemorosa*) with tall spikes of intense purple-blue flowers, or the similar but shorter *S.n.* 'East Friesland', which are all widely available. Less well known but just as lovely is *S. guaranitica* with deep purple flowers. The one exception is the lovely *S. uliginosa*, whose common name 'bog sage' gives a clue to its preferred conditions.

▷ *Height and spread: 40-90 × 40-60cm (1ft 4in-3 × 1ft 4in-2ft).*

Bouncing bette (*Saponaria ocymoides*) A vigorous ground-coverer covered in bright pink campion flowers in early summer, which is ideal for a dry sunny bank. It's sometimes sold as a rock plant but its vigour means it soon smothers other plants in the rock garden.

▷ *Height and spread: 15 × 75cm (6in × 2ft 6in).*

Ice plant (*Sedum spectabile*) Attractive for most of the year, with its low rosettes of fleshy, water-retaining pale blue-green leaves in spring, which grow through the summer into a mound of foliage. Then the flower stalks appear, carrying large flat heads of pale green buds which turn slowly from rose pink through salmon until they finally turn bronze in late autumn. You can leave the flower heads on through the winter – not only are they

*Lots of silver and blue used to great effect in this dry sunny border in a Dorset garden – *Nepeta × faassenii* with its small grey leaves and blue flowers, the filigree silver foliage of *Artemisia 'Powis Castle', the stems of *Perovskia atriplicifolia* which are so silver they are almost white, some frilly blue scabious flowers and clumps of the spiky steel blue evergreen grass *Helictotrichon sempervirens.*

attractive, but they help protect the new foliage coming through beneath. Butterflies and bees love it. 'Autumn Joy' is widely available; the slightly smaller 'Brilliant' with pinker flowers is a bit more difficult to find, but worth the trouble.
▷ *Height and spread: 50-60 × 50cm (2ft × 1ft 8in).*

Lamb's lugs (Stachys byzantina, still sold sometimes as S. lanata or olympica) Another excellent grey-leafed plant whose flowers are, with some exceptions, rather a disadvantage. The form 'Sheila McQueen' (sometimes sold as 'Cotton Boll') has attractive silvery flower spikes in midsummer, much prized by flower arrangers, while 'Silver Carpet' is non-flowering, making an excellent carpeter for the front of a border. 'Primrose Heron' is a fine, yellow-leafed variety, which was very fashionable among smart gardeners a few years ago.
▷ *Height and spread: 12-30 × 40cms (5in-1ft × 1ft 4in).*

Thyme (Thymus) Another Mediterranean plant that's perfect for a hot, dry spot, and there are any number of good ones to choose from, with flowers ranging from white through pink to mauve. Among the more upright bushy ones look out for 'Silver Queen', with variegated green and silver leaves, and *T. vulgaris* 'Golden King', while among the mat-forming ones, the dark green and gold variegated 'Doone Valley', the bright gold 'Golden Carpet' and the grey-leafed, pink-flowered *T. serpyllum* 'Pink Chintz' are widely available and good. A superb plant for attracting bees.
▷ *Height and spread: 5-30 × 30cm (2in-1ft × 1ft).*

Mullein (Verbascum) A stately plant for the back of a border and invaluable for adding almost instant height to a new border. Apart from the giant *V. olympicum*, with its huge woolly grey-white leaves and stems which can reach 2.8m (9ft), topped with clusters of yellow flowers, there are the smaller hybrids like the primrose-yellow 'Gainsborough', the rose-pink 'Pink Domino' and the white 'Mont Blanc'.
▷ *Height and spread: 1.1-2.8m × 40cm-1m (3ft 6in-9ft × 1ft 4in-3ft).*

Californian fuchsia (Zauschneria californica) As you would expect, this has flowers in late summer/autumn like a fuchsia's, except they are vivid scarlet. 'Glasnevin' has small, grey-green leaves, while the smaller and even tougher *Z.c. cana* (or *microphylla*) has grey leaves.
▷ *Height and spread: 30-40 × 45cm (12-15 × 18in).*

Grasses

Blue fescue (Festuca glauca 'Silver Sea') A compact powder-blue grass that revels in hot dry conditions. An ideal plant to provide a 'vertical' amid horizontal, mat-forming plants. *F. punctoria* is lower-growing, even tougher and copes with very hot dry conditions.
▷ *Height and spread: 15-25 × 20cm (6-10 × 8in).*

Avena (Helictotrichon sempervirens) Another blue grass, this has arching clumps of vivid grey-blue foliage, up to 45cm (18in) high, with plumes of silver-grey flowers up to 1.2m (4ft) tall in midsummer.
▷ *Height and spread: 1.2m × 60cm (4 × 2ft).*

Stipa gigantea A magnificent grass, throwing up clouds of pale gold flowers on stems over 2m (6ft) tall all summer long. An excellent way of introducing height into a new border.
▷ *Height and spread (of the leaves): 45cm × 1m (18in × 3ft 3in).*

Annuals

While most annuals like full sun, most of them also like moisture, so there isn't a huge selection that will grow well in these conditions. But among those that will, there are some spectacular ones.

Half hardy annuals

Gazanias In fact in their native habitat these are perennials, but rarely survive the winter here. They have large daisy flowers in yellow, orange, pink and rusty red, some of them single colours, many of them bi-colours. The flowers open only in bright sunshine. Look for G. 'Sundance'.
▷ *Height: 30 × 30cm (12 × 12in).*

Livingstone daisies (Mesembryanthemum) These daisy-like flowers also open only in bright sunshine, but they are produced in such

numbers that when they do open, they cover the fleshy, succulent foliage of the plant entirely. They come in glowing shades of pink, carmine, salmon, apricot and gold. You can buy them mixed or, if you prefer a single colour, look for the lovely yellow 'Lunette' (sometimes sold as 'Yellow Ice'), with a deep, rust-red eye.
▷ *Height and spread: 15 × 30cm (6 × 12in).*

Portulaca Another useful succulent with flowers in a similar range of 'hot' colours, only they are cup-shaped and stay open in dull weather.
▷ *Height and spread: 20 × 15cm (8 × 6in).*

Hardy annuals

These should be sown directly into the soil where they are to flower.

Star of the veldt (Dimorphotheca) Its flowers actually close in dull, wet weather – hence the plant's other common name, rain daisy. Among the best varieties to try are the Aurantica hybrids, in shades of white, lemon, gold, orange and salmon, or 'Glistening White', whose flowers are described perfectly by their name.
▷ *Height: 25-30 × 20cm (9in-1ft × 8in).*

Californian poppy (Eschscholzia) On hot, dry soils this will give you a dazzling display of red, orange, gold and even cream flowers. Good varieties include 'Monarch Art Shades' with semi-double flowers and 'Ballerina' with fluted, double and semi-double flowers.
▷ *Height: 25 × 15cm (10 × 6in).*

Nasturtiums (Tropaeolum) These are invaluable in this situation – in fact they flower more freely in poor thin soils than they do in richer, moister ones where their strength goes into producing foliage (see page 155).

Bulbs

Though many of the traditional spring-flowering bulbs don't enjoy being baked in summer, some of the more spectacular bulbs enjoy hot dry conditions.

Ornamental onions (Alliums) See page 155.

Peruvian lilies (Alstroemeria) With their long stems of small pink, orange and peach flowers, marked with distinct brown dashes, the Ligtu hybrids and the newer 'Princess' range are becoming increasingly popular as florists' flowers, and are worth trying in a dry, sunny spot, if you enrich the soil first and mulch them with more of the same once they're planted. They die back once flowering is over in late summer, and will need protection in winter.
▷ *Height: 75cm (2ft 6in).*

Nerines (Nerine bowdenii) A valuable, autumn-flowering bulb for a sunny, sheltered spot (the foot of a south-facing wall is ideal) in very poor soil, it carries a head of bright pink flowers with curly petals on a slender stem. The strap-like leaves follow the flowers, but die down in early summer. 'Mark Fenwick' is the most vigorous form.
▷ *Height: 50cm (1ft 8in).*

Tulips In the wild they grow mainly on sunbaked, rocky hillsides in the Balkans and Central Asia and so do very well in these conditions. Species tulips and the small hybrids are ideal for small gardens. For one thing they are more in scale, less likely to get flattened by hurricane-force April showers and, unlike most tall garden tulips, they can be left in the soil from one year to the next. Look for *T. kaufmanniana, greigii* or *fosteriana* which flower early and have attractive variegated leaves in many cases, as well as lovely flowers. Of the *kaufmanniana*, 'Heart's Delight', blush-white with carmine outside, 'Showwinner', a glowing cardinal red, and the creamy white 'Concerto' are all outstanding. Of the *greigii*, look for the deep rose 'Oratorio', the salmon-orange 'Toronto' with two or three flowers on each stem, and the vivid red 'Red Riding Hood'. Also lovely are *T. tarda*, whose butter-yellow flowers with a white edging open almost flat, the lovely, rounded, apricot-yellow *T. batalinii* 'Bright Gem', *T. saxatilis (bakerii)* with soft lilac flowers, and a true miniature, *T. linofolia*, with brilliant scarlet flowers on stems only 10-12cm (4-5in) high. This is lovely grown in window boxes, pots, or even between the slabs on a patio.
▷ *Height: 15-25cm (6-10in).*

BOGGY PLACES

As with so many 'problem' areas in the garden, a patch of boggy soil is often an opportunity because there are so many wonderful bog plants that need plenty of moisture to thrive: huge-leafed rodgersias, the exquisite candelabra primulas, hostas, many elegant irises, dramatic perennial lobelias, some of the small willows – the list goes on and on.

But again, it is possible to have too much of a good thing, and a large area of boggy soil in a small garden really is a problem. For a start, it is virtually impossible to have a decent lawn – unless you love moss and don't ever want to sit, lie, stand or play on it, and none of the usual alternatives are available either. You can't hard-landscape it because the paving or bricks would just sink into the morass, and ground cover isn't really a starter. A bog garden taking up most of your plot isn't exactly practical.

First of all, you need to look at the underlying causes of the boggy soil, and sometimes 'underlying' causes are exactly what they are. If the problem is on a lawn in a mature garden, you might find that the soil just below the surface is compacted, and so the water can't drain away. In that case, it's usually a relatively simple job to put it right. You need to go over it with a hollow-tined fork, which removes small cores of soil about 3in long, or, if it's only a small lawn, spike it every few inches with an ordinary garden fork, and then brush sharp sand (*not* builder's sand) into the

A planting of waterlilies, irises, astilbes and yellow-flowered trollius is dominated in early summer by the vivid flowers of Mimulus *'Wisley Red'.*

holes. To make sure the problems don't recur, do try and keep off the lawn when it's wet, since feet will compact wet soil. Try and keep the children off it, too, and if you need to take a wheelbarrow across it when it's wet, lay a path of scaffolding planks or use one of the new lightweight roll-up 'paths'. That might seem like a making a meal of it, but it's quicker to do that than have to cope with a waterlogged lawn again. Don't forget that worms are gardeners' allies and particularly so in this situation – their burrowing creates a succession of small drainage channels in the soil – so don't use a worm killer, not, of course, that you would anyway...

If you have problems with a waterlogged lawn in a new house, they are almost certainly due to the fact that you have only a few inches of top soil over a 'hard pan' (a layer of soil compacted into near-concrete hardness by the contractors' vehicles going backwards and forwards over the site while the house was being built) through which it is impossible for the water to drain away. If your house is built on land that was used for agriculture or market gardening, you might find the problem lies even deeper – about 25–30cm below the surface, the depth to which the farmer ploughed or rotovated the soil for many years. The answer here involves a lot more elbow grease. If you are to solve the problem permanently, the only answer is to start again. Kill off the grass and then double-dig the area – dig to two spades' depth or as deep as the hard pan allows – and then break it up with a fork, or even a pickaxe. Then reseed or returf the area, although do be sure the soil has had a chance to settle down before you do. Clay soils also often present drainage problems, but although hard work it's possible to solve them. (See page 120.)

If you have a very bad drainage problem throughout the whole garden, perhaps because the whole plot has a high water table, the answer may be to have a drainage system installed. This involves a herringbone of pipes, laid in narrow channels with gravel below and above them, under the lawn at a very slight gradient so that they carry the water away into a ditch or a specially dug soakway. You can do it yourself, but since it just won't work unless it's done properly, it might be worth getting an expert in to do it for you.

The cause of a small area of boggy ground could be a leaking drain or, if you're really unlucky, sewer under the soil. The only thing to do there is to investigate by digging down *carefully* – if you don't already have a cracked drain, you don't want one – and seeing if that's the problem. Or, if you are a sensitive soul, get someone in to do it for you. Another explanation could be that it's in the most low-lying part of the garden, into which all the water from the surrounding soil – not only in your garden but possibly from the neighbours' too – drains. One possibility there is to dig some grit into the soil to improve the drainage a little. The fact that it's low-lying could also mean it's a frost pocket (see page 99), so you need to bear that in mind when you're choosing plants and avoid those that are less than fully hardy. Or you could find that you have a natural spring beneath the soil, or even have a small stream running through the garden, which was the case with our 'problem place'. Where the geography –

and geology – of the garden is responsible for the boggy areas, the best advice is to go, literally, with the flow. If the spring or the stream runs all year you could create a pond by simply digging out a small area and planting water plants in the muddy bottom. If it tends to dry out in summer, you could create a pond using a butyl liner and underliner, which the spring would feed in winter and which could be topped up with a hose if it did dry out in summer. Easier still, you could create a bog garden, choosing plants that thrive in varying degrees of wetness from the damp to the positively sodden.

PERFECT PLANTS

Many bog plants have very dramatic leaves – think of the giant gunneras, the slightly smaller rodgersias and rheums, hostas, ligularias, lysichitons, ferns like the giant *Osmunda regalis* and the smaller but just as lovely shuttlecock fern (*Matteuccia struthiopteris*) – the effect of which is even more dramatic and beautiful when reflected in water.

The reason many of them have such large leaves is that there is always a constant supply of water to replace what they lose through their leaves, so why not? In the case of gunneras, rheums and rodgersias, though, it is worth pointing out that they need to be in a sheltered spot, out of full sun which might scorch their leaves, and certainly protected from strong winds which could reduce their fine foliage to tatters.

Bogside plants that grow in running water are often adapted to cope with the fact that nutrients are constantly leaching away. Alder, which actually grows in running water, has nodules the size of satsumas on its roots, which fix nitrogen from the air and provide nutrients for the plant that way.

Willows are also first-class plants for boggy situations and, although they will struggle a bit where it's very dry, they will also grow very happily in average soils. The reason that willows in the wild grow only where there's plenty of moisture is simple. Unlike that of most other trees, its seed is produced for just a short period in mid-summer and, unless it falls on to moist soil, it won't germinate. So the only way it can give its offspring a fighting chance of survival is to grow where moist soil can be guaranteed at the crucial time.

Some irises are also very good plants for water or boggy soils, but others actually need to have their rhizomes dry, baked by the sun, and since they all look roughly the same – broadly similar spiky leaves and broadly similar flowers – it can be a bit confusing. In fact the one thing practically all irises have in common is that they *must* have their heads in the sun. The plant needs as much sunlight as possible to build up reserves of food through its leaves and store them in its rhizome to produce next year's flowers. (That's how flowering bulbs function, of course, and in fact most irises are transitional plants – half-way between bulbs and herbaceous plants with fibrous root systems.) As a result of their various native habitats, they have all adapted to flowering early in the year, too. In the case of water irises, that's to enable them to make the most of the moisture before it dries up, and in the case of those that like it hot and dry, it means they will have flowered and in some cases their leaves will have died away before they can be scorched by the fierce midsummer sun.

As a general rule of thumb, the irises that like it hot and dry are the bearded type – they have a little 'beard' on the crest of their 'falls' (the three petals that curve downwards), and their rhizomes are fleshy and smooth and rot very easily in wet soil. Moisture-loving irises are all beardless, and have either a much hairier rhizome, or a small rhizome and a more fibrous root system, adapted to resist waterlogging.

OUR PROBLEM PLACE

Our problem place was very boggy soil on a bank between a very small stream (fed by a spring further up the hill, which runs through the end of the garden all year round), and the fence behind it, dividing the garden from the sloping field at the back. The stream itself was only about 20cm wide, and no more than 5cm deep in a gully about 25cm deep, but the lower part of the bank behind it was always boggy, partly because of the stream and partly because the water from the field drained down into it. In a gap in the fence was a young, healthy elm tree which the owners were particularly keen to keep, although it did cast quite heavy shade on one side. The banks were infested with weeds and couch grass, and although they had been dug out several times they always came back. The owners had tried some planting, but had had little success with that. A *Brachyglottis greyi* (*Senecio*, as was), which really needs dryish soil and full sun to thrive, was looking very sick indeed under the tree, and clearly not long for this world, and some newly planted ground-cover roses were still okay but they had only been in a couple of weeks and the prognosis wasn't good. The one shrub that was thriving was a viburnum, possibly *V. farreri*, though we wouldn't know for sure until it flowered.

The first thing to do was to clear the bank of weeds and couch. The most permanent solution was to use a weedkiller containing glyphosate. It becomes inactive on contact with the soil, so there was no danger of anything harmful leaching into the stream, but although the stronger, agricultural formulation of weedkillers containing glyphosate is cleared for use on waterplants like bulrushes because it does no harm to fish or any aquatic creatures, the formulation on sale to gardeners, which contains a different wetting agent, isn't. So you should take particular care when you're spraying close to water. To be safe, we covered the top of the gully with pieces of cardboard while we sprayed the weeds, and left it in place till the weedkiller had dried. Once the vegetation was dead, we cleared the bank and, to prevent weeds creeping in from under the fence again from the field behind, we sprayed the area immediately behind the fence, too – with the owners' permission, of course. If the weeds do start to creep through, then a more permanent solution would be to tack thick black polythene sheeting to the bottom of the fence, dig a narrow trench about a spade's depth beneath the fence, tuck the polythene into it to form a barrier underground and then fill in with soil. It would hardly be visible, especially once the plants have grown. It shouldn't affect the moisture in the soil on the bank either since the run-off from the field will simply penetrate the soil at a deeper level.

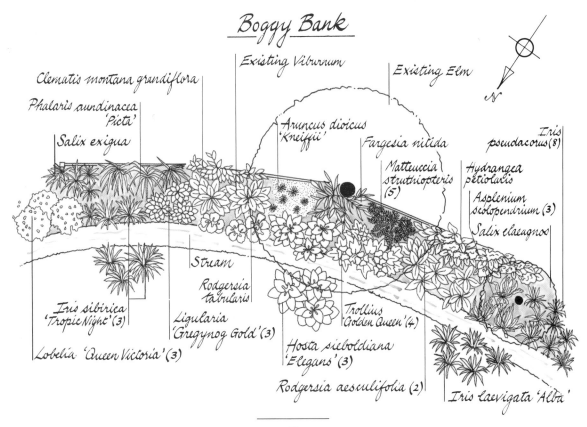

68

Before we started work, our boggy bank grew a fine crop of weeds and little else. By the end of the summer, the moisture-loving plants we'd chosen like ligularias, rodgersias, irises, and the spectacular Lobelia 'Queen Victoria' with its beetroot red leaves and startling scarlet flowers had transformed it.

We removed just a couple of the lowest branches from the elm tree to allow more light in, and then stained the new fence a subtle grey-brown shade with a plant-friendly woodstain to cover the existing rather garish orange-brown colour and to set the plants off to best effect. Then we were ready to plant.

We had three different situations to cope with: boggy shade, boggy sun (although the bank faced north, the garden was fairly open and so the area to the left of the tree got quite a bit of sun in the morning while the area to the right caught the evening sun) and the stream itself. While the soil on the bank was permanently moist with water running through it from the field behind and from the spring, it was in fact rather sandy and free-draining nature did mean that the soil lost nutrients very quickly, so we dug in plenty of bulky organic matter as we planted.

The fact that the bank sloped quite steeply meant we had a range of conditions to deal with – from moist at the top, then boggy, then muddy with shallow running water at the bottom – which meant we could grow a wide range of plants.

We started off with two climbers on the fence, one each side of the elm: a *Clematis grandiflora*, which likes moist but not water-logged soil, and a climbing hydrangea (*H. petiolaris*) which will put up with almost anything. We planted the silvery coyote willow (*Salix exigua*) at the back, a lovely graceful shrub which can be pruned back hard every year or two to keep it a reasonable size and to produce the most intensely silvery foliage. It is also an excellent background for the dramatic *Lobelia cardinalis* 'Queen Victoria', with deep beetroot-coloured leaves and vivid scarlet flowers in late summer, which we planted in front of it. Next to them are a group of ligularias – in this instance *L.* 'Gregynog Gold', a magnificent plant with huge dark green heart-shaped leaves and tall spires of orange-gold daisy-like flowers, up to 2m high. At the back against the fence we planted gardener's garters (*Phalaris arundinacea picta*), the cool green and white leaves of which also make a lovely contrast with the plants in front of it – a contrast in colour with the lobelia and in leaf shape with the rodgersias. It's true this grass can become invasive, but it's easily kept in check by chopping it back with a sharp spade, or even erecting a sub-soil barrier – just a piece of rigid plastic pushed into the soil around its rootball. In fact, the white variegations remain more vivid where its roots are confined, so that's another good reason for doing it.

Rodgersias are such good plants for boggy soil that we planted two different varieties. First, there's *R. tabularis* (now renamed *Astilboides tabularis*, but usually still sold as *Rodgersia tabularis*), which has large, round, soft green leaves with gently scalloped edges, which can grow to the size of dinner plates, and tall sprays of small white flowers in summer. Further along the bank, we planted *R. aesculifolia* – the Latin name means 'horse-chestnut leaf' and it's immediately obvious why. It has sprays of fragrant, tiny, pinkish-white flowers in midsummer. The rodgersias and the ligularias need a sheltered spot because wind can damage their large soft leaves easily.

Between the two clumps of rodgersias, we planted *Hosta sieboldiana elegans* with huge, blue-green leaves and sprays of white flowers in early summer. Technically the flowers are described as very pale lilac, but to the naked eye they look white and really gleam in the shady spot we'd given them under the elm and on the other side of the stream. Behind them, under the tree, we planted a bamboo (formerly *Arundinaria* now *Fargesia nitida*). It will grow in sun or shade and, though it won't grow as big in a shady spot, neither will its papery thin leaves curl as they would in full sun. We also planted a variety of goat's beard (*Aruncus dioicus* 'Kneiffii'), with lovely, lacy, much more finely divided leaves than its relative, and tiny white flowers in summer.

To the right of the elm, near the top of the bank we planted the lovely shuttlecock fern (*Matteucia struthiopteris*), which needs moist soil to produce its stunning, feathery, bright green fronds like shuttlecocks or ostrich feathers (another of its common names), and down near the water's edge another willow – the hoary willow (*Salix elaeagnos* or *rosmarinifolia*) this time. It gets its common name from the fact that when its young shoots and leaves first emerge they are covered in a silvery bloom, rather like a hoar frost. The shoots are dark reddish-brown underneath, and the leaves grey-green, long and slender, resembling a rosemary's. Like the coyote willow, it repays hard pruning every few years, because the young growth is the most attractive and it also keeps it compact. Below it we planted another moisture-loving fern, the smaller hart's-tongue fern (*Asplenium* or *Phyllitis scolopendrium*), which has glossy, evergreen undivided fronds.

In the stream itself, we planted irises – the common yellow flag iris (*I. pseudacorus*) and a white form of the Japanese iris (*I. laevigata* 'Alba') in the stream itself, and in the mud at the edge of the stream *Iris sibirica* 'Tropic Night' with stunning, velvety, deep blue flowers.

Just under two months later, when we went back for our final filming, the plants had settled in nicely. The vivid lobelia cardinals and the ligularias had flowered a little earlier than expected, but had been spectacular, and everything else was well-established, ready to take off next spring.

PLANTS

The following plants need permanently moist if not boggy soil to do well. Those that will actually grow in water are marked **W**. Many of the plants listed will grow in sun or part shade. As a general rule, the wetter the soil, the more sun they can tolerate. There are a few which really do need full sun or full shade and they are marked accordingly.

Trees

Most trees that will cope with heavy clay cope with moist soils, so those below are trees that will cope with boggy sites. Incidentally, poplars and large willows, classically the weeping willow, are often recommended for moist soils, and indeed they thrive in these conditions. But they are very vigorous trees and their roots do unspeakable things to drains and foundations, particularly on clay soils since a mature specimen can suck up to 100 gallons of water a day out of the soil, causing it to shrink and the foundations to move. The safe planting distance for trees like these on a clay soil (slightly less for sandy or chalky soils) is one and a half times their ultimate height, and since they can reach 25m that means they should be at least 38m away from any buildings or drains – which rules them out for all but large gardens.

Hawthorn (*Crataegus oxyacantha*) See page 90.
Mountain ash (*Sorbus aucuparia*) See page 91.

Climbers

Clematis Although clematis needs a plentiful supply of water, it doesn't like its roots being waterlogged. In a heavy, wet soil, improve the drainage in as wide an area as you can – not just the planting hole itself – before planting, by digging in grit and bulky organic matter. In lighter

The slender, elegant silvery leaves of the coyote willow, Salix exigua.

soil, dig in organic matter to improve the fertility. Try the smaller-flowered species like the spring-flowering *C. montana* or *C. alpina*, or the late-flowering virgin's bower (*C. flammula*). See page 30.

Golden hop (*Humulus lupulus* 'Aureus') A very fast-growing vigorous climber grown for its bright golden foliage. It dies down in autumn, when the dead growth needs to be cut back to about 25cm (10in) from the ground and then right back to ground level in spring if the winter frosts haven't done the job for you. It will tolerate very light shade, but in any more its golden foliage turns green.
▷ *Approx height and spread in 5 years: 3.7 × 3.7m (12 × 12ft).*

Climbing hydrangea *H. petiolaris*) This extremely accommodating self-clinging climber will cope with these soil conditions as well in anything from full sun to full shade. See page 30.

Shrubs

Snowy mespilus (*Amelanchier lamarckii*) This shrub (or small tree) is wonderful value, with masses of small white flowers in spring, at the same time as the new bronze-tinged foliage, which turns a brilliant fiery orange-red in autumn. It will grow in slightly alkaline soils, but the autumn colour is far more vivid on acid soils.
▷ *Approx. height and spread after 10 years: 5 × 5m (16 × 16ft).*

Sweet pepper bush (*Clethra alnifolia*)
See page 135.

Dogwood (*Cornus alba*) An excellent, accommodating shrub for small gardens since many varieties provide very attractive plain or variegated foliage in spring and summer, and vivid bark – scarlet or yellow – in the winter months. It's at its best in really moist soil, producing the lushest foliage then, but it will tolerate quite dry soil too, and though it does grow in full sun it is also quite happy in part shade. Good varieties include *Cornus alba* 'Elegantissima', which has beautiful pale green and white variegated foliage, and *C. a.* 'Spaethii', which has variegated gold and green leaves; both of these have brilliant red stems in winter. *C. a.* 'Westonbirt' has fresh green foliage and the brightest red stems of all. *C. stolonifera* 'Flaviramea' has soft green foliage which turns yellow in autumn, revealing butter-yellow stems – a good contrast to the red-stemmed varieties. The new *C. sanguinea* 'Winter Flame' has lovely orange-yellow autumn colour and winter stems that are gold at the base, deepening through orange to a fiery red at the tips. Its leaves are plain green. To get the best and brightest coloured bark, you need to prune the stems hard back each spring, which means that the shrub never grows bigger than the amount of growth it can make in one season. Since it flowers on two-year-old wood, hard pruning each year means you lose the flowers. If you want some flowers, then prune only half the stems hard back each year.
▷ *Approx. height and spread after 10 years (unpruned): 2.5 × 4m (8 × 13ft).*

Physocarpus opulifolius 'Luteus' or 'Dart's Gold' Another lovely golden-leafed shrub, which needs the same conditions as the golden elders to do well. 'Luteus' has clear yellow leaves, while 'Dart's Gold' has brighter golden yellow leaves and is smaller, growing to only about 1.2m (4ft) tall. As a bonus, they have rich mahogany-coloured bark in winter on growth made the previous season, so to get the best foliage and bark, prune at least some stems hard back in spring.
▷ *Approx. height and spread after 10 years (unpruned): 2.5 × 2.5m (8 × 8ft).*

Willow (*Salix*) This is the most accommodating family for these conditions, with members of all shapes and sizes, from the weeping willow (to be planted only by those with rolling acres to play with) right down to tiny, creeping varieties like *S. × boydii*, which is suitable for a rock garden or trough. Many have slender leaves which move in the gentlest breeze, and look wonderful reflected in water. Most have attractive catkins in spring, and some have brilliantly coloured bark in winter. Among the best small shrubby willows (up to about 1m 3ft in height and spread) are *S. hastata* 'Wehrhahnii', which has large silvery catkins on dark, reddish-purple stems, followed by rounded dark green leaves; *S. helvetica*, with narrow, pale yellow catkins, and grey leaves with silvery-white undersides; the woolly willow (*S. lanata*) with round, woolly grey leaves and small grey-yellow catkins; the black catkin willow (*S. melanostachys*), with dark purplish stems, and near-black catkins with brick-red anthers; *S. purpurea* 'Nana' or 'Gracilis', an elegant goblet-shaped shrub with very narrow purple-tinged dark green leaves and small, slender purple-silver catkins; and the low-growing *S. repens argentea*, which spreads up to 3m (10ft) across with round, silver catkins on top of the branches in early spring followed by grey-green leaves with silvery undersides.
▷ *Approx. height and spread after 10 years: 1 × 1.5m (3 × 5ft).*

Of the medium sized willows, the best for foliage are the hoary willow (*S. elaeagnos* or *rosmarinifolia*), which as one of its names suggests has long, very slender, grey-green leaves like rosemary. It is best pruned hard back every four or five years to keep it tidy and encourage it to produce the loveliest foliage. The coyote willow (*S. exigua*) has even longer, slender silver leaves which shimmer in the slightest breeze. For colourful winter stems, try the purple osier willow (*S. purpurea*), which as all its names suggest has deep purple stems, and benefits from hard pruning every few years. Its long, grey-green leaves are not wildly exciting, whereas members of the *S. alba* group, like 'Chermesina', with brilliant scarlet stems, and the golden willow, 'Vitellina', with bright golden stems, have more attractive silvery foliage from spring onwards. These last two will grow quite large (up to 4m/13ft, unpruned) but pruning them back in spring each year will keep them in check and give the brightest stems.
▷ *Approx. height and spread after 10 years: 4 × 3m (13 × 10ft).*

Elder (*Sambucus*) Another family of shrubs that produce their best foliage in very moist soils and, though most will grow happily in full sun or shade, light, dappled shade suits them best of all. Its plain green form is rather dull and grows very large, but there are a number of smaller varieties with either variegated or coloured foliage that are excellent specimens. *S. niger* 'Albovariegata' has sage-green leaves with creamy-white variegations, while *S.n.* 'Pulverulenta' has brighter green leaves mottled with white. *S.n.* 'Purpurea' has deep purple leaves, becoming more green as they age, and is at its best when the sun can shine through the leaves. The golden forms need just the right balance of sun and shade – too much sun, particularly at midday, can scorch the leaves, while too much shade means their wonderful sunshine-yellow leaves become more of an acid green. The most beautiful forms are the cut-leafed forms – *S. racemosa* 'Plumosa Aurea' and the slightly tougher 'Sutherland', which need hard pruning each year if they are to produce the biggest, brightest foliage. That means you lose the yellow flowers and red berries that follow, so if you want a bit of everything you must compromise, and cut back only up to half the stems each spring. There is a new, small, slow-growing form, *S. racemosa* 'Tenuifolia', the leaves of which are plain mid-green but very finely divided and lacy, not unlike a Japanese maple in both foliage and overall shape.
▷ *Approx. height and spread after 10 years (unpruned): 4 × 3.5m (13 × 12ft).*

Snowberry (*Symphoricarpos*) These very accommodating shrubs will grow in practically any soil, wet or dry, acid or alkaline, and in sun or shade, but produce more berries (the main reason for growing them) in moist soil and sun or part shade. Despite the common name, there are varieties with not only white berries but many shades of pink as well. Some forms produce lots of suckers which can be a nuisance, so make sure you go for a non-suckering variety like *S. × doorenbosii* 'Magic Berry', with small mauve-carmine berries, or *S. × d.* 'Mother of Pearl' which is a semi-weeping form with large, white, pink-tinged berries.
▷ *Approx. height and spread after 10 years: 2.5 × 2m (8 × 6ft).*

Blueberry/Cowberry (*Vaccinium corymbosum* and *vitis-idaea*) A good carpeter in an acid soil.
▷ *Height and spread: 10 cm × infinite (4in × infinite).*

Guelder rose (*Viburnum opulus*) This shrub will grow happily in really boggy soil, as well as in dry soil, in full sun or part shade, and is tolerant of acidity and alkalinity. See page 34.

Perennials

Sweet flag (*Acorus*) w Happiest in shallow water or very boggy soil, its narrow sword-like leaves and roots have a strong, sweet, spicy scent – hence its common name. The most attractive form is *A. calamus* 'Variegatus', which usually has one edge of the leaf striped white or cream.
▷ *Height and spread: 75cm-1m × 60cm (2ft 6in – 3ft 3in × 2ft).*

Anemone Several members of this family, from carpeters to the tall and stately ones, will grow in a shady spot in these conditions. For spring flowering, try the exquisite carpeting wood anemone, *A. nemorosa* (see page 39).

Goat's beard (*Aruncus sylvester* or *dioicus*) Like many plants that thrive in very wet soils, this has large, lush foliage – in this case deeply divided like a fern's – making a dense weedproof clump. It produces plumes of creamy-white flowers in midsummer – the male form, stocked by most nurseries, produces better flowers than the female form but misses out on the latter's glossy chestnut-brown seed pods in autumn. Even more attractive if you can find it is *A. d.* 'Kneiffii', which has the most delightful, even more finely divided leaves.
▷ *Height and spread: 1.2-1.6m × 90cm-1.2m (4-6ft × 3-4ft).*

Astilbe This large family, with its fern-like foliage and feather-duster-like plumes of flowers, does well in damp but not heavy soils, and while it prefers part shade it will stand full sun where there is plenty of moisture. The dwarf varieties are particularly lovely – look out for *A. simplicifolia* 'Bronze Elegance', the bronze-tinged foliage of which is a perfect foil for the tiny salmon pink and cream flowers; *A. chinensis* 'Pumila' with rosy-

mauve flowers which fade to a warm buff in winter; and *A.* 'Sprite' with dark green fern-like foliage and delicate shell-pink flowers which turn into rust-coloured seed heads in autumn. None of these reaches much more than 40cm (16in) in flower. Among the taller varieties, look for *A. taquetti* 'Superba', which has rosy-mauve flowers later than most, and some of the wonderful hybrids, with plumes of flowers in white and many shades of pink and red. Among the older varieties try the deep red 'Fanal', the bright pink 'Bressingham Beauty' and the new rose-pink 'Catherine Deneuve', launched at Chelsea in 1993.
▷ *Height and spread: 50-90 × 60cm (1ft 8in-3ft × 2ft).*

Bog arum (*Calla palustris*) w A low-growing water plant, rather like a miniature lysichiton. It has semi-evergreen glossy heart-shaped leaves, and large white arum-like spathes in spring, often followed by red berries. A good plant for a pond edge.
▷ *Height and spread: 25 × 30cm (10 × 12in).*

Kingcup or Marsh marigold (*Caltha palustris*) w Another plant that's happy in shallow water or very boggy soil. Both the single- and the double-flowered form, *C.p.* 'Plena', have a mound of shiny round leaves, and very attractive, long-lasting golden flowers in spring. The white form, *C.p.* 'Alba', is very different in that it's happier in boggy soil than water and starts producing its pure white flowers as early as February and carries on till early summer. It has the same attractive leaves and makes good pond-side ground cover for the rest of the summer.
▷ *Height and spread: 30-40 × 25-45cm (12-16 × 10-18in).*

Bugbane (*Cimicifuga*) Best in moist shade, this lovely late-summer/early-autumn flowering per-ennial deserves to be more widely grown. It has elegant, glossy, divided leaves, and tall narrow stems bearing plumes of white flowers like slender bottle brushes. *C. simplex* 'Elstead Variety' has dark foliage, almost purple stems and buds before the warm white flowers open. *C.s.* 'White Pearl' has lighter green leaves and green-tinged, creamy-white buds which open to pure white.
▷ *Height and spread: 1.2m × 60cm (4 × 2ft).*

Meadowsweet (*Filipendula*) Not unlike the astilbe, with its handsome jagged leaves and plumes of tiny flowers in shades of red and pink from midsummer onwards. Good varieties include *F. palmata* 'Elegantissima' and *rubra* 'Venusta', and the new dwarf form from Japan, *F.* 'Kakome'. There is a variety with wonderful golden-yellow foliage – *F. ulmaria* 'Aurea'. It does have white flowers in midsummer but these are insignificant, so cut them off when they appear to encourage the plant to produce fresh new foliage instead.
▷ *Height and spread: 30cm-2m × 30-60cm (1-6 × 1-2ft).*

Water avens (*Geum rivale* 'Leonard's Variety') Another moisture-lover with divided leaves, it has unusual bell-like flowers in coppery-pink from May onwards. *G.r.* 'Lionel Cox' is similar with soft green foliage and creamy-apricot flowers.
▷ *Height and spread: 30 × 30cm (1 × 1ft).*

Gunnera manicata The colossus of the bog garden, it has huge leaves like mega-rhubarb, up to 1.5m (5ft) across, and produces club-like spikes of insignificant flowers in early summer, followed by orange seed pods. The usual advice is plant it only in wide open spaces, but I have seen it grown to spectacular effect in a small shady London garden. Although you'd think it was big enough to look after itself, in fact it isn't fully hardy, so bend its own leaves over the crown in autumn and only remove them in spring.
▷ *Height and spread: 2 × 2.2m (6 × 7ft).*

Day lilies (Hemerocallis) As the common name suggests, they have flowers that last only for a day, but they are produced in such profusion over many weeks, from June onwards, that it doesn't matter. They also produce weed-smothering clumps of bright green strap-like leaves that look very good next to water. There are many, many different ones – indeed there is even a Hemer-ocallis Society – but a few good varieties that are widely available include the old variety, *H. flava*, with very sweetly scented, clear yellow flowers; the pale primrose 'Whichford' which is also sweetly scented; and the warm peachy-pink 'Pink Damask'. There are some new dwarf varieties that are well worth trying – 'Stella d'Oro' with masses

of golden yellow flowers for months, 'Little Wine Cup', a burgundy-red with a yellow throat, and the scented 'Cream Drop' with exquisite small, creamy-yellow flowers.
▷ *Height and spread: 75 × 50cm (2ft 6in × 1ft 8in). Dwarf varieties: 50 × 45cm (1ft 8in × 1ft 6in).*

Plantain lilies (hostas) Ideal plants for damp shade. See page 35.

Houttuynia cordata **'Chamaeleon'** A real eye-catcher, this one, in either shallow water or very moist soil, with its heart-shaped leaves boldly variegated in green, cream and red. It achieves the most dramatic coloration in part shade. It also has small white flowers in summer, but they're not the reason you grow it. Once established, it can become invasive, but you can keep it in check with ruthless use of a sharp spade.
▷ *Height and spread: 15cm × infinite (6in × infinite).*

Iris There are so many superb irises for these conditions, in a sunny spot, that it's hard to know where to start – or, indeed, stop! There are some that grow very happily in water like our native flag iris (*I. pseudacorus*) with its clear yellow flowers in June. There is a form with larger, deeper yellow flowers, *I.p.* 'Bastardii'; and a superb variegated form, *I.p.* 'Variegata', whose new growth is creamy-yellow, retained as margins as the leaves develop their green colour and gradually fading away as the summer wears on, leaving the leaves plain green. It will also grow on dry land, surprisingly, but will only reach about half the size. *I. laevigata* is that one iris that must grow in water, though it must be shallow, not much more than 10-12cm (4-5in) deep, or in extremely boggy soil that *never* dries out. If it does, the plant will die. Its flowers are soft lavender-blue, though there is also a lovely white form *I.l.* 'Alba'; another, 'Snowdrift', with double white flowers; a beigy-rose pink, 'Rose Queen', and one with elegant green and cream variegated leaves, *I.l.* 'Variegata'. *Iris sibirica*, with its slender, rush-like foliage and elegant flowers in many shades of blue and white – 'White Swirl', the powder-blue 'Papillon', the rich velvet 'Tropical Night' or the blue and white veined 'Flight of Butterflies' – is lovely at the water's edge, though not with its feet in water. It

will tolerate slightly less moist soil in part shade. *Iris ensata* (which used to be known as *I. kaempferi*) is slightly fussier. In an ideal world, indeed in its native habitat, it would have its feet in warm water in summer but would be dry in winter, and so it's probably best grown in moist soil. Although it is meant to dislike lime, a friend has it growing happily in his chalky soil. There are many hybrids to choose from in colours ranging from white through pink to purple.

No irises like to be planted too deeply, even those growing in water. The top of the rhizome should just be showing through the mud at the bottom of the pool or stream.
▷ *Height and spread: 75cm-1.2m × 30cm (2ft 6in-4ft × 1ft).*

Ligularia Another family of perennials ideal for these boggy conditions, with wonderful lush dramatic foliage, as well as flowers in late summer. Not for the faint-hearted is *L. clivorum* 'Desdemona', which has large heart-shaped, bronzy-green leaves veined in purple, and with almost beetroot-red backs, and large branching heads of orange flowers. Even more dramatic is 'Gregynog Gold' which forms mounds of big heart-shaped leaves and throws up very tall (2m/6ft) spikes of rich yellow flowers, while *L. stenocephala* (or *przewalskii*) 'The Rocket' also has large leaves, only with very jagged edges this time, and spikes of bright yellow flowers on almost black stems.
▷ *Height and spread: 1.2-2m × 60cm (4-6 × 2ft).*

Lobelia 'Queen Victoria' Not the modest, small, blue, edging and hanging basket plant, but the real show-off of the family, with vivid red flowers and deep, purple-red foliage. There is another very similar variety, 'Bees' Flame'. They are not totally hardy in colder areas and so benefit from protection of a mulch throughout the winter, or (belt and braces) take cuttings or save seed, just in case you lose it.
▷ *Height and spread: 1m × 30cm (3ft 3in × 1ft).*

Bog arum (*Lysichiton americanus*) A dramatic plant for the water's edge, just in or just out, with bright yellow spathes appearing through the mud in early spring to be followed by huge shiny leaves which, as leading British plantswoman

Beth Chatto rightly says, look like giant spinach. There is a smaller, white-flowered form, *L. camtschatcensis*, whose flowers and leaves are about two-thirds the size of *L. americanus*, which doesn't like to be planted in water.

▷ *Height and spread: 60cm-1.2 × 1m (2-4ft × 3ft 3in).*

Loosestrife (*Lysimachia*) The summer-flowering yellow loosestrife (*L. punctata*) which carries its bright golden flowers the whole length of its stem,

The rounded globes of Trollius *'Yellow Beauty' brighten the bog garden in late spring or early summer.*

can be invasive, so plant it only in a part-shaded spot where there's plenty of room. The low-growing ground-cover variety, creeping jenny (*L. nummularia*), sends out long stems of rounded, light green leaves, studded with bright golden buttercup flowers. The gold-leafed form, *L.n.* 'Aurea', needs protection from overhead sun to

prevent its bright gold leaves from scorching. Less well known but very attractive is the tall *L. chlethroides* which has curving, terminal spikes of tiny white flowers.
▷ *Height and spread: 75cm-1m × 60-90cm (2ft 6in-3ft 3in × 2-3ft).*

Monkey musk (*Mimulus*) An attractive family of spreading perennials for this situation, though since some can become seriously invasive you might be safer growing members like the new hybrids 'Malibu' in a range of colours from red to ivory, and the speckled 'Viva F 1' as annuals. Look for *M. luteus*, with yellow snapdragon-like flowers all through the summer, the larger *M. guttatus*, with similar flowers only the lower parts are spotted with red and brown, while *M.* 'Whitcroft Scarlet' and 'Wisley Red' have vermilion and blood-red flowers respectively.
▷ *Height and spread: 30-60 × 30-60cm (1-2 × 1-2ft).*

Water forget-me-not (*Myosotis palustris* or *scorpioides*) w This native plant is happy in water or in the mud on the edge of a pond, and has the same small bright blue flowers from May or June onwards as its land-based relative.
▷ *Height and spread: 15 × 30cm (6 × 12in).*

Knotweed (*Persicaria*, formerly *Polygonum*) See page 35.

Pickerel weed (*Pontaderia cordata*) w An attractive foliage plant for the shallow water at the edge of a pond or slow-moving stream, with elegant, smooth, elongated, heart-shaped leaves in a light glossy green. In late summer it produces intense blue flowers, like fluffy grape hyacinths.
▷ *Height and spread: 60-75cm × 45cm (2ft-2ft 6in × 18in).*

Primula This is another huge family, flowering from early spring almost right through till late summer, with many members that thrive in boggy soil. Look for the lovely candelabra primulas (so called because their flowers are arranged in whorls up their tall stems) like *P. beesiana*, *P. bulleyana* (try growing one each of the former close together and seeing what stunning hybrids you get), *P. chungensis*, *P. helodoxa*, *P. japonica* (look for 'Postford White' or the pure red 'Miller's Crimson')

and *P. pulverulenta*, which come in a wide range of colours from deep red to pale pink and white, palest yellow to rich orange and a range of blues. The drumstick primulas (*P. denticulata*), which take their name from a tight ball of flowers on the end of the stem, have flowers in shades of blue – from palest lavender through to rich red-purple, as well as white. They all need a very moist neutral or acid soil to do well and most prefer dappled shade. The auricula primulas with their lovely rich bi-colour flowers – vibrant reds, blues with gold markings – are also supposed to dislike lime, but I have seen them growing beautifully on limy soil. The common primrose (*P. vulgaris*) will grow almost anywhere as long as the soil is rich and moist. The largest of the family, the giant Himalayan cowslip (*P. florindae*), has as its common name suggests heads of sweetly scented flowers like the cowslip's writ large, on stems that can reach up to 1.2m (4ft) or more! It is usually soft yellow, but you can find it with warm, copper-coloured flowers. It's later-flowering than the rest of the family – in July and August.
▷ *Height and spread: 25-60 × 30cm (10in-2ft × 1ft).*

***Rheum palmatum* 'Atrosanguineum'** This ornamental cousin of rhubarb creates wonderfully lush jungly effects with its large, deeply cut leaves which are reddish-purple when they first unfurl in spring, before turning deep green, while their undersides remain pinky-red throughout the season. They throw up tall spears of fluffy crimson flowers in May. They need protection from drying winds and hot sun, so part shade suits them very well, and while they like moist soil they don't like it too wet or the crowns will rot.
▷ *Height and spread: 2 × 2m (6ft 6in × 6ft 6in).*

Rodgersia This is another first-rate family of large, handsome foliage plants for positions near water. It will tolerate very wet conditions better than the rheum but, like it, needs protection from winds and midday sun. As with many plants in this category, the wetter the soil, the more sun it can tolerate. There are several excellent varieties like *R. aesculifolia*, which has large leaves like a horse-chestnut's and sprays of pinky-white flowers in midsummer, and *R. podophylla* with more jagged leaves which are bronze when they first

unfurl, and creamy-white flowers, while the less common *R. tabularis* has huge round leaves with just slightly scalloped edges and tall spikes of small starry white flowers.
▷ *Height and spread: 1-1.2 × 1m (3ft 3in-4ft × 3ft 3in).*

Smilacina racemosa See page 139.
Trillium See page 139.

Globe flower (*Trollius europaeus*) This attractive perennial has masses of round, lemon-yellow flowers in spring, above clumps of deeply divided mid-green leaves. There are several very good cultivars of *T. × cultorum* in colours from palest creamy-yellow (*T.* 'Alabaster'), through soft yellow ('Lemon Queen'), bright yellow ('Canary Bird' or 'Golden Queen') to hot orange ('Etna' or 'Orange Princess'). They flower in early summer and sometimes again in the autumn.
▷ *Height and spread: 60-75 × 45cm (2ft-2ft 6in × 1ft 6in).*

Typha minor w Our native bulrush is far too invasive for most garden pools or streams, but this miniature version is much better behaved. It has slender leaves and the same rusty-brown poker-like seed heads at its larger relative.
▷ *Height and spread: 45-60 × 30cm (1ft 6in-2ft × 1ft).*

Arum lily (*Zantedeschia aethiopica*) Very fashionable in 1993 – prominently featured in many gardens at the Chelsea Flower Show – this is an exotic-looking plant with its waxy cream-white flowers and large, lush, spear-shaped green leaves. It thrives in shallow water or mud, and needs a sunny spot. Good named varieties are 'Crowborough' which has slightly smaller leaves and flowers, and 'Green Goddess' which has white-throated green flowers. It's not reliably hardy and will benefit from a mulch in winter.
▷ *Height and spread: 45cm-1m × 45-60cm (1ft 6in-3ft 3in × 1ft 6in-2ft).*

Grasses and reeds

As people begin to realize what good and easy garden plants many ornamental grasses are, so their popularity is spreading, and you can find an increasing number of varieties in garden centres.

For a wider selection you may well have to buy by mail order from a specialist like P. W. Plants in Norfolk (0953 888212) or Beth Chatto in Elmstead Market near Colchester. (0206 822007)

Bamboo (*Arundinaria* or *Sinarundinaria* or *Pleioblastus* or *Pseudosasa* or *Fargesia*) The names of bamboos have been changed so much in recent years that it's all rather confusing. There are some lovely varieties that will grow in moist conditions, though since they do not like waterlogged soil they're best placed on a bank above a pond or stream. Good varieties for small gardens include the dwarf golden variegated *A.* (or *P.*) *viridistriata*, which gives its best colour in full sun, though it will grow in part shade. The young foliage is the brightest gold, so cut the old canes to ground level in spring. There is a subtler green and white striped one, too, *A. variegata*. Good taller varieties which are not too invasive include *A.* (or *F.*) *nitida*, with dark purple stems and slender leaves green on top and grey-green underneath, and the graceful, arching *A. murieliae* (now *Fargesia spathacea*) which will reach 3m (10ft) or more in a sunny spot. I have it in a damp shady corner in my own garden and six years on, it's less than 2.5m (8ft) tall.
▷ *Height 75cm-3m × 2m-infinite (2-10ft × 6ft-infinite)*

Arundo donax In warmer climates than ours, this giant reed reaches 4.5m (15ft) or more. Here, in milder areas, it reaches a more manageable 2.5m (8ft). It has stout stems and long blue-grey leaves, and would benefit from some winter protection in colder areas. There is a variegated form, *A.d.* 'Variegeta' or 'Versicolor', with blue-green leaves with ivory stripes, but is less hardy than its relative.
▷ *Height and spread: 1.2-2.5m × 60cm (4-8 × 2ft).*

Sedge (*Carex*) Sedges are excellent plants for damp soils in a sunny spot and they look wonderful near water. *C. morrowii* 'Evergold' has narrow bright gold leaves with narrow green margins erupting from the centre of each clump, while the much taller *C. stricta* 'Aurea' or 'Bowles' Golden' has lovely bright gold foliage.
▷ *Height and spread: 25-60 × 15-20cm (10in-2ft × 6-8in).*

Instant water gardening at the 1993 Chelsea Flower Show with irises, hostas, and Zantedeschia.

Tufted hair grass (*Deschampsia cespitosa*)
Despite its foreign-sounding botanical name this is one of our native grasses and one of the most beautiful too, with narrow arching leaves and tall plumes of tiny silvery flowers, which look just as attractive in winter after they have died. It's happiest in sun or part shade. Look for *D.c.* 'Gold Veil' or 'Bronze Veil,' or the newer 'Golden Dew' with much shorter flower spikes.
▷ *Height and spread 75cm-1.2 × 30cm (2ft 6in-4 × 1ft).*

Glyceria maxima **'Variegata'** Good in sun or part shade in damp, heavy soil at the water's edge, the broad green, yellow and white strap-like leaves of this grass are tinged pink when they first appear in spring. It can be invasive, but the deft wielding of a sharp spade keeps it in check.
▷ *Height and spread: 60cm × infinite (2ft × infinite).*

Woodrush (*Luzula maxima* 'Marginata')
Excellent for evergreen ground cover in sun or shade, especially where the soil is moist, though it will tolerate drier soil too. It's a particularly good plant for a boggy bank since its roots can hold the soil together. Its rich green leaves are striped with white and, in summer, it has drooping sprays of tiny golden brown flowers.
▷ *Height and spread: 45cm × infinite (18in × infinite.*

Bowles' Golden Grass (*Milium effusum* 'Aureum') This well-known evergreen grass provides a splash of sunlight in any shady spot particularly in winter. Beth Chatto grows it spectacularly with the purple-leafed *Viola labradorica* and snowdrops.
▷ *Height and spread: 40 × 25cm (16 × 10in).*

Miscanthus A family of tall elegant grasses which will put up with quite dry conditions, although they are at their best in rich moist soil. Among the best plain ones are *M. sinensis* 'Gracillimus' with very dark green narrow leaves, and *M.s.* 'Silver Feather', so called after the silvery plumes up to 2.4m (8ft) tall. Of the variegated kinds '*M.s.* 'Variegatus' is good, while the unusual horizontally striped *M.s.* 'Zebrinus', with gold bands across its dark green leaves, is very attractive indeed. Their slender canes are an excellent contrast with the huge solid leaves of rodgersia or rheum.
▷ *Height and spread: 1.2-2m × 45cm (4-6ft × 1ft 6in).*

Molinia caerulea **'Variegata'** A beautiful neat little grass, with subtle cream and green variegated leaves which turn a warm pale buff colour, along with the plumes of tiny flowers, in autumn.
▷ *Height and spread: 45 × 30cm (1ft 6in × 1ft).*

Gardener's Garters (*Phalaris arundinacea* 'Picta') In a moist soil, and a shady spot, this evergreen green and white grass looks very cool

and light indeed. The down side is that it is invasive, so either be prepared to chop it back regularly, or grow it in a confined space.
▷ *Height and spread: 1m × infinite (3ft × infinite).*

Ferns

Many ferns like moist soil (see pages 38–39), though considerably fewer like it really wet. Those that do are among the most spectacular, so that is some consolation.

Shuttlecock or Ostrich plume fern (*Matteuccia struthiopteris*) One of the most beautiful of all ferns, this has the most delicate divided fronds arranged just like the flights on a shuttlecock. It needs really damp soil to do well and looks stunning mirrored in water.
▷ *Height and spread: 1m × 45cm (3ft × 18in).*

Sensitive fern (*Onoclea sensibilis*) A very attractive fern for a very damp soil, forming a mound of fresh green, leathery, almost triangular fronds, which have a pinkish tinge when they first unfurl and turn golden-yellow before they die back in autumn.
▷ *Height and spread: 45 × 45cm (18 × 18in).*

Royal fern (*Osmunda regalis*) If you have space, and a lime-free soil, this is *the* most magnificent fern, virtually twice the size of the shuttlecock fern, with long, oval, finely divided, bright green fronds. You can well believe it was able to hide the daughter of the Saxon chief, Osmund, from the Danes – hence its name. It can cope with a sunnier spot than many ferns, provided the soil is really wet.
▷ *Height and spread: 1.2-2 × 1m (4-6ft 6in × 3ft 3in).*

Annuals

There are very few which like boggy conditions, but the few that do are invaluable.

Himalayan balsam (*Impatiens glandulifera*) This tall annual has pale pink or white flowers with a very distinctive perfume in the evening, which look more like an orchid's than the Busy lizzies we all know and love. It self-seeds like

crazy so only plant it where there is lots of room, or if you don't mind getting busy with the hoe.
▷ *Height and spread: 75 × 45cm (2ft 6in × 1ft 6in).*

Monkey flower (*Mimulus*) See page 39.

Bulbs

Again, there are very few bulbs that will survive, never mind thrive, in these conditions – they are more likely to rot. But there are a few that can cope with moist soil, as long as it's not too heavy.

***Arum italicum* 'Pictum'** A member of the same botanical family as lysichitons and zantedeschias. See page 39.

Snowdrops (*Galanthus nivalis*) These bulbs, the first to flower in late winter, will grow in a moist shady spot. There are many different varieties to choose from, differing slightly in leaf shape, flower size, whether double (like *G.n.* 'Flore Plena') or single, some with beautiful green markings on the petals (like *G.n.* 'Viridapicis'). *G.n.* 'S. Arnott' has larger flowers. They are best planted 'in the green', after flowering, but while the leaves are still green – you can buy them in pots from many garden centres now. Dried bulbs take longer to establish and, besides, planting 'in the green' makes absolutely certain that you aren't buying bulbs dug up from the wild in places like Turkey where native bulbs are becoming endangered.
▷ *Height and spread: 10-25 × 5-8cm (4-10 × 2-3in).*

Spring and summer snowflake (*Leucojum vernum* and *aestivum*) These members of the same family as the snowdrop thrive in the wild on the banks of streams, and are valuable garden plants for this situation. The spring snowflake flowers in March and is very like a snowdrop in size and overall appearance with the same distinctive green spots on the tip of each petal. Despite its common name, the summer snowflake flowers in April and May, is much taller than its relatives – up to 90cm (3ft) – and its flowers are a bit like lily-of-the-valley, each petal tipped with green spots, though its leaves are more like a daffodil's. Look for 'Gravetye Giant'.
▷ *Height and spread: 10-15 × 10cm (4-6 × 4in).*

WINDY PLACES

 Although a nice gentle breeze is welcome in the garden – dispersing pollen, even dispersing seeds in some cases and helping to prevent fungal diseases developing, besides creating soothing, relaxing, rustling sounds – a Force 10 gale is something entirely different. There are lots of situations where winds can be a problem for gardeners. Perhaps seaside gardens are the first to come to mind, but the problem there is complicated by several other factors. For a start, the winds are usually laden with salt, and sometimes sand too, which is obviously damaging to many plants, but on the plus side there's the fact that their proximity to the sea keeps winter temperatures slightly higher than those inland, and so more tender plants can survive. For that reason, it makes sense to deal with seaside planting later in a chapter of its own, although obviously some of the perfect plants will feature in both categories.

As you'd expect, any garden on a hill is exposed to winds, but because they gust over and around the hilltop, it's liable to suffer damage from turbulence as well. The same applies to urban gardeners who have only a roof top or a balcony high up in a tower block for example. Other gardeners may not be in an exposed position, but may find that their garden or part of it is in a wind tunnel. They could be in a valley, between hills or even between tall buildings which funnel the wind, increasing both its strength and its speed.

Anyone who drove around southern England in the weeks after the hurricane of October 1987 will be in no doubt about how much damage wind can do to plants. Thousands of huge, mature trees were ripped up by their roots like so many seedlings. Many more that were left standing had their roots so seriously weakened that they had to be cut down for safety's sake. That wind was exceptional, but ordinary strong winds can do a lot of damage, not just bringing branches off trees but actually affecting, long-term, the way a tree will grow, bending it permanently away from the prevailing wind, pruning it, almost, by damaging the growth on the windward side. You sometimes see trees on cliffs or the tops of hills that look like rather large bonsai. Smaller plants can be damaged too, and some tall perennials, like delphiniums, smashed flat. Wind can actually rock plants from side to side, too, loosening their roots, leaving pockets for water to enter and freeze in winter, killing some of the roots if not the plant. That's one reason for half-pruning roses in autumn in a windy garden. It reduces the superstructure, making it less vulnerable to wind-rock.

Apart from the mechanical damage it can do, wind also has a drying effect. Both the warmth of the wind and the speed with which it blows increase the amount of moisture lost from the leaves (and even, though to a much lesser extent, from the bare wood). In very windy spots, some plants with shallow root systems just can't replace the moisture lost fast enough. Then some evergreens, conifers particularly, suffer very badly from the effects of drought, with their foliage turning brown and dying. In winter, when the ground is frozen and the moisture in it has turned to ice and is not available to plants' roots, the damage can be even more severe.

As always, the approach to the problem is two-pronged. While there are plants that will grow in the teeth of a gale, the truth is that they are, as you'd expect, mainly tough old workhorses, and it seems a shame to settle just for those when by providing a bit of shelter, and breaking the force of the wind, the number of plants you can grow well increases dramatically.

There are a number of ways of creating windbreaks. What you don't want is an impenetrable barrier like a wall or even a solid fence because that creates more problems than it solves. When the wind hits solid structures, the air is forced upwards and over them, creating an area of low pressure immediately in their lee. The air is then pulled downwards to fill the vacuum that's been created and creates turbulence, which will knock the plants about from all sides and do at least as much damage as the full force of the wind would have done.

If you already have such a wall, then the best thing to do, if possible, is plant a hedge on the windward side. What this will do is slow down and diffuse the wind *before* it hits the wall, so that the resulting turbulence on the other side will be greatly reduced.

If you are creating your windbreak from scratch then you want something that is not much more than 50 per cent solid. A ranch-style fence is ideal, or loose-woven hurdles that allow the wind through, or a living windbreak – a hedge or an informal planting of shrubs – can do the job just as well. If you've got quite a bit of wide open space in your garden, you'll need to think about several windbreaks at intervals. It's known that a windbreak of, say, 2m can slow the wind down by up to 75 per cent for up to 4m (twice its height) on the far side of it. Even at a distance of 10 times the height of the windbreak, the reduction is still 50 per cent but that effect then diminishes quite quickly the further you go, so that 30m away, it's only 20 per cent. In a large garden, ideally you should put up a series of windbreaks at a distance of 10 times their height. This doesn't mean that your garden has to resemble the Grand National course at Aintree, though. You can create a series of different windbreaks – maybe a hedge, then an informal planting of shrubs, even a screen of espalier fruit trees – and not all of equal width, either, so that you can break up your garden in a way that is visually interesting as well as practical in diffusing the force of the wind. At least that way you'll create some more sheltered areas where you can grow more delicate plants. Do remember, though, that wind whips round the end of any windbreak, so the most sheltered areas will be in the middle or, if it adjoins another boundary – a wall, fence or hedge – at right angles, in the corner.

Creating a shelter belt for a very large exposed garden involves the careful planting of several staggered rows of large tough trees like sycamores and Austrian pines, with smaller trees and shrubs between them. But for the vast majority of us who don't have very large gardens, that isn't an option. For most of us, a screen of evergreen shrubs – either conifers or some large-leafed shrubs – is the best bet. If possible the screen should be more than one shrub deep to filter the wind effectively but if space really is at a premium then that will do.

A newly planted windbreak will need a windbreak itself initially – young trees will be whipped about by the wind which, as I've already said, can extract moisture from the foliage of young evergreens (and conifers in particular) faster than the plant can replace it from the soil, with the result that the leaves suffer the effects of drought and turn brown.

Young trees should be staked, and current thinking is that a short stake, no more than one-third the length of the trunk, is more effective than a taller stake reaching

Above: *Whether clipped into topiary, or left alone, holly is a good choice for a windy spot.*

Right: *A range of colourful flowering rock plants and tough rhododendrons thrive on a windy Welsh hillside.*

to the top of the trunk, because the former allows the top of the tree to flex in the wind, and so encourages it to develop a thicker trunk and a stronger root system more quickly. Do use a proper tree tie to attach the tree to the stake – ties cost very little, and will prevent chafing and therefore

damage to the tree. They are also easily adjusted so that you can loosen them as the trunk expands.

For newly planted conifers and other evergreens, you need to put up a windbreak of netting or special mesh, tacked on to wooden posts or, if you only have a small group of plants to protect, even woven hurdles. Netting is probably cheapest, though you need to use it double for the greatest protection. It has to be said that none of these man-made windbreaks looks particularly attractive, but bear in mind that they are only temporary – in most places you need them only for the first winter – and without them, your living windbreak will take much longer to get established (if indeed, it gets established at all!).

You might have a windy corner of the house, where the draught fairly whistles round. A tough evergreen shrub – an almost spineless holly (on account of people walking by) such as 'J. C. van Tol' or 'Pyramidalis', for example, or, in a sunny or part-shaded spot, if there was enough room, even Mexican orange-blossom (*Choisya ternata*) – would be good planted just on the more sheltered side of the corner because it's out of the full blast of the wind but will slow it down as it whips round the corner and offer protection to plants growing further along.

For a high roof garden or even a large balcony, you'll need some kind of screening. You want something that isn't solid, like rigid square trellis, loosely woven bamboo screening or, if the budget allows, a row of glass screens with gaps in between them, for several reasons. Firstly, they filter the wind rather than try and block it entirely so they are less likely to be damaged in a gale. Secondly, as we know, solid screens create turbulence that will damage plants. And finally, solid barriers could make the garden feel very claustrophobic, so it's important psychologically to be able to see out and know that you're on a roof or a balcony.

PERFECT PLANTS

The sort of plants that will cope with a windy site are those which offer less resistance to the wind, either because they are very flexible and so bend rather than break, or very open in their habit allowing the wind to pass through, or low-growing – and that applies to everything from trees to perennials. The mountain ash (*Sorbus aucuparia*), which as its name suggests is often found on windy hillsides if not mountains exactly, has an open habit, which allows the wind to filter through, and flexible branches, while something like *Robinia pseudoacacia* 'Frisia' is stiffer and more brittle, and so easily damaged in a windy spot. It's also worth remembering that in a windy spot, trees and shrubs won't reach anything like the size they would in more favourable, sheltered conditions.

Some smaller conifers like the common Christmas tree (*Abies picea*) and the mountain pines (*Pinus mugo*) are excellent in these conditions because they are open in habit, and so are bushy, twiggy, deciduous shrubs like potentillas, deutzias, pernettya and mock orange (*Philadelphus*). Again, the wind passes through the shrub and none of the individual twigs is thick enough to offer any serious resistance, and so is not at risk of being snapped. Tall grasses and bamboos are also very good in windy spots because they are so fine that they simply bend – sometimes horizontal – but don't break.

When it comes to leaves, small (or narrow like grasses), is more likely to remain beautiful. Large thin leaves, like rodgersias, ligularias, or rheums, will get ripped to shreds by strong winds, while small leaves like those of berberis, cotoneaster or potentilla, or leathery leaves like holly or euonymus, or very thin, leathery needles like those of the mountain pine, will survive much better. They are not at risk of physical damage by the wind because of their size, and their tough texture means that they aren't likely to be desiccated by it either. Other leaves which look at first sight as though they might be vulnerable to wind damage, like dogwood (*Cornus alba*), actually survive quite well because they are just about small enough to offer little resistance, and since this plant can tolerate dry conditions surprisingly well, its leaves are unlikely to suffer from drought.

Obviously, the lower-growing a perennial plant is, the less likely it is to be damaged by wind. Tall spikes like those of delphiniums or hollyhocks are much too vulnerable in an exposed windy garden to be worth the risk. Even if you stake them, as you'd have to, they can still be snapped by strong winds. But obviously a variation in height makes a border more interesting and again there are some tallish perennials that will bend rather than break. Some taller yarrows (achillea), for instance, have attractive flat heads of small flowers that are not as weighty as, say, delphiniums and so will support themselves. 'Coronation Gold' is a vivid golden yellow while 'Moonshine', which is slightly smaller, has sulphur-yellow flowers. Common old red valerian (*Centranthus ruber*) is another good tallish plant that thrives in an exposed spot, and Japanese anemones are worth trying

too because their tall wiry stems will sway rather than break, but it must be said that a stiff breeze can remove their petals. Obviously, most low-growing alpines would grow very successfully in this situation (see page 106–107).

OUR PROBLEM PLACE

Our windy spot was a half-moon-shaped bed in the corner of a garden on a farm, facing south-west, the direction from which the prevailing wind blows. Since the owners reckon this bit of the garden is the highest point between there and the Bristol Channel, you can imagine that the wind fairly whistles through it. They've tried any number of plants there over the years, and its present state was a very clear demonstration of the Survival of the Fittest theory. All that had survived was one very old, big box-leafed honeysuckle (*Lonicera nitida*) clipped into a pill-box shape, which dominated the border, a clump of ordinary lemon balm, masses of bugle (*Ajuga reptans*), a patch of *Sedum spectabile*, and a lovely golden *Euonymus japonicus* 'Ovatus Aureus', which, although not as hardy as the *Euonymus fortuneii* varieties, had survived extremely well both its exposed position and, when it reached the top of the wall, a regular pruning by passing cows. And on top of that, there was a fair sprinkling of ground elder, couch grass and assorted annual weeds.

We decided to keep the euonymus, and a bit of the lemon balm. The sedums were moved to another part of the garden. Taking out the box-leafed honeysuckle was a difficult decision to make because it had been there for years and birds nested in it in winter. It was so old, though, that opening

it up revealed that behind a few inches of foliage there was a mass of dead tangled wood inside. To reduce it to a sensible size for its position would have meant removing every trace of greenery, and hacking back really hard into the old wood, and while it would have regenerated eventually it would have looked such a mess in the meantime that we decided it wasn't worth it. There was no shortage of alternative nesting sites in the garden, and if the owners particularly wanted another *Lonicera nitida* in the garden it would make sense to plant a new one because it is relatively quick-growing and this time, if it was cut back as soon as it reached a sensible size and kept trimmed, the problem with dead wood in the centre would not arise again.

Our windy corner looked pretty dull before we started work. Now a variety of tough but attractive plants like the yellow-flowered potentilla 'Elizabeth', the blue grass, Festuca glauca, *and the mountain pine,* Pinus mugo, *will give interest all through the year.*

Having cleared the ground of weeds and dug in plenty of compost – one of the big plusses of being on a farm that keeps cows is that there is a free and plentiful supply of well-rotted manure – we then covered the ground with Plantex. This woven membrane acts like a black polythene mulch in that it suppresses weeds and keeps the moisture in. But the important difference is that while you can't water through black polythene, Plantex allows water through. Given that the winds dry out the soil, as well as the foliage of plants, we used it primarily for its moisture-conserving properties, with a distinct lack of weeding as a very definite bonus.

The plants we chose were all those which could stand up to windy conditions for a variety of reasons – twiggy, small-leafed potentillas and deutzias, and the tough, very dense globe of *Viburnum opulus* 'Compactum', evergreens like the rugged little mountain pine, the tall, bushy evergreen berberis 'Wallich's Purple' (*B. wallichiana purpurea*), with blue-green undersides to its purple leaves, the low, tough, winter-flowering *Erica carnea* 'Heathwood', with very dark green foliage with a bronzy tint and deep lilac pink flowers, and the small blue grass, *Festuca glauca*. Hardy geraniums can cope with a windy spot, although they may lose their petals in a real blow, so we

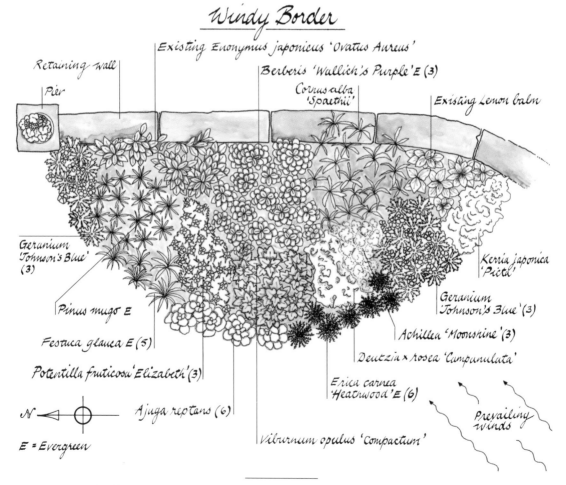

Windy Border

Existing *Euonymus japonicus* 'Ovatus Aureus'

Retaining wall

Berberis 'Wallich's Purple' E (3)

Pier

Cornus alba 'Spaethii'

Existing Lemon balm

Geranium 'Johnson's Blue' (3)

Kerria japonica 'Picta'

Geranium 'Johnson's Blue' (3)

Pinus mugo E

Achillea 'Moonshine' (3)

Festuca glauca E (5)

Deutzia × rosea 'Campanulata'

Potentilla fruticosa 'Elizabeth' (3)

Erica carnea 'Heathwood' E (6)

N

Prevailing winds

Ajuga reptans (6)

E = Evergreen

Viburnum opulus 'Compactum'

planted *G.* 'Johnson's Blue' both on the sheltered side of the bed and the windy side. It survived in both. The result was a bed with just the right balance of evergreen and deciduous plants to give colour and interest all through the year, without requiring much attention from its owners. The final touch was to cover the Plantex with something more attractive. Organic materials like shredded bark would be scattered to the four corners of the garden in the first major sou'wester, and it would have been expecting too much even of cocoa shells to stay put. So we opted for a thin layer of gravel, which wouldn't blow about and which toned in perfectly with the pale honey-coloured Cotswold stone of the garden wall.

When we went back two months later at the beginning of September, a few days after a Force 8 gale, the bed had survived extremely well. The geraniums were beginning to form a clump, the achilleas were still in flower, and the leaves of the small viburnum were taking on their rusty autumn colour. What with the Plantex *and* the gravel, no weed had stood a chance!

PLANTS

Shelter-belt plants

Since most of us do not have huge gardens where giant forest trees like sycamores (*Acer pseudoplatanus*) and the Corsican pine (*Pinus nigra maritima*) are necessary to create an effective windbreak, I shall list only smaller trees and shrubs that would be suitable for solving the problem in average sized gardens. Although you could grow any of them as specimen trees or shrubs, in most cases they are chosen for their toughness rather than for their beauty. Obviously evergreens act as good windbreaks all year round, but some of the twiggier, bushier trees and shrubs still give some protection even when they're not in leaf.

Birch (*Betula*) Our native silver birch needs to be planted in a group for maximum windbreak effect and for maximum visual impact, and few of us have the space for a copse. Of the smaller birches, *B. pendula* 'Fastigiata' is a good bet. It has an upright, columnar shape, dark green leaves and, as the tree matures, its bark takes on the characteristic silver colour.
▷ *Approx. height and spread after 10 years: 10 × 3m (32 × 10ft).*

Hazel or Cobnut (*Corylus avellana*) A useful quick-growing shrub for this situation, with attractive light green, veined leaves turning gold in the autumn, yellow catkins in late winter and nuts in the autumn. It's particularly useful as it will grow in sun or deep shade, and in any type of soil. It can be pruned if it outgrows its allotted space, and to encourage the growth of strong new wood. Cut out only a proportion of the old wood each year, so that it retains its screening function. There are more interesting golden-and purple-leafed varieties (*C.a.* 'Aurea' and *C. maxima* 'Purpurea'), but they really need to be cut back hard almost to ground level every five years or so to get the best and brightest foliage, which defeats the object of the exercise. Another unusual and attractive variety is Harry Lauder's walking stick (*C.a.* 'Contorta') with twisted stems and twigs, which come into their own in winter along with yellow catkins, but rarely any nuts. It's much smaller and slower-growing than the parent.
▷ *Approx. height and spread after 10 years: 4 × 5m (13 × 16ft).*

Ilex (Holly) See page 31.

May, Hawthorn, Quickthorn (*Crataegus monogyna*) A very tough, bushy small tree, with attractive small glossy green leaves, white flowers in May – or even June in colder areas – and red berries in the autumn. It responds well to being cut hard back to keep it bushy and within its allotted space.
▷ *Approx. height and spread after 10 years: 6 × 3m (20 × 10ft).*

Mountain pine (*Pinus mugo*) These tough little pines are excellent plants for the average sized

garden, and are also useful as an informal hedge. There are lots of dwarf cultivars like 'Gnom' and 'Mops' around which only grow to a metre or two, but in this instance it is the ordinary *Pinus mugo* you want.
▷ *Approx. height and spread after 10 years: 3-5 × 5-8m (10-15 × 15-25ft).*

Alder buckthorn (*Rhamnus frangula*) A large tough shrub that forms dense thickets which make useful windbreaks in large country gardens. Its oval green leaves turn yellow in the autumn and, as well as cream flowers, it also has red berries in autumn.
▷ *Approx. height and spread after 10 years: 2.5-3.5 × 1.5-2m (8-11ft × 5-6ft 6in).*

Mountain ash (*Sorbus aucuparia*) These tough little trees really do grow where little else will, and what's more they are a lot more attractive than we have a right to expect from something this tough. Apart from the attractive fern-like leaves, which colour well in autumn too, there are creamy-white flowers in spring and scarlet berries from mid to late summer on.
▷ *Approx. height and spread after 10 years: 5 × 2.5m (16 × 8ft).*

***Thuja plicata* 'Atrovirens'** A much better hedging plant than the overplanted, all too often overgrown Leyland cypress because it has a more attractive deep green colour, and isn't quite as vigorous. It can be clipped to make an excellent formal hedge. If left unpruned it can reach 10m (30ft) or more. *Thuja* 'Smaragd' can be grown as a hedge too, but can also be used as a specimen or planted in an informal group to provide screening. Its name means 'emerald' and that gives you a clue to its colour.

Viburnum Some of the large evergreen viburnums, like *V. rhytidophyllum*, can stand up to a battering from the wind (see page 34).

Shrubs

Bamboo (*Arundinaria japonica* now officially *Pseudosasa japonica*) A good screening plant to filter wind in particular areas the garden – on a windy corner or at the end of a windbreak to slow the wind down as it whips round the end.
▷ *Approx. height and spread after 10 years: 3m × infinite (10ft × infinite).*

Spotted laurel (*Aucuba japonica*) This tough old reliable will also cope here. See page 30.

Berberis julianae A real toughie this one, with small, slender glossy evergreen leaves, bright yellow flowers in late spring/early summer, blue-black berries in autumn, it also has very sharp thorns which make it an effective, if somewhat anti-social hedging plant. It's happy in sun or shade, and will cope with most soil conditions except extreme dryness.
▷ *Approx. height and spread after 10 years: 3 × 3m (10ft × 10ft).*

Calluna See page 134.
Cotoneaster *C. dammeri* and *C. microphyllus* are good here. See page 42.

Elaeagnus* × *ebbingei A fast-growing shrub, subtle rather than showy, with long, leathery evergreen leaves that are silver underneath and so look very attractive when they move about in the wind. Mature plants have sweetly scented, bell-shaped silver-white flowers in autumn. See page 31.

Erica carnea These winter-flowering, low-growing heathers come from the Alps and with their very small, narrow evergreen leaves are well adapted to windy conditions. Unlike their summer-flowering relatives, they will tolerate a degree of lime in the soil. They all have white, pinky-mauve or red flowers, but in many cases it's their foliage that is outstanding – from the orange gold of *E.c.* 'Ann Sparks' to the deep bronzy-green of 'Vivelli'.
▷ *Approx. height and spread after 10 years: 50 × 80cm (1ft 6in × 2ft 6in).*

Spindle (*Euonymus fortunei*) See page 31.
Hippophae See page 114.

St John's wort or Rose of Sharon (*Hypericum calycinum*) It has leathery almost evergreen leaves, and large gold cup-shaped flowers with very

prominent golden anthers all summer.
▷ *Approx. height and spread after 10 years: 30cm × 2m + 2m + (1 × 6ft 6in +).*

Box-leafed honeysuckle (*Lonicera nitida*)
A very useful evergreen. Try the green 'Yunnan' or the golden 'Baggeseus Gold'.
▷ *Approx. height and spread after 10 years: 2 × 3m (6ft 6in × 10ft).*

Shrubby cinquefoil (*Potentilla fruticosa*)
First-class flowering shrubs for this situation, producing masses of flat-faced buttercup-like flowers all summer long in a range of shades from white through cream to pale yellows, golden yellows, apricots, oranges and, more recently, pinks and reds. There are so many good ones to choose from that it's very much a matter of personal choice. My favourites include *P.* 'Abbotswood' with pure white flowers and grey-green foliage and 'Tilford Cream', both of which are smaller than most, 'Daydawn' with soft apricot flowers, and 'Katherine Dykes' with soft yellow flowers. *P.* 'Princess' is a pretty soft pink, but it fades in hot weather and dry spells to an off-white, while 'Red Ace' needs light shade to maintain the best colour.
Approx. height and spread after 10 years: 1.2 × 1.2m (4 × 4ft). .

Pyracantha (Firethorn)
One of the few wall shrubs for this situation, since its growth is stiff enough not to be blown down, or off the wall. See page 73.

Willow (*Salix*)
The slim, whippy stems and slender leaves of some of the medium-sized willows – the coyote willow (*S. exigua*) or hoary willow (*S. elaeagnos* or *rosmarinifolia*) make them a good choice for a windy situation. See page 73.

Spiraea
Good, tough twiggy bushes for this situation. Some people find the combination of the gold foliage of some varieties like 'Gold Flame' and the smaller 'Golden Princess' and their bright pink flowers in early to midsummer a bit too much. Like most golden-leafed shrubs they need some overhead shelter from the hot summer sun or else their leaves may scorch. Other good varieties include *S.* × *bumalda* 'Anthony Waterer' with dark green leaves veined in wine-red, a shade which tones well with the pinky-red flowers, the dwarf 'Little Princess' with light green leaves and pinky-red flowers, and the curious 'Shirobana', which has flowers that are either pink or white or half and half. Most benefit from being cut hard back in early spring.
▷ *Approx. height and spread after 10 years: 60 × 70cm (2ft × 2ft 3in).*

Gorse (*Ulex europaeus*)
This tough, prickly customer, which has no leaves, is grown for its yellow pea-flowers which are produced for months on end from early summer onward. It's useful for growing on poor soil in exposed sunny spots – ideal on a dry, inaccessible bank for example since its very sharp thorns make handling it a hazardous business. *U.e.* 'Plena' has lemon-yellow double flowers, and is smaller.
▷ *Approx. height and spread after 10 years: 1.5 × 2m (5 × 6ft).*

Guelder rose (*Viburnum opulus*)
Another tough branching shrub that will grow in most conditions and is useful for screening. For a small windswept area, try the small round *V.o.* 'Compactum' which grows to well under half the size of its relative. See page 34.
▷ *Approx. height and spread after 10 years: 3 × 3m (10 × 10ft). V.o. 'Compactum': 1.2 × 1.5m (4 × 5ft).*

Perennials

Yarrow (*Achillea filipendulina*)
Some of the taller yarrows like the bright gold 'Coronation Gold' and the softer yellow 'Moonshine' have stems that sway rather than snap, and their flat heads of small flowers offer less resistance to the wind. The newer, shorter hybrids, like 'Anthea' with creamy-yellow flowers stand up to the wind pretty well, too, and have attractive divided foliage.
▷ *Approx. height and spread: 60cm-1.2m × 60cm (2-4ft × 2ft).*

Bugle (*Ajuga reptans*) See page 42.

Japanese anemone (*Anemone × hybrida*)
Another plant whose stems bend rather than break in strong winds, though its larger petals are more

likely to get blown away. Hedge your bets and choose one of the shorter, sturdier varieties, like the deep pink 'Bressingham Glow' or *A. hupehensis*, which are only two-thirds the height of most.
▷ *Approx. height and spread: 75-90 × 60cm (2ft 6in-3 × 2ft).*

Mountain cornflower (*Centaurea montana*) A rather floppy perennial, this, with attractive cornflower-blue blooms in early summer. The petals are rather curious, almost skeletal – ideal for allowing strong winds to pass through.
▷ *Approx. height and spread: 50 × 60cm (1ft 8in × 2ft).*

Red valerian (*Centranthus ruber*) A lovely old cottage garden plant that seems happiest growing in poor conditions – like on top of stone walls. It soon forms dense clumps of attractive green leaves and has heads of deep pinky-red flowers right through the summer.
▷ *Approx. height and spread: 60-90 × 45-60cm (2-3ft × 1ft 6in-2ft).*

Grasses

Some ornamental grasses are good for windy gardens because they sway and bend rather than break, though since the wind dries out the soil go for those that like drier conditions.

Blue fescue (*Festuca glauca* 'Silver Sea') See page 62.

Blue oat grass (*Helictotrichon* or *Avena sempervirens*) This grass has lovely vivid blue-grey evergreen leaves with plumes of tiny flowers much the same colour. The new *H.s.* 'Sapphire Spray' has even more vivid foliage.
▷ *Height and spread: 1.2m × 60cm (4 × 2ft).*

Miscanthus See page 80.

Golden Oats (*Stipa gigantea*) An excellent evergreen grass for bringing instant height to a newly planted border, since its plumes of oats, which

Tall grasses like Miscanthus sinensis *are perfect for a windy spot as they bend rather than break.*

are more silvery than golden, reach 2.5m (8ft) or more. Like other grasses, they remain attractive in winter once they have died, especially when rimed with frost.
▷ *Height and spread: 2.5 × 1m (8 × 3ft).*

Alpines

Many of these are well adapted to windy sites. See pages 106–107.

Annuals and biennials

Again, height is the key factor in choosing annuals here – you would be a little ambitious to think of trying to create a cottage garden effect with sunflowers or hollyhocks in this situation (though one or two annuals that reach 60cm (2ft) or so in height can put up with a bit of buffeting).

Pot marigold (*Calendula*) These are lovely old cottage garden annuals in a range of colours from

creamy-yellow to burnt-orange. Good varieties include 'Pacific Beauty' and the smaller mixed-colour 'Fiesta Gitana' or, if you want just gold or just orange, go for 'Baby Gold' or 'Baby Orange'.
▷ *Height and spread: 30-60 × 30-60cm (1-2 × 1-2ft).*

Cornflower (*Centaurea*) These now come in a range of colours, but to the traditionalists among us they still look best in deep, rich blue. The best tall variety is 'Blue Diadem', while 'Baby Blue' has similar flowers but grows to less than half the size, which makes it a better choice for this situation.
▷ *Height: 30-75cm × 15-30cm (1ft-2ft 6in × 6in-1ft).*

Chrysanthemum carinatum One of the few members of the family to retain the name 'chrys-anthemum', this fast-growing bushy annual has delicate feathery foliage and daisy-like flowers, in a range of colours. 'Monarch Court Jesters', for example, have red or white flowers zoned with a contrasting band of yellow or red. If you prefer a single colour, try *C.c.* 'Golden Gem' which has semi-double yellow flowers.
▷ *Height and spread: 30-60 × 30cm (1-2 × 1ft).*

Clarkia An upright annual that produces double flowers in shades of red, pink and white that could pass for carnations at a distance. The new 'Elegans Love Affair' has large double flowers in a wide range of colours on very sturdy, compact plants – a plus in this situation.
▷ *Height: 50-60 × 30cm (18in-2 × 1ft).*

Sweet william (*Dianthus barbatus*) The best bet here is probably the dwarf varieties like 'Round-about' or 'Indian Carpet', with masses of flowers in shades of red, pink and white, some single-coloured, some bi-colours.
▷ *Height and spread: 15 × 20-30cm (6 × 8-12in).*

Viper's bugloss (*Echium vulgare*) The dwarf hybrids are tough, bushy little plants with masses of small tubular flowers in a range of blues, mauves, pinks and white, which are attractive to bees. 'Blue Bedder' has deep blue flowers, while 'Moody Blues' has flowers in a range of blues from pale to deep.
▷ *Height and spread: 30 × 20cm (12 × 8in).*

Californian poppy (*Eschscholzia*) See page 63.

Iberis umbellata (**Candytuft**) This has clusters of small flowers in lavender, carmine and white. It's easy to grow and flowers for months. 'Fairy Mixture' (or 'Mixed') is a good variety.
▷ *Height and spread: 22 × 20cm (8 × 8in).*

Mallow (*Lavatera trimensis*) A stunning, easy-to-grow plant for the middle of a border, pro-ducing large trumpets of pink or gleaming white flowers for months on end. 'Silver Cup', a rich silver-pink, and 'Mont Blanc', a pure white, are both old favourites, while a new, paler pink variety 'Pink Beauty' seems set to join them.
▷ *Height and spread: 60 × 45cm (2ft × 1ft 6in).*

Poached egg plant (*Limnanthes douglasii*) Another self-seeder, this has yellow-centred white flowers all summer, and feathery light green leaves.
▷ *Height and spread: 15 × 10cm (6 × 4in).*

Scarlet flax (*Linum grandiflorum* 'Rubrum') Grown for its brilliant, scarlet flowers that really do have a satiny sheen.
▷ *Height and spread: 45 × 15cm (18 × 6in).*

Alyssum (*Lobularia maritima*) Once you've sown it you've always got it, for it seeds itself freely every year. The largest-flowered variety is 'Snow Crystals' but 'Carpet of Snow' is good.
▷ *Height and spread: 15 × 30cm (6 × 12in).*

Honesty (*Lunaria*) This biennial is probably appreciated more for its round, flat, papery seed heads in late summer than its purple flowers, but it's a useful space-filler in difficult situations. Even more attractive are the white form if you can find it, and the form with variegated leaves.
▷ *Height and spread: 75 × 30cm (2ft 6in × 1ft).*

Bulbs

Obviously, this is not the ideal site for tall daffodils and tulips, which would simply get knocked flat but there is no reason why you can't grow dwarf varieties, and of course any of the small bulbs, like *Anemone blanda*, glory-of-the-snow (*Chionodoxa*), crocus, hardy cyclamen, dwarf fritillarias, snow-drops, scilla and so on.

COLD PLACES

 Cold can affect plants and gardens in all sorts of different ways. In a cold garden the soil takes longer to warm up and so it takes longer for the plants to start into growth. Few plants will actually grow, as opposed to merely staying alive, in temperatures below 5°C, which is why many alpines are so slow-growing. It means the growing season is shorter, so plants don't grow as large and aren't as productive as they would be in a warmer garden. It also means that tissue on shrubs and perennials that are borderline for hardiness has less chance to harden, and they are less likely to survive the winter.

There are all sorts of reasons why your garden might be a cold garden. You might live high up on a hillside, and the higher you go, the colder it is. If you live in the north of Scotland, you'll find it cold because obviously the further north you go, the colder it gets, too. You might live on the east coast of Britain, where there is nothing between you and the Urals to block those icy easterly winds.

But it's not always that straightforward. If you live on the west coast of Scotland, you'll find you have more in common with gardeners in Cornwall or the Scilly Isles than with your neighbours fifty miles inland because the Gulf Stream warms the west coast in winter, keeping minimum temperatures just that crucial bit higher, which allows tender plants to survive. A visit to the wonderful gardens at Inverewe, near Inverness, will prove that point. Even on the east coast of Britain, despite those Siberian winds which can make it *feel* extremely cold,

the proximity of the sea keeps temperatures higher than they would be even a little further inland. In fact, the lowest temperature ever recorded in England was −26°C in Newport, Shropshire, in 1982 – only a degree or two higher than the lowest recorded temperature for the whole of the British Isles (in Braemar, in Scotland). The reason why Newport is so cold is not just that it's about as far from the sea as you can get in any direction, it's also because it lies in a large frost hollow or frost pocket. While frost pockets can be large enough to contain a whole town, they can also be much smaller – small enough to contain just one garden, or even one small part of a garden. Frost hollows or pockets appear in dips or at the bottom of hills. What happens is that on still nights, cold air, which is denser and therefore heavier than warmer air, rolls down slopes – in what the meteorologists call, delightfully, 'a katabatic wind' – and if it hits a barrier of any kind, whether it's rising ground on the other side, a wall, a fence, or even a hedge, then it has no escape and simply lies there, getting colder and colder. And frost can kill plants - as you'll know if you've ever got carried away in late spring and put your bedding plants out too early. Ground frost – technically, when temperatures of 0°C are recorded at ground level – can damage newly planted bedding or vegetable plants like runner beans or courgettes, blackening the foliage, setting them back a few weeks or even killing them altogether. What happens is that the water inside the plants' cells turns to ice, and ruptures them. In

new growth, the cell walls are very soft, sappy and easily damaged, whereas in older plants they are tougher, woodier, and therefore less likely to be damaged by ice crystals.

Over a long period, frost can damage larger, more mature plants too. When the ground is frozen hard, it has the same effect as drought – the moisture in the soil is locked up, unavailable to the plants. Particularly vulnerable are evergreens like conifers because they are still losing water through their leaves, but can't replace it from the soil since they are shallow-rooted, especially when they are newly planted, and it's the top few inches of soil that are frozen. Plants with deeper roots are usually unaffected because they can tap into water further down in the soil that remains unfrozen, though a long period of intense cold, combined with strong winds and clear

Above: *Alpine plants which grow on mountainsides in the wild thrive in this cold Scottish garden.*

Right: *The tough evergreens in this almost magical winter landscape may droop in the cold, but will survive unscathed.*

skies – both of which mean that leaves lose water rapidly – can damage mature evergreens. It can also damage deciduous shrubs and trees, because even twigs lose some moisture, though not as much as leaves, and so the damage isn't as great.

Although grass provides insulation and prevents the soil losing too much heat, it actually causes the air above it to cool down more rapidly, so that trees and shrubs planted in the lawn are more susceptible to damage from frost than those planted in bare soil.

Air frosts – when the temperature is 0°C at 1.2m (4ft) above the ground – can be

even more damaging, particularly in early spring, when they can kill blossom (and on fruit trees, that means the year's crop is destroyed) and new shoots. The most devastating combination is a mild spell which starts everything into growth, followed by an air frost, which freezes the soft new tissue and destroys it. Plants may escape permanent damage if they are allowed to thaw very slowly, which is why shrubs like camellias are safer in a north-facing border than in an east-facing one. In the latter, the early morning sun thaws the buds or flowers much too quickly, and in the process larger ice crystals are formed which rupture the delicate cell walls of the petals and kill them. The brown staining is dead tissue.

If you live in a cold area, then there's not much you can do other than move, or choose plants that can cheerfully put up with the cold. Native plants, or plants from northern Europe, the north of North America and other temperate regions with a very similar climate to our own, will normally do well in cold gardens. All native trees and many of their hybrids – like some maples, birches, hornbeams, hawthorns and rowans – will tolerate these conditions. You might think that because trees are woody, and therefore not vulnerable to frost damage, any tree would cope in a cold garden. But that's not so. A tree that's native to a warmer climate may well go on producing new growth well into late summer, and that new growth is then vulnerable to the first frosts. It would probably survive a couple of years of this treatment but would eventually become weakened and die. Equally trees from a much colder climate are vulnerable here too. They might be lured out of dormancy by a mild spell early in the spring – something that

wouldn't happen in their native habitat – and then have the new growth cut back by late spring frosts. Again, this would weaken the tree and eventually kill it.

Shrubs that can stand cold conditions inland are very tough and in many cases can stand up to other hardships as well, like shade and lack of moisture. The evergreens usually have tough, leathery leaves – holly (*Ilex*), *Elaeagnus* and the very accommodating *Euonymus fortunei*. The leaves are not usually very large (though of course there are exceptions, like *Viburnum rhytidophyllum* whose leathery leaves are up to 25cm long) and sometimes very small indeed like those on the low-growing evergreen cotoneasters and some berberis, for instance, and sometimes, virtually non-existent, like those on gorse (*Ulex*). The reason here is drought, only this time caused, not by heat but by extreme cold which freezes the water in the soil and makes it unavailable to the plant. Small leaves and tough leathery ones lose water less rapidly than large, softer, thinner ones.

One group of plants you would expect to thrive in cold gardens are alpines. True alpines (as opposed to rock plants, which are virtually any small plants that are in scale with a rock garden, and can include lovers of Mediterranean conditions like thymes and helianthemums) are plants whose native habitat is the side of a mountain, and which spend their winters under a blanket of snow. Ironically that acts as insulation against very low temperatures, keeping what warmth there is in the soil, preventing it from freezing. But of course that's only part of the story. They also grow in very thin, poor, free-draining soil, often no soil worthy of the name at all – just the crevice of a rock or virtually pure gravel -

with plenty of water in spring, as the snow melts, and then hardly any more for the rest of the growing season. Most of them grow in brilliant sunshine, though there are some that prefer the shady side of a rock, always in circulating air and often exposed to very strong winds. And they are well adapted to these conditions. They are very hardy, usually very small – few true alpines are more than 15cm tall, though their flowers may be taller – and their compact, creeping habit means they are in little danger of damage from strong winds or from heavy falls of snow. The fact that they get little moisture during the growing season, apart from the spring thaw, means their leaves are adapted to cope with lack of moisture just like those of drought-lovers – so they are either very small, like raoulia, very narrow, like *Armeria maritima*, very fleshy, like houseleeks (sempervivums) and stonecrops (sedums), or very woolly, like edelweiss (*Leontopodium alpinum*).

What they can't cope with, though, is wet, either in the soil or on their leaves. Try to grow them in heavy soil and you'll find that many of the choicer alpines will just rot. If yours is very sticky clay, you can still grow alpines, provided you open it up first with lots of organic matter and grit. On really heavy soil, you're better off growing them in a raised bed, which could be as simple as an area edged with single railway sleepers, and filled with the light, gritty compost alpines love. Given they are mostly very shallow-rooting, 15cm will be plenty deep enough.

Some, particularly those with hairy leaves, will also rot if they get too much rain or, just as bad, a blanket of wet leaves sitting on top of them in autumn, so do make sure you clear any dead leaves as soon

as they fall. One way to solve the problem is to grow the vulnerable alpines in a raised bed or a trough and make a simple cover on legs from rigid PVC and wood to sit over the top during the winter months. This will keep the rain off but allow air to circulate and keep the plants cold. If you only have a few, then you can make individual shelters from small pieces of window glass supported on metal clips or, if they're all growing together, cover them all with one larger sheet of glass supported by three bricks on each side, two underneath the glass and one on top, to hold it in place.

Frost pockets

If the problem is a frost pocket then there might be something you can do, at least to alleviate the situation if not to solve it completely. If your garden is on a slope, and what traps the cold air in is a hedge, wall or fence across the lower end of the garden, then think about removing part of the hedge, putting a gate in the wall, or raising the fence a few inches off the ground to allow the cold air an escape route.

If your garden is actually situated in a hollow, then it might be worth thinking about diverting the cold air by putting in some kind of barrier – a formal, or informal hedge or a copse of trees or shrubs – part-way across the slope *above* your garden. You'd still get some cold air rolling into your garden, but at least you'd protect part of it so that you could grow some slightly more tender plants in that area. If only a part of your garden is in a frost pocket, you might find a raised bed, or just raising the level of the soil a bit, solves the problem.

The type of soil you have plays a part here, too. Wet soils are less likely to suffer

from frost than free-draining ones – they are better conductors of heat and so can draw on heat stored lower down to resist frost more easily – but plants that are slightly tender actually stand a better chance of survival in the latter than the former. The reason is simply that there is less water available to the plant, less water to freeze inside its stems and leaves and do damage to the cell structure, less water to turn into a solid block of ice around its roots. So if you have a heavy soil, improving the drainage with organic matter and grit will help improve the plants' chances of survival. It's also worth noting that potassium and sodium, both important plant nutrients found in organic matter, both lower the freezing point of sap, so plants which are grown in soil rich in organic matter stand a better chance of survival than those that aren't. Obviously, if you can't live without a particular shrub or perennial that is on the borderline for hardiness, then give it the warmest, most sheltered spot you can find in the garden, and be prepared to take additional measures in winter.

Protection from air frost

To protect small freestanding borderline shrubs like pittosporum, small-leafed hebes and the lovely tri-coloured sage (*Salvia officinalis* 'Tricolor'), take two pieces of chicken wire, one slightly smaller than the other, and make a sandwich with a filling of straw, dead leaves, evergreen prunings, loft insulating material (though you'd need

Left: *The crimson leaves of* Parthenocissus tricuspidata, *stunning in autumn, will brighten up a cold north wall.*

Below: *The tough leathery evergreen leaves of* Bergenia crassifolia *look lovely rimed with frost.*

to put it inside a plastic sack first to prevent it becoming soggy with rain) or even newspapers. Then bend them into a circle around the plant and wire the edges together. Alternatively you can use two layers of fine plastic garden mesh to sandwich the insulation, although you would need four long stakes or canes pushed into the soil around the plant to support it. Even simpler is a wigwam of bamboo canes, into which you push dry bracken or straw, and then wrap string around the outside in a spiral to keep the material in place.

For slightly tender shrubs planted against walls and climbers like the Chilean potato

vine (*Solanum crispum*), and the Chilean glory flower (*Eccremocarpus scaber*), the same principle applies. Fix two layers of plastic netting to the wall or fence on either side of the plant using wooden battens or metal eyes screwed into the fence. The inner layer should fit snugly across the plant, while the outer one should be just slightly looser. Then fill in between the two layers with one of the same materials as before. Alternatively, pile some brushwood or twiggy sticks around the base of the plant to give at least some of the top growth protection. If you have a wall-trained peach, pear or apple trees then a hard frost while they're in flower can be devastating, so take a broad piece of polythene long enough to stretch across the front of the tree and fix it to two posts – wood, metal, or even plastic drainpipe would do. When frost threatens, unroll your makeshift screen and prop the two posts against the wall or fence, one on either side of the tree. Remove it again in the morning. In the old days, fruit farmers used to protect orchards and vineyards against spring frosts by lighting bonfires between the trees. Indeed Thomas Hill, who was born in 1529, wrote in *The Gardeners' Labyrinth*:

If the careful Gardener would withstand the force of frost approaching, then let him burn store of chaffe if such plenty be there or near at hand, but for lack of the same, may he use the dry weeds plucked up out of the Garden or Field and the bigger Thistles or other waste fruits in many places of the same, especially toward that way which the wind bloweth, for on such wise handled, that the evil nigh or at hand is adverted.

A number of shrubs which produce new shoots from just below or at ground-level can survive cold weather even though their top growth is killed off by frost, *provided* their roots are insulated. Among them are fuchsias, like 'Mrs Popple' and *F. magellanica*, 'Versicolor', the lovely blue hardy plumbago (*Ceratostigma willmottianum*) and climbers like passion flower, the Chilean potato vine and Chilean glory flower, though if you can protect the top growth of the latter in the way suggested above, they will flower at least a month earlier next year. Spread a 15cm layer of dead leaves, straw or bark over the root area. If you just leave it, you may find the birds scattering it everywhere, as they pillage the heap for nest-building materials, so cover it with fine plastic mesh netting and peg it down with stout twigs. Alternatively, if you've been pruning conifers or evergreens like rhododendrons and laurel, pile the prunings over the roots instead. In a very wet, mild winter, there is a chance that the insulating material could rot, and therefore encourage the crown of the plant to rot, so do keep an eye on it and, if it does appear very wet, then replace it with dry material. Alternatively you could put a piece of chicken wire, bent very slightly into a curve, over the crown, just clearing it, and pile the insulating material on top of it. That way, the material isn't actually in contact with the crown, but it's close enough to it for the insulation to be effective.

Newly planted specimen conifers and shrubs like evergreen ceanothus, escallonia, Japanese maples and rock roses (cistus) can be badly damaged, if not killed, by bitingly cold winter winds, so protect them with a windbreak. For individual shrubs, take four stakes long enough to be a few inches taller than the shrub when they've been hammered into the ground, then tack or staple special plastic windbreak mesh (available from garden centres) to them, so that the shrub is completely surrounded, though open at the top. Leave it in place till late March or later in very cold areas.

If you forget all about protecting your shrubs until a severe frost is forecast for that night, don't panic – all is not lost. If you have any spun polypropylene 'floating cloche' material or even an old net curtain handy, drape it over the most vulnerable shrubs. It will afford a surprising amount of protection against air frost. Failing that, wrap the plant in clear bubble plastic for the night or, if you don't have any, take a large plastic rubbish bag with the bottom slit open and four long stakes or canes. Push them into the ground around the plant, then slide the plastic bag over them and stuff straw, if you happen to have any, or crumpled newspapers around the plant inside. If you don't have any canes to hand, then simply slip a carrier bag or dustbin bag (depending on the size of the shrub) over the plant and push crumpled newspapers up inside between the bag and the plant. That way, if the condensation on the inside of the bag does freeze, the paper will protect the foliage from it. Do remember that plastic bags really are a last resort, though, and only a very temporary measure, since plants inside them can't breathe and will soon suffer. If it looks as if we're in for a long, cold spell, then take more permanent precautions as soon as possible.

Most perennials are hardy, but in very cold gardens it's worth leaving the dead foliage on till spring to provide some insulation for the crown of the plant. A few perennials, like red hot pokers (*Kniphofia*), agapanthus, and the arum lily (*Zantedeschia aethiopica*) are vulnerable to frost damage,

and so benefit from additional root insulation. Pile a good 15–20cm of straw, bark, bracken, evergreen prunings or even grit or ashes over the crown of the plant. With red hot pokers, though, it's best to tie their strappy leaves together first and pull them clear of the protective layer. If you cover them with it, they may rot and kill the plant that way.

It's also worth remembering that snow can damage some trees and shrubs. The sheer weight of it on branches can either snap them off in the case of slightly brittle varieties like the golden *Robinia pseudoacacia* 'Frisia' or, in the case of conifers, bend them down permanently and ruin the shape of the tree. Hedges are particularly vulnerable. A heavy fall of snow can break them open, particularly if they haven't been trimmed so that they are narrower at the top than the bottom. If you've got a new hedge, do make sure you trim it that way, and so minimize the risk of snow damage in the future. As soon as practical after it has snowed, preferably before it's had a chance to freeze, shake the snow off the branches of shrubs and trees and off hedges, or knock it off with a long cane.

PLANTS

Plants that can cope with cold conditions tend to be the extremely tough, hardy ones which can put up with other, less than ideal conditions, too, so many of them are listed in other sections.

Trees

Common Maple (*Acer campestre*)
See page 111.
Acer negundo See page 143.
Betula See page 90.
Ilex See page 31.

Juniper (*Juniperus communis, J.×media, J. horizontalis* etc) Most junipers are extremely hardy. See page 144.
Laburnum See page 123.
Whitebeam (*Sorbus aria*) See page 143.
Rowan or Mountain ash (*Sorbus aucuparia*) See page 91.

Conifers

Mountain pine (*Pinus mugo*) See page 90.
Corsican pine (*Pinus nigra maritima*) See page 90.
Yew (*Taxus baccata*) See page 146.
Thuja occidentalis See page 146.

Climbers

Ivy (*Hedera*) Surprisingly, perhaps, not all ivies are fully hardy, but plain green varieties of common English ivy (*H. helix*) like 'Baltica' and the cheerful variegated *H.h.* 'Goldheart', and the larger-leafed Irish ivy (*H. hibernica*) and Persian ivy (*H. colchica*) and their cultivars can cope with very cold spots. See page 30.

Climbing hydrangea (*Hydrangea petiolaris*) This toughest of climbers will tolerate cold, too. See page 30.

Virginia creeper (*Parthenocissus tricuspidata*) See page 30.

Clematis Many species. See *alpina* particularly and large flowered hybrids are surprisingly tough. See page 30 and 146.

Shrubs

Bearberry (*Arctostaphylos uva-ursi*) See page 134.

Right: *Of all the dogwoods with colourful winter bark, Cornus alba 'Westonbirt' has the most vivid, sealing-wax red stems of all. Plant it where it catches the winter sun for the most dramatic effect. Cut it back hard each spring for the brightest colour.*

Left: *The hawthorn, Crataegus mono-gyna, is one of the toughest trees that will grow happily in a whole range of problem places. It makes a very good, animal-proof hedge and is a good shelter-belt tree for places exposed to wind, salt spray or pollution.*

Berberis See page 51 and 91.
Buddleia See page 52.
Scotch heather (*Calluna vulgaris***)**
See page 134.
Japanese quince (*Chaenomeles japonica***)**
See page 126.
Dogwood (*Cornus alba* **and** *stolonifera***)**
See page 73.
Cotoneaster See page 42.

Smoke tree (*Cotinus coggygria***)** In a sunny spot and moderately fertile but free-draining soil, these are lovely shrubs, grown primarily for their coloured foliage and their clouds of tiny pinkish flowers in late summer which look like billowing smoke, and which give the group its common name. The slight dilemma with the coloured foliage forms is that you get the best colour leaves if you cut them hard back, but if you do prune them hard, you lose that season's flowers. Perhaps the best compromise is to prune every few years, or prune out some stems each year so that you get some of each. Among the best are 'Flame' with dark green leaves turning brilliant orange-red in autumn, and showy plume-like purplish-pink flower heads, while the best purple form is probably 'Nottcutt's Variety', the leaves of which keep their wonderful translucent purple colour right through till autumn.
▷ *Approx. height and spread after 10 years (unpruned): 3 × 3m (10 × 10ft).*

Deutzia See page 148.
Elaeagnus commutata See page 31.
Euonymus fortunei and *japonicus* See page 31.
Gaultheria mucronata (formerly *Pernyetta mucronata*) See page 135.
Hippophae rhamnoides See page 114.

Hydrangea paniculata 'Grandiflora' One of the hardiest hydrangeas, this one needs a fertile, moist but well-drained soil in sun or part shade. Again, the more moisture in the soil, the more sun it can take. From late summer, it has large candles of creamy-white flowers that fade to pink.
▷ *Approx. height and spread after 10 years: 3 × 3m (10 × 10ft).*

Kerria japonica 'Variegata' See page 32.
Mahonia aquifolium See page 32.
Mock orange (*Philadelphus*) See page 127.
Pieris floribunda See page 138.
Potentilla fruticosa See page 92.

Rhododendron The wild rhododendron *R. ponticum* is very hardy – in fact it's become a menace in some parts of the country where it has taken over! Obviously not a plant for a small garden. The lovely dwarf *R. yakushimanum*, which grows in the wild on windswept mountainsides in Japan, is also very hardy. See page 138.

Willow (*Salix*) See page 73.
Spiraea See page 92.
Snowberry (*Symphoricarpos albus*) See page 74
Tamarix See page 106 (all varieties).
Gorse (*Ulex*) See page 92.
Wayfaring tree (*Viburnum lantana*) See page 115.
Guelder rose (*Viburnum opulus*) See page 34.

Perennials

Elephant's ears (*Bergenia cordifolia*) See page 34.
Siberian bugloss (*Brunnera macrophylla*) It has sprays of forget-me-not-like flowers in spring, and large heart-shaped leaves. Good under trees
▷ *Height and spread: 45 × 45cm (18 × 18in)*
Cranesbill (*Geranium*) See page 43.
Christmas rose (*Helleborus niger*) See page 35.

Dead-nettle (*Lamium maculatum*) See page 35.
Pachysandra terminalis See page 32.
Knotweed (*Persicaria* – formerly *Polygonum* – *affinis*) See page 32.
Phlox See page 152.
Primrose (*Primula vulgaris*) See page 78.
Lungwort (*Pulmonaria officinalis* and P. *saccharata*) See page 37.

Foamflower (*Tiarella wherryi*) A small relative of the true foamflower, *T. cordifolia*, this forms small mounds of similar heart-shaped green leaves that are flushed with deep red along its veins in winter. In early summer it has spikes of very small fluffy white or very pale pink flowers. It's a woodland plant and so likes reasonably moist soil and partshade.
▷ *Height and spread: 10 × 15cm (4 × 6in).*

Alpines

Many of these tough little plants from mountainous regions are good in this situation. Unless stated otherwise, all these plants need a sunny spot.

New Zealand burr (*Acaena*) The very low-growing alpines are grown for their virtually evergreen foliage and curious reddish-brown burrs in autumn which follow the flowers. Look for *A. inermis* 'Copper Carpet' with copper-coloured leaves and reddish-orange burrs, or 'Blue Haze' with steel-blue foliage and deep pink-red burrs.
▷ *Approx. height and spread: 5-10 × 50-75cm (2-4in × 1ft 8in-2ft 6in).*

Yarrow (*Achillea*) The best alpine variety is probably *A × lewisii* 'King Edward' which has delicate ferny grey-green foliage and primrose-yellow, daisy-like flowers from June to September.
▷ *Approx. height and spread: 15 × 25cm (6 × 10in).*

Arabis ferdinandi-coburgii 'Variegata' Its name is almost larger than it is! This plant forms low mounds of very attractive green and white variegated foliage and has white flowers in summer. There is now a gold and green variegated form, *A.f-c.* 'All Gold'.
▷ *Approx. height and spread: 10 × 30cm (4 × 12in).*

Thrift (*Armeria*) Good, very low-growing varieties of this evergreen cushion plant include *A. caespitosa* 'Bevan's Variety' which has bright pink flowers and deep green foliage and *A.c.* 'Alba' with white flowers. Both flower in May.
▷ *Approx. height and spread: 6 × 15cm (2-3 × 6in).*

Bell flower (*Campanula*) The C. cochleariifolia hybrids are valuable summer-flowering alpines, taking over when the many spring-flowering ones have finished. They'll grow in part shade as well as full sun. *C. poscharskyana* and *C. portenschlagiana*, with starry blue-mauve flowers, both spread like crazy but will grow practically anywhere - in sun or shade in very poor soil, in the cracks of paving or steps. If it gets over-ambitious, just pull out its long flower-covered runners by the handful. It does the plant no harm.
▷ *Approx. height and spread: 10-15cm × infinite (4-6in × infinite).*

Maiden pinks (*Dianthus deltoides*) Although some other dwarf dianthus like 'Pike's Pink' are lovely, the mat-forming maiden pinks like *D. deltoides* 'Brighteyes' (white with a red 'eye') and *D.d.* 'Flashing Light' (brilliant cerise) with masses of flat-faced flowers are probably a better bet in a windy spot.
▷ *Approx. height and spread: 10 × 10-20cm (4 × 4-8in).*

Cranesbill (*Geranium*) Among the best alpine varieties are *G. cinereum* 'Ballerina', with lilac-pink flowers veined with red from May to July, *G.* 'Laurence Flatman' with soft, mauve-pink flowers mottled with magenta from May to September, *G.c. subcaulescens*, with crimson flowers with a black eye from May to July, and the delicious pale pink *G. sanguineum lancastriense* with very finely divided bright green leaves.
▷ *Approx. height and spread. 10-15 × 30cm (4-6 × 12in).*

Alpine phlox (*Phlox subulata*) Another good carpeting plant for this kind of site, with mats of evergreen mossy foliage and masses of tiny flowers in early summer in red pink, white and blue. Good varieties include 'White Delight', 'Oakington Blue' and the rose-pink 'Marjory'.
▷ *Approx. height and spread: 10 × 20cm (4 × 8in).*

Sedum Try the mat-forming, evergreen S. *spathulifolium* with fleshy silver leaves, suffused with wine-red. The leaves of *S.s.* 'Cape Blanco' are suffused with purple, giving the plant a more steely colour. Both forms have bright yellow flowers and will spread indefinitely. S. *lydium* has very small fleshy leaves often stained bright red and clusters of tiny white flowers, and is much more restrained. Do avoid the native stonecrop, *Sedum acre*, unless you have a huge mount of space to fill, since it is dreadfully invasive and will regrow from the smallest piece left in the soil.
▷ *Approx. height and spread: 10cm × infinite (4in × infinite).*

Houseleeks (*Sempervivum*) People become addicted to these and build up huge collections. Their rosettes of fleshy leaves in a range of colours are very striking, as are their spikes of flowers in June-July, and they grow in almost any dry sunny spot, even on roofs - hence their common name.
▷ *Approx. height and spread: 10-15 × 20-30cm (4-6 × 8-12in).*

Annuals

Most common hardy annuals will do well in cold gardens, *provided* the soil is not too heavy and wet. What they won't tolerate is a combination of cold *and* wet so if yours is a sticky clay soil you must improve the drainage first (see page 119). Also remember not to plant any half-hardy bedding out until all danger of frost has past, which will probably be later than average in your garden, even as late as mid June.

Bulbs

Crocus A huge choice from large-flowered Dutch hybrids to small species crocus, like *C. chrysanthus* 'Blue Pearl' or *C. tommasinianus*.
▷ *Height and spread: 10 × 5cm (4 × 2in).*

Winter aconite (*Eranthis hyemalis*) See page 39.
Snowdrops (*Galanthus nivalis*) See page 40 and 81.
Narcissi See page 156.
Grape hyacinths (*Muscari*) See page 40.
Tulips The small species tulips are all very hardy. See page 63.

SEASIDE PLACES

Seaside gardens differ from windy gardens inland in two very important respects. First, winds off the sea are laden with salt, which means that not only is the air very salty, leaving a white crusty deposit on leaves, but the soil becomes salty too, and the plants absorb it through their roots. And second – a plus this time – because of the sea, winter temperatures on the coast are just a few degrees higher than those inland, which means that

a number of tender plants which wouldn't survive even ten miles inland will thrive.

In recent years, salt has become not just a problem for seaside gardens but for some inland gardens too, where local authorities use salt or salt-based compounds rather than grit to treat icy roads in winter. You only have to drive along some busy roads to see the damage done to hedges – deciduous hedging plants like beech, some conifers like Leylandii and thuja, evergreens like laurel – which are slowly dying.

The reason is that salt is highly toxic to some plants, as you'll know if ever you've sprinkled it on the centre of a dandelion or other weed between paving stones, and watched it slowly shrivel and die. Salt extracts water wherever it can, and so it drains moisture out of some leaves, causing drought damage. The resulting salt solution also burns the leaf chemically.

With a seaside location, where the milder temperatures start plants into growth earlier than inland only for them to be killed by the next salt-laden gale, the first thing to do is create a tough wind-filtering and salt-resistant barrier. Appealing though a 2m wall may seem initially, it's not a good idea, so your best bet is a permeable screen, and ideally a living one (see page 83).

Given the job these shelter-belt plants have to do, the most important quality to go for is toughness. By and large this means

Left: *The rowan,* Sorbus aucuparia, *is another tough attractive small tree for a wide range of problem places.*

Right: *Film director, Derek Jarman's extra-ordinary seaside garden, near Dungeness in Kent.*

they will be fairly ordinary trees and shrubs which you wouldn't choose to grow in more favourable circumstances, and which are never going to reach even their limited true potential, because strong winds will stunt their growth and tear their leaves, which could also be scorched by the salt. Even they will need some sort of man-made windbreak themselves when they're first planted (see page 86) to give them a real chance of getting established.

Of course, if your garden overlooks the sea directly, presumably the sea-view was one of the reasons you want to live there, and so you don't want to block it out entirely with a shelter belt. The answer then is to put up a partial barrier, creating some more sheltered areas in the garden, and at the same time framing the view.

As for gardens suffering from roadside salt pollution, the solution to the problem is similar. You need to create a salt-tolerant and salt-resistant barrier to keep out the air-borne salt. You can't do much about the salt in the soil, but that's not too much of a problem since it's unlikely to spread beyond the strip closest to the road where you'll be planting your barrier anyway.

Plants that grow naturally on the shore line have to be very tough indeed, to cope with growing in more or less pure sand with little in the way of nutrients. And, like those growing near the sea, they have developed strategies to cope with salt. Pines, for example, like the Austrian pine (*Pinus nigra maritima*), which have very fine, leathery needles, can shrug off salt spray with no ill-effects, while the softer foliage of other conifers, like junipers and piceas, will quickly brown at the tips and die.

Other shrubs, like the evergreen New Zealand native *Griselina littoralis* (littoralis means 'of the coast') have evergreen leaves with a very tough, shiny surface, off which salty water runs, and through which salt cannot penetrate. Other non-maritime evergreens like holly, aucuba, *Elaeagnus × ebbingei* and euonymus are equally useful in this situation and inland, while slightly more tender subjects like Mexican orange blossom (*Choisya ternata*), escallonia and some cotoneasters will be fine by the sea, but are less likely to thrive in colder areas.

Many plants with silver foliage do well by the sea because the small dead hairs which give the leaf its silver colour, and which protect it from the drying effects of both the sun and the wind, also trap the salt particles and keep them off the surface of the leaf. The daisy bush (*Olearia macrodonta*) adopts a belt and braces approach here by having leaves that are tough and shiny on the top, but silvery and felted underneath. Plants with very small leaves – leathery evergreens like the box-leafed honeysuckle (*Lonicera nitida*) or tiny slender leaves like tamarisk or broom, or no leaves at all, like gorse, also do well, because they offer the salt little surface area on which to settle and penetrate.

Also worth trying are some of the tough, deciduous shrubs like elder, sea buckthorn (*Hippophae rhamnoides*), the common dogwood (*Cornus sanguinea*) spiraea and the guelder rose (*Viburnum opulus*), which shed their leaves in winter when there's more likely to be more salt around, and woody stems won't be damaged by it in the same way that foliage can be.

Roses on the whole don't like salt much, but there are a few species that cope with it very well. In fact, as a result of long-term trials, the Department of Transport recommends some roses for central reservation planting on main roads. The native sweet briar or eglantine (*Rosa rubiginosa*) has exquisite buds opening to small, scented single pink flowers, small red hips in the autumn and, unusually, foliage that is even more richly scented than the flowers.

▷ *Rosa rugosa* has wrinkly leaves (*rugosa* means 'wrinkly') and tough spiny stems which shrug off salt well – indeed although it's not a native, you now find it naturalized around the coast of Britain from Kent to the north of Scotland. There are some attractive hybrids, too, flowering throughout the summer. Another rose which stands up to salt and wind very well is the Scotch or burnet rose (*Rosa pimpinellifolia*) and its hybrids, though they only flower once, in May–June. Other species roses, like *R. moyesii* with its bright geranium-red flowers, and *R. glauca* (formerly *rubrifolia*) will tolerate some salt.

Once you have got your salt-resistant barrier in place, then you will be able to grow a wide range of smaller shrubs and perennials, limited only by the aspect and the type of soil you have. But if such a barrier is impossible, there are some perennials that will do well in these conditions – mainly those whose native habitat is the seashore and their relatives. Not surprisingly, many have 'sea' in their common name like 'sea thrift', and *maritima* in their Latin name like *Armeria maritima*. Again, they tend to have very tough leaves, like the very spiky sea holly (*Eryngium maritimum*), very slender leaves like sea lavender (*Limonium vulgare*, known to dried-flower arrangers as 'statice' – or as my local flower seller calls it, 'status'), or very small leaves like sea thrift. There are also some lovely wild plants for this situation, as you'll know if you saw Plantlife's

remarkable seaside garden at the Chelsea Flower Show in 1993, which not only won a gold medal but also the award for the best garden in the show.

Most ordinary summer bedding plants will survive salty conditions reasonably well, as will spring-flowering bulbs – especially if they are planted deeply enough to escape the top salty layer of soil. Winter and early spring bedding – pansies and wallflowers, for example – is more likely to suffer damage from salt.

Many plants that grow naturally near the sea are used to very free-draining, poor conditions, so they would not be able to cope with boggy or heavy soil. But it's true to say that plants that do well in these impoverished conditions would do even better with a bit more moisture and nutriment, so it's worth digging some bulky organic matter into the soil before you plant.

PLANTS

Plants that will put up with only seaside conditions are marked **S**. Those that are suitable only for roadside planting in colder places inland are marked **R**. Those marked **SR** are suitable for both.

Salt-resistant shelterbelt trees for small gardens

Field maple (Acer campestre) R The only true British native maple, this low-branching round-headed tree will tolerate most soil types and conditions, though it will grow more slowly in poor conditions. Its leaves are a simplified version of the more beautiful varieties of maple, but it does have spectacular golden autumn colour.
▷ *Approx. height and spread after 10 years: 5 × 5m (16 × 16ft).*

Quickthorn/Hawthorn (Crataegus monogyna) SR See page 90.

False acacia (*Robinia pseudoacacia*) R It has good salt tolerance inland, but the fact that its branches are rather brittle and prone to wind damage means it's not a good tree for a seaside garden. The golden-leafed version, *R.p.* 'Frisia', is unlikely to do as well since its leaves have less chlorophyll than the plain variety and are less tough. ▷ *Approx. height and spread after 10 years: 8 × 5m (26 × 16ft).*

Common osier or Basket willow (*Salix viminalis*) RS This has long narrow green leaves, the undersides of which are covered in silvery hairs that help protect the leaves from salt. It produces golden catkins before the leaves in March. It is very quick-growing, but since it's grown to produce materials for basket-making, it can be cut back with no ill effects to its health – only to its appearance. ▷ *Approx. height and spread after 10 years: 5-6 × 5m (16-20 × 16ft).*

Above: *Tamarisk, with its plumes of tiny pale pink flowers in summer, looks too delicate to stand up to salt-laden winds, but it does with ease.*

Right: *This garden on a Devon clifftop shows how the slight increase in temperatures by the sea allows a tender plant to thrive – a rare relative of the yucca, and even a Japanese banana plant,* Musa basjoo.

Whitebeam (*Sorbus aria*) RS An attractive upright tree whose leaves – bright green on top, and a downy silver underneath – need a breeze to show them to advantage. It also has good autumn colour. *S.a.* 'Lutescens' is one of the best, with leaves that start silvery on top as well before turning green. For small gardens *S × hostii*, which will only reach 3–4m (10–13ft) in 10 years, is a good choice. It has the same sort of leaves, and pink flowers in May. ▷ *Approx. height and spread after 10 years: 6 × 4m (20 × 13ft).*

Shrubs

Bamboo (*Arundinaria* etc) s See page 79.

Berberis s Some of the deciduous berberis, like *B. thunbergii*, and some of the tough leathery evergreens like *B. darwinii* and *B. julianae*, make good boundaries for seaside gardens. They will also put up with roadside conditions where salting is done occasionally, rather than regularly. See page 40.

Brachyglottis (formerly *Senecio* 'Sunshine') s See page 52.

Pea tree or Salt tree (*Caragana arborescens*) RS As one of its common names suggests, this small tree or large shrub with feathery bright green foliage and masses of pea-flowers can tolerate salt very well. The weeping version, *C.a.* 'Pendula', on either 1.5m (5ft) or 2.5m (8ft) stems is very attractive, as is the smaller *C.a.* 'Walker' grafted on to 1m (3ft), 1.5m (5ft) or 2m (6ft) stems.
▷ *Approx. height and spread after 10 years: 4 × 4m (13 × 13ft).*

Common dogwood (*Cornus sanguinea*) R Another tough native that can withstand roadside pollution, it has plain green leaves, and attractive red-green stems in winter. It must be said, it's not as attractive as the many variegated forms, but the variegation means that the leaves aren't quite as tough as the plain ones, and so they're not likely to survive as well.
▷ *Approx. height and spread after 10 years: 2.5 × 4m (8 × 13ft).*

Oleaster (*Elaeagnus angustifolia*) SR This is probably the toughest member of the family, and scored highly in the Department of Transport's tests. *E.* ×*ebbingei* and *E. commutata* (see page 31) will do well in seaside locations and will tolerate roadside conditions too, though not quite as well.
▷ *Approx. height and spread after 10 years: 2-3 × 2m (6-10 × 6ft).*

Escallonia A good seaside hedging plant, it will remain evergreen in mild conditions, and lose some of its leaves in colder spots, though they will reappear in spring. There are several good hybrids – anything with 'Donard' in its name is worth growing – and they all have pink flowers in June, ranging from the palest blush to a deep pinky-carmine. Also good is 'Iveyi', with large deep green leaves and white flowers in August rather than June.
▷ *Approx. height and spread after 10 years: 3 × 4m (10 × 13ft).*

Euonymus fortunei (formerly *japonicus*) s These tough little evergreens are valuable in this problem place, as in so many others. Some plain green varieties of *E. fortunei*, like 'Dart's Blanket' and the larger-leafed *E. japonicus*, are so tolerant of salt spray that they can cope with salty conditions inland as well. Variegated varieties, which have less chlorophyll in their leaves, are less tough. See page 31.

Shrubby veronica (*Hebe*) A number of these evergreen New Zealand natives do really well in the slightly milder winter conditions on the coast. Three in particular are worth trying – *H. brachysiphon*, a rounded bush with dark leaves and stubby spikes of white flowers in late summer, the larger *H. salicifolia*, which (as its botanical name suggests) has willow-like leaves and the very palest mauve, almost white flowers in midsummer, and hybrids derived from *H. speciosa*, like the deep blue 'Alicia Amherst' (sometimes sold as 'Veitchii') and the magenta 'La Séduisante'.
▷ *Approx. height and spread after 10 years: 1.2 × 2m (4 × 6ft).*

Sea buckthorn (*Hippophae rhamnoides*) RS A real toughie this, it will survive almost anywhere, including sand dunes. It's also more attractive than you might expect, with slender silvery willow-like leaves, and, if you plant a male plant with some females, bright translucent orange-yellow berries from September to February. It can be grown as a hedge.
▷ *Approx. height and spread after 10 years (unpruned): 4 × 4m (13 × 13ft).*

Ligustrum ovalifolium (Privet) RS Not the most exciting of shrubs in its plain green form, but useful here. See page 42.

Duke of Argyll's tea tree (*Lycium barbarum*) A useful salt-resistant shrub that ought to be better known, it has long, grey-green leaves and clusters of small, purple, trumpet-shaped flowers in late spring/early summer which are followed by round orange-red berries. In a sunny spot, it forms a broad arching shrub.
▷ *Approx. height and spread after 10 years: 2 × 3m (6ft 6in × 10ft).*

Daisy bush (*Olearia × haastii*) s Another Antipodean which benefits from the milder winter temperatures on the coast. *O. × haastii* is probably the hardiest, with grey-green leaves and masses of white scented daisies from midsummer on. *O. macrodonta*, the New Zealand holly, is also good, but larger with holly-shaped leaves and similar heads of white flowers in early summer.
▷ *Approx. height and spread after 10 years: 1.2-2 × 1.2-2m (4-6 × 4-6ft).*

Firethorn (*Pyracantha*) RS See page 32.

Sweet briar or Eglantine, Scotch or Burnet rose (R. rubiginosa, R. pimpinellifolia and R. rugosa) SR *R. rubiginosa* has scented pink flowers in midsummer, and apple-scented foliage too, released when the leaves are bruised – after a shower of rain, for instance. The smaller *R. pimpinellifolia* has single, creamy-white or sometimes palest pink flowers in midsummer. The hybrid *R.p.* 'Double White' has double flowers, and *R.p.* 'Grandiflora' has much larger flowers. Also worth trying are *R.p.* 'Stanwell Perpetual' which produces pale pink scented double flowers throughout the summer, and *R.p. harisonii* with scented, double sulphur-yellow flowers.
▷ *Rosa rugosa* flowers throughout the summer. Look for hybrids like 'Alba', 'Blanc Double de Coubert', which are both white, the lovely clear pink single 'Fru Dagmar Hastrup' (or sometimes sold as 'Frau Dagmar Hartopp') and deep crimson 'Roserie del' Hay'.
▷ *Approx. height and spread after 10 years: 1-2.4 × 1.2-2.4m (3-8 × 4-8ft).*

Spanish broom (*Spartium junceum*) RS See page 56.

Snowberry (*Symphoricarpos*) RS See page 74.

Common tamarisk (*Tamarix gallica*) s This species can be found growing wild along the coast now, so clearly it can stand any amount of exposure to salt-spray and winds. It combines very slender, whippy branches that bend in the wind with very tiny leaves that salt can't damage.
▷ *Approx. height and spread after 10 years: 2.5 × 2.5m (8 × 8ft).*

Gorse (*Ulex*) s See page 92.

Wayfaring tree (*Viburnum lantana*) R A stout native, with clusters of white flowers in spring followed by red berries that turn black, and large leaves, felted underneath to protect the leaf from salt, which turn deep red in autumn. The guelder rose will also cope with salt spray.
▷ *Approx. height and spread after 10 years: 3 × 2.5m (10 × 8ft).*

Yucca s All do well in seaside gardens though some varieties, like *Y. filamentosa* and *Y. flaccida*, are hardy everywhere. See page 57.

Perennials

Again, once you have created a salt-proof windbreak you can grow a wide range of perennials, limited mainly by your soil type and aspect. Those listed below will cope where it's not possible to put up such a screen, or while you're waiting for it to become established. Their natural habitat is poor, sandy soil, or sometimes just sand, free-draining and very low in nutrients, so to cope with that as well as windy and salty conditions, they really do have to be tough.

Sea thrift (*Armeria maritima*) A good low-growing plant for this situation, with its narrow grass-like foliage and round heads of tiny flowers, rather like miniature cloves, for weeks throughout the summer. *A.m.* 'Alba' is a pure white form, while 'Dusseldorf Pride' has deep pink flowers.
▷ *Approx. height and spread: 10 × 15cm (4 × 6in).*

Sea holly (*Eryngium*) RS The perennial members of the family are very dramatic plants for very free-draining soil in full sun. See page 58.

Red hot pokers (*Kniphophia*) s These marginally tender perennials do well in milder coastal gardens – indeed they are now to be found growing wild along the shoreline and now come in a range of lovely subtle colours as well as the basic red and orange, like the lemon-yellow 'Citrina', the dwarf 'Little Maid', which has cream flowers with a soft orange tip, or a new variety, 'Bressingham Cobra'.
▷ *Height and spread: 60cm-1.2m × 45-50cm (2-4ft × 1ft 6in-1ft 8in).*

Sea lavender (*Limonium latifolium*) This clump-forming perennial has clouds of small blue-mauve flowers in late summer, which are often dried.
▷ *Approx. height and spread: 30 × 45cm (12 × 18in).*

Evening primrose (*Oenothera biennis*) Through-out the summer, the biennial evening primrose has a succession of butter yellow flowers, lasting only a day, which are richly scented when they open in the evening. However, it seeds itself like

crazy, so although it's biennial, once you've got it, you're likely to have it for keeps.
▷ *Approx. height and spread: 1m × 30cm (3ft × 10in).*

Knotweed or Bistort (*Persicaria bistorta*) RS
See page 35.
Phormium S See page 35.
Double sea campion (*Silene maritima* 'Flore Pleno') RS
A seashore plant with grey-green leaves and branching heads of white pompom flowers in summer.
▷ *Approx. height and spread: 20 × 20cm (8 × 8in).*

Lamb's lugs (*Stachys byzantina* or *lanata* or *olympica*) S The hairs that give the leaves their silver colour also keep the salt off. See page 62.

Annuals

Most summer-flowering annuals are tolerant of seaside conditions and, since they are extremely unlikely to get doused by the council's salting lorries during their growing season, they are useful for roadside planting inland, too. Winter bedding – wallflowers, pansies and so on – which would get drenched in salty water during the icy road season will not survive.

Bulbs

Most dwarf bulbs will do well in seaside conditions though obviously the taller daffodils and tulips would get battered by the wind, so go for low-growing, sturdy varieties. Most will also tolerate

Left: *A small formally laid out seaside garden, with salt-tolerant plants growing in beds edged with box. Tall spires of* acanthus mollis *and of red hot pokers,* Kniphofia, *can clearly withstand sea breezes.*

Right: *Gorse with its minimal, tough spiny leaves, and sea campion,* Silene maritima, *are both perfectly adapted for growing in the wild on a cliff face in the Channel Islands.*

roadside planting, too – think how cheerful verges planted with daffodils and crocuses look in spring. Although the mucky, salty spray from passing traffic doesn't improve their appearance, it doesn't actually do the bulbs any harm.

Wildflowers Plants that are native to the seashore will obviously thrive in seaside gardens, and while you may not choose to grow them where other more beautiful cultivated garden plants will thrive, in a situation where beggars can't be choosers they will do very nicely indeed. The Department of Transport recently produced a booklet on wild-flower planting on roadside banks and verges, and their advice is not to plant any wildflowers within 45cm (18in) of the kerb because the amount of grit, muck and salt thrown on to them makes their survival unlikely.

Obviously you mustn't take any plants from the wild. Instead buy seed or small plants from specialist seedsmen like John Chambers 0933 652562 or Chiltern Seeds 0229 581137.

It's worth pointing out that many of these plants, the creeping ones especially, have a quite different habit and quite different dimensions when they are grown alone and not in grass. Those I have given below refer to their height and spread in a border.

Kidney vetch (*Anthyllis vulneraria*) This low-growing biennial has curious heads of flowers yellow or orange-red. It will grow on the very poorest soil.
▷ *Approx. height and spread: 50 × 30cm (20 × 12in).*

Sea wormwood (*Artemisia maritima*) Like all the artemisias, this has silvery, finely divided, strongly aromatic foliage and curious yellow flowers that look a bit like a boiled egg with the top cut off.
▷ *Approx. height and spread: 25-50 × 20cm (10-20 × 8in).*

Harebell (*Campanula rotundifolia*) s This long-lived perennial has pretty blue bell-shaped flowers and can withstand being cut down, so a good choice for naturalizing in grass.
▷ *Approx. height and spread: 20-30 × 20-30cm (8-12 × 8-12in).*

Greater knapweed (*Centaurea scabiosa*) s This tall perennial has purple cornflower-like flowers, and jagged green leaves. Does well on very dry poor soils.
▷ *Approx. height and spread: 90 × 45cm (3ft × 1ft 6in).*

Common centaury (*Centaurium erythraea*) s This low-growing member of the gentian family has sprays of small pink flowers in summer.
▷ *Approx. height and spread: 10 × 10cm (4 × 4in).*

Hound's tongue (*Cynoglossum oficinale*) s This tall biennial, which smells of mice, has downy grey-green leaves and heads of small maroon flowers throughout the summer. The seeds are covered in burrs and so stick to your clothing.
▷ *Approx. height and spread: 60 + × 30cm (2 + × 1ft).*

Viper's bugloss (*Echium vulgare*) s See page 94.

Yellow horned poppy (*Glaucium flavum*) s An attractive perennial with large yellow flowers from June to September and grey-green leaves, this grows wild along the south and east coasts of Britain.
▷ *Approx. height and spread: 60 × 20cm (2ft × 8in).*

Oxeye daisy (*Leucanthemum vulgare*) The large white, gold-centred daisies appear from May to September, and the jagged leaves are evergreen. It's fairly short-lived.
▷ *Approx. height and spread: 70 × 20cm (2ft 4in × 8in).*

Common toadflax (*Linaria vulgaris*) This ever-green perennial has yellow flowers like a snap-dragon's except they have a spur at the base from July to October.
▷ *Approx. height and spread: 50 × 10cm (20 × 4in).*

Tansy (*Tanacetum vulgare*) This strongly aro-matic plant has clusters of small yellow button flowers from midsummer till autumn.
▷ *Approx. height and spread: 60 + × 20cm (2ft + × 8in).*

Wild thyme (*Thymus praecox* or *drucei*) A low-growing, mat-forming evergreen shrub with aromatic leaves, just like its garden relatives, and small mauve or deep pink flowers in summer.
▷ *Approx. height and spread: 10 × 30cm (4 × 12in).*

CLAY SOIL

 There's no doubt that a heavy clay soil is a big problem. It's the most difficult type of soil to work initially because when it's wet, it's a sticky, slimy morass and when it's dry, it's as hard as concrete, and neither of these states is particularly hospitable to plants. That's the bad news. The good news is that, once you've alleviated the problems as much as possible – and I'd be doing you no favours if I didn't say that it involves a fair bit of hard work – a clay soil will grow far better plants than very light, sandy soils ever can because it holds on to essential moisture and nutrients far better than they are able to.

The main problem with heavy clay soils (and with silt soils) is very bad drainage. That's because the particles that make up these soils are the smallest there are, so unlike the larger particles of sandy or gritty soils, there are no air spaces between them to allow water to drain through. Instead, when water is added they bind together to form a cohesive sticky mass, and a wet airless environment means that many fine roots will drown and rot. When the soils dry out, they form a bone-hard, solid mass, which allows no water to penetrate, or they crack, and the water pours uselessly into those cracks, so roots near the surface are starved of both air and water. The one plus here is that clay soils are the last to feel the effects of long-term drought at a lower level, although if you're one of those unlucky people whose home suffered from sub-sidence during the drought years of the 80s, you'll known that even they can dry out in extreme conditions, too.

It's not just that these soils in both con-ditions are inhospitable to plants – they don't exactly embrace the gardener with open arms either. Digging a clay soil when it's wet is a thankless task since it will stick like superglue to your spade and your boots, weighing you down, as well as testing your back and your temper almost to destruction. In some parts of the country a particularly sticky clay is known as 'the loving earth' because if you have it, it will never let you go. Digging it when it's baked hard is no more rewarding, either, and certainly no easier. I have known gardeners, desperate to plant something, resort to a crowbar.

The best time to tackle a heavy clay soil is when it's drying out but still moist. Given what hard work digging a clay soil is, it's sensible to tackle it a bit at a time, but then there won't be all that many days when it's at its optimum for digging, so you need to use a bit of common sense.

Ideally, you should dig it over roughly in the autumn and leave it for the winter frosts to work on. As it dries out, it cracks and when water gets into those cracks and freezes, it forces them wider apart, breaking the soil down into smaller and smaller clods. With a bit of luck and a few good hard frosts, you'll find that when the spring arrives it is a much less daunting task. And since slugs seem to like clay soils, opening them up this way and exposing the slugs and their eggs to the frosts can have a beneficial (to us gardeners anyway) effect on their numbers. Incidentally you should *never* walk on heavy soils when they are wet, since you are simply compounding the problem. If for some reason, you simply have to walk on a heavy clay, you should always put down wide scaffolding planks, to spread the weight.

There are various chemicals on the market which claim to improve clay soils. As with so many other things in life, the idea of a magic, pain-free solution to a problem is extremely appealing, but as with so many other 'magic solutions', they are rarely all they seem. Certainly adding lime to the soil will help the particles to 'flocculate' – stick together to make larger crumbs – and so create more spaces through which air and water can pass. But if yours is an acid soil, and you want to grow acid-loving, lime-hating plants, lime clearly isn't a good idea. It's also worth remembering that these chemical treatments will only affect the top few inches, and that the soil underneath will remain as sticky as before.

There's no doubt the best way to improve an averagely sticky clay or silt soil is to incorporate grit and organic matter to open it up, and the most efficient way of doing that is to double-dig it (digging the soil to two spades' depth – See illustration) and in the process work in about one barrowload of coarse grit and one of organic matter to every two or three square metres of soil. The grit will open up the soil, its much larger particles creating spaces which allow air and water to pass more freely through it. The organic matter helps to open up the soil too, but in the case of well-made garden compost, or well-rotted animal manure, it also contains essential plant nutrients and provides a home for the millions of soil organisms that are vital to plant growth. If you aren't very young and/or fit, or the area really is too large for you to tackle, it might be worth paying someone to do it for you, but do make sure they know what 'double digging' means, and check that they actually do it. When the double-digging is finished, spread a thick layer of organic matter over the area. It will soon get worked into the top few inches of soil by the rain and the worms. As for the type of organic matter to use, it depends on what's available locally and how much it costs, because if you're working on the whole garden you're

Double Digging

Soil from first trench

Direction of digging

Movement of soil into trenches

Right: *One of the most sweetly scented flowering shrubs, Philadelphus will cope very well with clay soil. This particular variety, 'Belle Etoile', is smothered in large single white flowers, each with a purple blotch at its base, from late spring to early summer.*

going to need large quantities. Your own garden compost is ideal, and free, but you'll have to have been making it for a long time to have anything like enough.

If you have a farm or riding stables locally, you can use farmyard or horse manure, provided it's well-rotted. You could also use spent mushroom compost – a mixture of well-rotted horse manure and peat, which also contains a small amount of lime. That's fine if your soil is already limy or if you want to use it on the vegetable patch, since vegetables prefer a slightly alkaline soil, but not if you have an acid soil and want to grow acid-loving plants. It doesn't contain many plant nutrients by the time you get it, either, so you will have to add those in the form of fertilizers. You might live near a crisp factory and be able to buy potato waste, or wool shoddy or some other local waste product that would do the job.

Cocoa shells are now widely available. They have a slight acidifying effect on the soil, are full of nutrients and, a bonus for chocoholics, smell powerfully of chocolate, but they are quite expensive. Peat contains no plant nutrients at all, is very expensive and also controversial, since it is non-renewable and much of it is extracted from Sites of Special Scientific Interest – habitats of threatened wild life and plants. 'Green' gardeners don't use it for soil conditioning, if at all, since there are many other excellent products around now, but some people still do so the choice is yours.

If you really can't face double-digging, and can't afford to pay someone to do it for you, you can still improve the soil quite a lot by digging grit and organic matter into the top layer, or even just by spreading organic matter on the surface and waiting for worms and weather to work it in for you. Obviously it takes longer this way, but it's a great deal better than doing nothing.

By adding all this organic matter and grit to the soil, you are also raising the level of your borders slightly, which will also help the soil to drain more freely.

Planting as much as you possibly can helps too, because the plants' roots open up the soil as they grow as well. Once the plants like annuals or vegetable crops have died off, remove the top growth and compost it down, but leave the roots in the soil because they will still perform that service. So if you can, aim to keep the soil covered with plants all the time.

One word of warning. On a clay soil it can seem very tempting just to dig a hole where you plan to plant, fill it with decent top soil or compost and put the tree or shrub in that. Don't. What you are doing is creating a sump into which water from the surrounding soil will drain, so that your newly planted tree or shrub will be sitting with its roots in water, and it will almost certainly die. If you are sowing annuals into a clay soil, it's worth making quite deep drills with a sharp stick and filling them with seed compost before you sow, so that the very delicate new roots of the germinating seedlings have something a bit more sympathetic than a slab of cold wet clay in which to start life. By the time they are ready to push their roots out a bit further they will be bigger and stronger, and better able to cope.

The kinds of plants that do well on clay soils are very hardy and can cope with a range of problem places, so they are likely to appear elsewhere in the book, too. Though some will also put up with dry conditions, most of them prefer a moist soil. But it's the combination of cold and wet that kills plants, so a shrub or perennial that would withstand the cold in a well-drained soil may well succumb in a heavy clay soil.

PLANTS

Trees

All the trees listed here are suitable for small or medium sized gardens.

Field maple (*Acer campestre*) See page 111.

Variegated box-leafed maple (*Acer negundo* 'Variegatum') A tough, open-branched tree, more attractive than its plain green relative, which can also be grown as a large shrub by cutting it back hard each year.
▷ *Approx. height and spread after 10 years: 7 × 6m (23 × 20ft).*

***Acer pseudoplatanus* 'Brilliantissimum'** A very slow-growing small tree (which makes it very useful for small gardens), with stunning spring foliage, which opens deep shrimp-pink, becoming paler flesh pink, then creamy-yellow and pale green before assuming its summer mid-green. The downside is it's rather dull the rest of the year.
▷ *Approx. height and spread after 20 years: 4.5 × 3.5m (14ft × 12ft).*

Silver birch (*Betula pendula*) See page 90.

Hornbeam (*Carpinus betulus*) This is a poor man's beech in that it will make a very acceptable hedge in these conditions where beech won't. Like beech it hangs on to its dead leaves well into the winter.
▷ *Approx. height and spread after 20 years (untrimmed): 16 × 12m (50 × 39ft).*

Hawthorn (*Crataegus*) See page 90.

Laburnum Grown for its spectacular chains of golden yellow pea-flowers in spring, this tree will cope with clay soils though it isn't long-lived in any situation. The most widely grown variety is *L × watereri* 'Vossii', but the weeping *L. alpinum* 'Pendulum', which doesn't reach much more than 3m (10ft) in height is also very attractive. Since the seeds of all laburnums are very poisonous, it's not a tree to plant if you have children or are planning to.
▷ *Approx. height and spread after 20 years: 7 × 5m (23 × 16ft).*

Crab apple (Malus)

Many varieties of ornamental crab are excellent for small gardens – on the most favourable types of soil, as well as sticky clay, because they have a long season of interest, with masses of flowers in spring, in some cases attractively coloured foliage, and bright coloured fruits in autumn which you can turn into jelly or leave for the birds. Here are a few personal favourites.

The Japanese crab (*Malus floribunda*) A stunning sight in spring, when it has a three-colour effect, with masses of deep red buds, newly opened pale pink flowers and more mature blush-white ones, all at the same time. It has a semi-weeping habit and branches on mature specimens can almost reach the ground. In autumn it has small, cherry-like fruits.
▷ *Approx. height and spread after 20 years: 8 × 6m (26 × 20ft).*

Malus sargentii One of the smallest crabs, it has masses of scented white flowers (tinted yellow in bud) with golden stamens. In autumn it has bright red, currant-like fruits, and its leaves turn yellow. It can be grown as a standard tree or a shrub.
▷ *Approx. height and spread after 20 years: 5 × 2m (16 × 6ft).*

***Malus* 'Profusion'** A spreading tree, it has coppery-crimson young foliage which slowly turns green through the summer, as well as purply-red flowers which fade to pink, and oxblood-red fruits.

***Malus* 'Red Jade'** A small, weeping crab, with bright green leaves which turn yellow in autumn, blush-white flowers followed by small, bright red fruits.
▷ *Approx. height and spread after 20 years: 3 × 5m (10 × 16ft).*

Flowering cherries, plums and almonds (Prunus)

This species offers an even wider choice than the ornamental crabs, but some grow very large and have little to offer after their flamboyant show of lurid pink flowers in late spring. In small gardens, especially, when there's probably only room for one or two trees, they must really earn their keep so make sure you choose one that has something to offer after the blossom has gone. Some breeders are now offering Japanese flowering cherries grafted on to dwarfing rootstocks, which means the final height and spread of the tree are reduced.

Prunus 'Accolade' A superb small tree with a graceful, open, spreading habit, and in early April clusters of deep pink buds opening into semi-double, hanging, light pink flowers up to 4cm

(1½in) across, with fringed petals. It goes on flowering for weeks.
▷ *Approx. height and spread after 20 years: 8 × 8m (26 × 26ft).*

Sargent's cherry (Prunus sargentii) This eventually makes a rather flat-topped tree which offers a long season of interest. It has masses of single pink flowers in early spring, followed by new leaves which are coppery-red when they first appear, turning green in summer, then, as early as September in some areas, turning brilliant vermilion and scarlet.
▷ *Approx. height and spread after 20 years: 9 × 10m (30 × 32ft).*

Autumn cherry (Prunus subhirtella 'Autumnalis') This produces semi-double white flowers on bare stems from November intermittently right

Left: Chaenomeles is a superb shrub for early spring when there is little else in this vibrant red in flower to cheer up the garden. It is available in a whole range of colours, but among the best bright red varieties to look for are C. × superba 'Nicoline' or the lower-growing 'Rowallane'

Right: While the individual flowers of Magnolia × soulangeana are superb, the sight of a mature tree in full flower in mid spring takes your breath away. Though it seems unlikely that something so beautiful will survive in a sticky clay soil, it will, provided you improve it as recommended first.

through the winter to April, depending on the weather. A really cold snap can delay the flowers, but a spell of mild weather will bring them out. It has good, golden autumn colour too. There is also an attractive variety with pink flowers, *P.s.* 'Autumnalis Rosea'.
▷ *Approx. height and spread after 20 years: 7 × 7m (24 × 24ft).*

Prunus 'Shirotae' or 'Mount Fuji' This stunning tree has fragrant, single or semi-double pure white flowers, and fresh, light green leaves, turning orange-red in autumn, with distinctive fringed edges. It forms a wide-spreading tree and, in mature specimens, some of the horizontal branches may touch the ground.
▷ *Approx. height and spread after 20 years: 8 × 8m (25 × 25ft).*

Weeping cherries

***Prunus × yedoensis* 'Shidare Yoshino'** In early spring this has masses of pale pink flowers, fading to white, on branches that weep to the ground. *P. yedoensis* 'Ivensii' has fragrant snow-white flowers and a similar habit. They are not so easy to find as Cheal's weeping cherry (*P.* 'Kiku-shidare Sakura' or *P. subhirtella* 'Pendula') but specialist nurseries have them and they are well worth the extra effort involved in finding them.
▷ *Approx. height and spread after 20 years: 5 × 6m (16 × 20ft).*

Weeping willow-leafed pear (*Pyrus salicifolia* 'Pendula') Its long, silvery willow-like leaves are covered in a silky white down until early summer. It does have small white flowers in April, but it

is grown primarily for the dense mound of silvery foliage it eventually forms.
▷ *Approx. height and spread after 20 years: 4 × 3m (13 × 10ft).*

Willow (*Salix alba*) See page 73.
Mountain ash and **Whitebeam (*Sorbus aucuparia* and *aria*)** See pages 91 and 143.

Conifers

Although most conifers dislike heavy soils and the waterlogging that often goes with them, a few will tolerate these conditions. Some are very slow-growing, so that while they will reach only 2–3m (6–10ft) in 10 years or so, they will go on growing slowly and eventually reach 15m (50ft) and more. It depends how concerned you are about the potential problems you may be leaving a gardener of your grandchildren's generation!

Korean fir (*Abies koreana*) A neat conical conifer with glossy green needles which are grey-white underneath, and long purplish cones in winter, even on young plants.
Approx. height and spread after 10 years: 2 × 1.2m (6ft 6in × 4ft).

Yew (*Taxus baccata*) Common yew will tolerate these conditions after the drainage has been improved. See page 146.

Thuja plicata 'Atrovirens' The best hedging conifer for these conditions, with dark glossy foliage. See page 91.

Climbers

Golden hop (*Humulus lupulus* 'Aureus') See page 72.

Vitis coignetiae This ornamental vine has colossal leaves - up to 30cm/12in across - which turn the most brilliant shades of orange and red in autumn. It has very small but sweetly scented flowers in June and July, and small purple grapes. It is very vigorous, so prune it if it outgrows its allotted space.
▷ *Height: 9m + (30ft +).*

Shrubs

Abelia (*Abelia × grandiflora*) An attractive shrub with masses of small fragrant blush-white flowers in late summer/early autumn on wood that's 3 years old or more, so be patient. *A. × g.* 'Francis Mason' has golden foliage and slightly pinker flowers, but is not as hardy as the type.
▷ *Approx. height and spread after 10 years: 1.5 × 1.5m (5 × 5ft).*

Spotted laurel (*Aucuba*) See page 30.
Berberis See page 40.

Japonica (*Chaenomeles*) Valuable late winter/early spring-flowering shrubs whose bright flowers provide a real splash of colour. The *speciosa* hybrids, like the apple-blossom-pink 'Moerloesii', the larger than average 'Nivalis' with pure white flowers and the low-growing 'Simonii' with semi-double, dark crimson flowers, are good for training on walls, while the × *superba* hybrids like 'Knap Hill Scarlet' with large translucent red flowers, 'Fire Dance' with bright scarlet blooms, 'Pink Lady' and the white 'Jet Trail', make excellent free-standing shrubs. For something out of the usual colour range, try 'Lemon and Lime', with ivory buds turning into, well, lemon and lime flowers.
▷ *Approx. height and spread after 10 years: 1.2 × 1.5m (4 × 5ft).*

Cornus See page 73.
Hazel (*Corylus avellana*) See page 90.
Cotoneaster See page 42.
St John's Wort or Rose of Sharon (*Hypericum calycinum*) See page 91.

Box-leafed holly or Japanese holly (*Ilex crenata*) More tolerant of these conditions than most hollies, these are useful small evergreens. *I.c.* 'Helleri' forms a low rounded mound in full sun or part-shade, while the larger gold-leafed *I.c.* 'Golden Gem' needs a degree of shade to prevent scorching of its leaves, but not too much or the golden fades to a less interesting yellow-green.
▷ *Approx. height and spread after 10 years: 80cm × 1.5m (2ft 6in × 5ft).*

Kerria See page 32.

Magnolia Some of these stately shrubs, especially *M. × soulangeana* and its hybrids, with their exquisite cupped flowers, either pink or white flushed with pink, will cope with a heavy clay soil. They need a sunny position, but avoid planting them where they catch the early morning sun.
▷ *Approx. height and spread after 10 years: 4 × 4m (13 × 13ft).*

Mock orange blossom (*Philadelphus*) This gets its common name from its sweet scented white flowers, borne in profusion in June and July. Again there are a number of good varieties, though those that grow to 3m + (10ft +) are not ideal for small gardens. Among the best small varieties are 'Belle Etoile', which forms an arching shrub covered in superbly scented, large single white flowers, *P.* 'Lemoinei' with arching branches of exquisitely scented flowers and the smallest of all, 'Manteau d'Ermine (Ermine Overcoat!) whose twiggy branches are smothered in fragrant, creamy-white double flowers.
▷ *Approx. height and spread after 10 years: 1-1.5m × 1-1.5m (3-5 × 3-5ft).*

Cherry laurel (*Prunus laurocerasus*) Useful evergreens that will tolerate a whole range of problem places, including deep shade and the edge of tree canopies where they get dripped on, but they don't like extremely dry and/or extremely limy soil. *P.l.* 'Otto Luyken' has glossy deep green foliage and, in spring, candles of small creamy-white flowers. There is a newer, lower-growing variety which is also good if you can tolerate the Wagnerian pun – it's called 'Low 'n' Green'.
▷ *Approx. height and spread after 10 years: 1.5 × 2m (5 × 6ft).*

Firethorn (*Pyracantha*) See page 32.
Flowering currant (*Ribes*) See page 32.

Roses The received wisdom is that roses do best in a clay soil, and so they do *provided* it's not a very sticky, waterlogged, airless clay. They should do well once the drainage of such a soil has been improved with organic matter and grit. There are thousands to choose from, with new ones coming on the market every year, so it really is a question of personal choice. I'm not a lover of hybrid teas,

or floribundas (though I make an exception for the deliciously scented blush-white 'Margaret Merrill') so this is merely a selection of some favourites among the other types of roses.

Among the old scented roses which have a long flowering period throughout the summer and autumn, try 'Buff Beauty' with warm apricot flowers, 'Felicia' with clear, pink flowers and 'Cornelia' with copper-apricot flowers fading to pink.
▷ *Approx. height and spread: 1.5-1.8 × 2.2m (5-6 × 7ft).*

The new English roses, which combine all the merits of old roses with the vigour, repeat-flowering and compact habit of modern hybrids, are the perfect choice for a mixed border in a small garden. And there are some real stunners - the soft shell-pink 'Heritage', for instance, the deeper pink 'Pretty Jessica', the yellow 'Graham Thomas' and the new blush-pink 'Sharifa Asma'.
▷ *Approx. height and spread: 1-1.5m × 1-1.5m (3-5 × 3-5ft).*

Even smaller are the dwarf or patio roses, which can be grown very successfully in containers or in a mixed border. One of the very best is the old variety 'The Fairy' with glossy, dark green leaves, and masses of small clear pink rosettes well into the autumn. The range of colours available in patio roses is increasing all the time. In 1992 the brightest vermilion yet was introduced, in 'Top Marks', and there are now oranges ('Duchess of York'), peaches ('Sweet Dream'), deep, almost cerise, pink ('Rosy Future' which is also fragrant, something rare in dwarf roses), yellows ('Minilights', only 25cm/10in tall and 50cm/20in across), and white ('Hakuun'). Or try 'Snow Carpet', which is only about 25cm (10in) tall but will spread about 75cm (2ft 6in) and form dense ground cover that will smother any weeds at birth.
▷ *Approx. height and spread: 30-60 × 30-60cm (1-2 × 1-2ft).*

Willow (*Salix*) See page 73.
Skimmia See page 73.

Bridal wreath (*Spiraea × arguta*) This elegant shrub is stunning in late spring when its long curving branches are packed with small white flowers.
▷ *Approx. height and spread after 10 years: 2 × 2m (6ft 6in × 6ft 6in).*

Snowberry (*Symphoricarpos*) See page 74.

Lilac (*Syringa*) These are beautiful shrubs for late spring and early summer-flowering in a sunny spot on any soil, though they do best on a chalky one. There are many excellent named varieties, but many of them grow into very large shrubs or trees, so for small gardens you need to look for a 'compact' one, like the pure white S. 'Vestale', the dark lilac-red 'Congo', and the pale yellow S. 'Primrose'.
▷ *Approx. height and spread after 10 years:*
1.5 × 1.2m (5 × 4ft).

Alternatively, you could try one of the dwarf lilacs - the very slow-growing Korean lilac (S. *meyeri* 'Palibin' or 'Velutina') which produces numerous sweetly scented, pinky-lilac flowers on a bush which reaches no more than 80cm (2ft 6in) in 10 years. Slightly larger is S. *microphylla* 'Superba', which has rose-pink flowers in May and June and often again in the autumn.
▷ *Approx. height and spread after 10 years:*
80 × 50cm (2ft 6in × 1ft 6in).

Viburnum The good old warhorses of the family, and the guelder rose (V. *opulus* - see page 34) and the evergreen V. *tinus* will do well on a heavy clay soil, though its hybrid 'Eve Price' is smaller and

Below: *The warm golden, black-eyed flowers of* Rudbeckia *'Goldsturm' add warmth to the garden from late summer through till autumn.*

Right: *The graceful* Viburnum plicatum *'Mariesii' in full flower.*

more attractive. Of the deciduous varieties, the summer-flowering *V. plicatum* 'Mariesii' is stunning with fresh green deeply ribbed leaves and, in time, a distinctly layered habit, so the 'lacecaps' of white flowers that appear on the tiered branches make them look as though they are covered in snow. It also has berries in autumn and good autumn colour.

Lesser periwinkle (Vinca minor) See page 34.

Weigela This deciduous shrub has pretty white, pink or red foxglove-like flowers in May and June. For flowers, the ruby-red-flowered 'Bristol Ruby' and the scarlet 'Evita' are both good, while for the longest possible season of interest look for *W. florida* 'Foliis Purpureis' (Latin for 'purple leaves'), the smoky tone of which is the perfect foil for the paler purply-pink flowers, and, perhaps

best value of all, *W.f.* 'Variegata', which has pale pink flowers and very attractive cream and green variegated foliage. If you have a very small garden, look for *W.f.* 'Variegata Compacta', which has slightly whiter variegations and is just over half the height and spread of *W.f.* 'Variegata'.
▷ *Approx. height and spread after 10 years: 1.8 × 1.8m (5ft 6in × 5ft 6in).*

Perennials

Bugle (Ajuga) See page 42.
Anemone × hybrida See page 34.

Michaelmas daisies (Aster amellus) These offer valuable autumn colour in a sunny border. The tall ones come in a range of colours; white and pink as well as the usual blue-mauve, and good trouble-free varieties include 'Violet Queen' and

the pink 'Pink Zenith'. Good *A. novae-angliae* hybrids include 'Rosa Sieger' with branching heads of salmon-pink flowers. The dwarf Michaelmas daisies (*A. novi-belgii*) come in a similar range of colours, plus red - 'Dandy'. Good varieties include the soft lavender-mauve 'Lady in Blue', the warm coral pink 'Alice Haslem', and the semi-double bright pink, 'Little Pink Beauty'. If you have room for only one perennial aster, go for the elegant, self-supporting, mildew-resistant *A. × frikartii* 'Mönch' which, from July, carries large lavender-blue flowers with a gold centre.
▷ *Height and spread: 30-90cm × 40-50cm (1-3ft × 1ft 4in-1ft 6in).*

Elephant's ears (*Bergenia*) See page 34.
Crocosmia See page 58.
Foxgloves (*Digitalis*) See page 42.
Hemerocallis See page 75.
Dead-nettle (*Lamium maculatum*) See page 35.

Lysimachia clethroides This member of the family ought to be better known, with its lovely curved racemes of small white flowers, looking rather like geese's heads, in late summer. As an added bonus, its foliage turns red in autumn. The better-known yellow-flowered creeping jenny (*L. nummularia*) and the tall *L. punctata* will also cope with clay soils.
▷ *Height and spread: 90 × 90cm (3 × 3ft).*

Persicaria See page 35.

Jacob's ladder (*Polemonium caeruleum*) This old cottage garden favourite gets its common name from its ladder-like bright green foliage, and has clusters of mid-blue flowers throughout the summer. It has a tendency to self-seed very freely, but *P. foliosissimum* is more restrained in this respect.
▷ *Height and spread: 70 × 50cm (2ft 3in × 18in).*

Rodgersia See page 78.

Annuals

Few annuals like heavy clay, but if you improve the soil generally as recommended and put out largish plants, you should be able to grow most common annuals - though avoid those that need very free-draining conditions, like petunias, dianthus and any of the 'everlasting' flowers. Alternatively, try sowing the seed of hardy annuals in drills filled with seed compost, where they are to flower.

***Helianthus* (Sunflower)** A real giant annual, this one, reaching 3m (10ft) in height, though it's unlikely to get quite so large in this type of soil. And it's not only worth growing for its own sake - such a large plant needs a deep and extensive root system to sustain it and, even after the plant has died, those roots help open up the soil and improve the drainage.
▷ *Height and spread: 3-20m × 30-45cm (3-10ft × 1-1ft 6in).*

Bulbs

Again, few bulbs like heavy clay soils because they are more likely to rot in all that rather airless moisture. Improving the soil generally will help, as will putting a layer of fine grit or sharp sand at the bottom of the planting hole and sitting the bulbs on that. Even then, it's not worth risking anything too rare and therefore expensive, so stick to the cheapest varieties of the borderline bulbs.

Camassia leichtlinii This rather exotic-looking bulb actually prefers a quite heavy soil. It puts up a tall, leafless stem in summer on top of which is a dense spike of white or very pale mauve starry flowers. It has a tuft of rather untidy looking leaves at the base which die away with the rest of the growth by late summer, so it's best planted in among low-growing shrubs or perennials to disguise it.
▷ *Height and spread: 1-1.5m × 20-30cm (3-5ft × 8-12in).*

Eranthis hyemalis See page 39.

Daffodils (*Narcissus*) There is always the chance that they will rot in a really sticky clay soil, so if you really must have daffodils, go for tough, cheap varieties like 'Golden Harvest' or the small 'W. P. Milner' which is about half its size.
▷ *Height: 20-45cm.*

ACID SOIL

Any gardener rash enough to *complain* about having an acid soil can expect absolutely no sympathy at all from other gardeners whose soils are limy and who would give their eyeteeth to be able to grow with ease spectacular acid-loving plants like camellias, pieris and rhododendrons. And while there are some beautiful plants that will thrive on their limy soils, just to rub salt into the wound, there are hardly any of them that won't grow well enough on your acid soil, too.

The acidity or alkalinity of a soil is measured in terms of its pH – the measure of the concentration of hydrogen ions – on a scale of 0–14. A pH of 7 is neutral, less than 7 is acid and more than 7 is alkaline, though you are very unlikely to come across a soil more acid than about 3.5 or more alkaline than about 8.5, even in the wild. Most plants do best in a very slightly acid soil with a pH of about 6.5, although most – apart from the real lime-haters – will tolerate a pH up to about 7.5.

Extremes of acidity and alkalinity affect which nutrients in the soil are available to plants. Too acid and it reduces the amount of phosphate available to help soil bacteria convert nitrogen from the air into food. It also makes other plant nutrients in the soil too soluble in water so that they leach out of the soil before the plants can make use of them. That means that very acid soils need lots of added nutrients. Too alkaline, on the other hand, and it locks up vital trace elements in the soil – not only phosphate but potassium, manganese and iron as well. It's a lack of iron – and magnesium – that makes the leaves of acid-loving plants growing in a limy soil turn yellow and die.

While all that may sound a bit technical, it's really the first thing you need to know about your soil. It may sound over-dramatic to say it's a matter of life or death, but to a plant it is! Plant an acid-loving plant in a lime soil, and it will slowly die. Simple as that. The good news is that a very easy-to-use lime testing kit, that costs about a pound and can be bought from any garden centre, will tell you all you need to know.

Acid soils come in a variety of forms, from heavy clay to spongy peat to a very free-draining sand. Ironically, you may find that a sandy soil that was originally limy, and is over limestone, may in fact be quite acid because lime is easily dissolved in water and rain may have washed much of it out of the top, free-draining layer. And of course the texture of the soil affects what you need to do to make it more hospitable to plants. You also need to be clear about whether you want to maintain its present acidity or make it a bit less acid – for growing vegetables for example.

With a heavy clay soil, you need to improve the drainage by opening it up (see page 120), but if you plan to grow acid-lovers make sure you use a lime-free grit and organic matter like composted bark, garden compost, well-rotted animal manure and leaf mould which are all naturally slightly acid, or composted pine bark or cocoa shells which are particularly so, with a pH of 5-5.5. Spent mushroom compost which contains lime would be fine if you want to decrease the acidity, but not if you plan to grow acid-loving plants, although some growers are now skimming off the top layer containing the lime before they sell it on, so it's worth checking when you buy.

A naturally peaty soil is wonderful for acid-loving woodland plants, but it does have a tendency to dry out in hot weather, and it can then be difficult for water to penetrate – as you'll know if you've ever used a peat-based compost in containers and allowed it to dry right out. Digging in some grit to open it up a bit will help, as will adding some good garden soil, though make sure it's slightly acid to neutral, and doesn't contain any lime.

If you have a very acid soil, you might want to reduce its pH a little to grow

vegetables. Most fruit and vegetables grow well enough in a soil between pH 5.5 and 7.5. Some, like raspberries, gooseberries and apples, like it slightly more acid, while brassicas (cabbage, broccoli), peas and beans and pears, cherries and plums like it more alkaline, and asparagus, leeks and spinach like it even limier still.

Making an acid soil more alkaline is relatively simple. You add lime to the soil – either quick-acting gardener's lime if you're not organic or, if you are, magnesian lime-stone or 'Dolomite lime', which is much slower-acting and lasts for up to 18 months. Calcified seaweed, a sort of coral, is also good and slow-acting, but it is expensive.

To raise the pH from 5.5 to 6.5, you need to add about 240 grammes of lime to the square metre on a sandy soil, and double that amount on a heavy clay soil, where of course, it will also help form the soil into larger 'crumbs' (see page 120). Do stick to the recommended amounts because this is a case where the extra bit for good luck can actually do harm, locking up essential trace elements in the soil. Unless yours is a really acid soil, you'll probably only need to treat the area where you plan to grow brassicas – preferably in the spring or autumn, a good few weeks before you want to sow or plant and never after you have just added manure to the soil. The two would combine to produce ammonia in gas form and that would release much of the valuable nitrogen in the manure into the air. If possible, add lime in autumn and manure in spring.

Left: Camellia *'Inspiration'*.

Right: *This acid-lover,* Enkianthus campanulatus, *is worth growing for its vivid crimson autumn colour alone. Its pretty peachy-pink flowers in late spring are a bonus.*

As for ornamental plants, well, the world is your oyster and you can grow virtually anything you like, whether they're acid-lovers or not – though it would be perverse not to grow some of the spectacular plants that must have an acid soil to thrive. Just one word of warning, though. Many of the most eye-catching acid-lovers – azaleas and rhododendrons, camellias – are woodland shrubs and therefore mostly flower in spring before they have to complete with the trees for light, water and nutrients, so unless you're careful you'll wind up with a garden that's magnificent for a few weeks in spring, and frankly rather dull for the rest of the year. So be sure to include a few later-flowering shrubs like the calico bush (*Kalmia latifolia*) or the sweet pepper bush (*Clethra alnifolia*) or of course any of the many other shrubs that are happy in acid soils as well as other types.

PLANTS

The trees and shrubs listed below are those that *must* have an acid soil to thrive. Some may not die where there is lime in the soil, but will not fulfil their true potential if there is.

Trees

Katsura tree (*Cercidiphyllum japonicum*) A small tree or large shrub, it has very attractive small heart-shaped leaves that are bright pinky-red when they emerge, turning a rather smoky green before they turn brilliant red and gold in the autumn. It will grow in a more alkaline soil, but the autumn colour – the main reason for growing it – will be nothing like as stunning.
▷ *Approx. height and spread after 20 years: 12 × 9m (39 × 30ft).*

Nyssa sylvatica Another tree grown primarily for its spectacular autumn colour, this one won't tolerate any lime. It eventually makes a broad columnar tree. *N.s.* 'Jermyns Flame' is a selected form, with the most brilliant leaf colour in autumn. *Nyssa sinensis* is a smaller, more conical tree with more slender, pointed leaves but the same superb autumn colour.
▷ *Approx. height and spread after 20 years: 10 × 8m (33 × 26ft).*

Shrubs

Japanese maples (*Acer japonicum*, *A. palmatum* and *A.p.* 'Dissectum') These are among the most beautiful small foliage shrubs there are, with either gold (*A.j.* 'Aureum'), bright green, or wine-red leaves (*A.p.* 'Atropurpureum', *A.p.* 'Dissectum Atropurpureum' or 'Garnet'). *A. japonicum*'s leaves are deeply lobed and maple-like, while *A. palmatum*'s more hand-shaped, and those of *A.p.* 'Dissectum' are very finely divided. Many have very good autumn colour.
▷ *A. palmatum* varieties form small umbrella-shaped trees – very small trees in the case of *A.p.* 'Dissectum' – and their bare branches offer an attractive outline in winter months. Apart from a lime-free soil, they need shelter from cold winds and late spring frosts, and dappled shade to protect them from the strong midday sun which can scorch the foliage and cause quite serious damage.
▷ *Approx. height and spread after 10 years: 1.2-5 × 5m (4-16 × 5-16ft).*

Bearberry (*Arctostaphylos uva-ursi*) This evergreen, low-growing, arching shrub has intertwining stems of small bright green leaves covered in urn-shaped pinkish-white flowers in summer, which are followed by scarlet berries.
▷ *Approx. height and spread after 10 years: 10 × 50cm (4in × 20in).*

Heathers (*Calluna vulgaris*) These lime-hating summer-flowering heathers come in a range of colours – flowers in white, pink, red or purple and foliage in green, gold, grey, orange and, in the case of *C.v.* 'Winter Chocolate', chocolate brown in winter. Planted in groups, they quickly make an attractive carpet. If you don't have an acid soil and want to grow heathers, grow the winter-flowering kinds – *Erica carnea*. They come in as

wide a range of flower and foliage colour, but they are happy on neutral and slightly limy soils – or you could grow the summer-flowering types in containers in special lime-free compost.
▷ *Approx. height and spread after 10 years: 5-50 × 30cm (2-18 × 12in).*

Camellia Perhaps because of *The Lady of the Camellias*, these exquisite flowering shrubs are often thought of as exotic and therefore tender, but in fact as long as they are sheltered from icy winds and the early morning sun, many will grow happily enough outside. They produce masses of single, semi-double or double flowers in a whole range of colours from white through many shades of pink to blood-red, and even a few multi-colours like the pink and white striped *C.* 'Lady Vansittart'. They start flowering between February and April, depending on the variety, and keep their flowers for several weeks. Once the flowers have fallen, their elegant glossy green leaves are attractive in their own right – making it a good host perhaps for a small, late-summer flowering clematis like *C. viticella* (see page 146).

Good varieties include *Camellia japonica* 'Alba Plena' (double white), the soft pink semi-double *C.j.* 'Lady Clare', the clear rich pink *C.j.* 'Leonard Messel' and, perhaps the most widely grown and most popular of all, *Camellia × williamsii* 'Donation', with an abundance of large, semi-double clear pink flowers from February onwards. Among the red-flowered varieties, look for the large semi-double deep crimson *C.j.* 'Mercury' and *C.j.* 'Adolphe Audusson' whose semi-double, blood-red flowers have conspicuous gold stamens.
▷ *Approx. height and spread after 10 years: 1.5 × 1.5m (5 × 5ft). Japonica types: williamsii's grow larger – up to 3 × 1.5m (10 × 5ft).*

Sweet pepper bush (*Clethra alnifolia*) A useful late-flowering shrub, with fluffy spikes of scented creamy-white flowers in August and September. It's a woodland native and so prefers light shade but will put up with anything from full sun to medium shade. *C.a.* 'Pink Spire' has spikier, pink flowers.
▷ *Approx. height and spread after 10 years: 1.2 × 2m (4 × 6ft).*

Creeping dogwood (*Cornus canadensis*) A lovely woodland ground-cover plant that eventu-ally forms mats of pale olive-green leaves that turn wine-red in autumn, with four-petalled white bracts surrounding insignificant flowers in summer. It needs woodland conditions to do well – a light moist acid soil and light to medium shade.
▷ *Approx. height and spread after 10 years: 20cm × 2m (8in × 6ft 6in).*

Chinese or Japanese dogwood (*Cornus kousa*) Another lovely woodland plant, but this time a tall elegant shrub or, in perfect conditions even a small tree. It has four-petalled white bracts in late spring/early summer, and pale olive-green leaves, slightly crinkled, which turn a wonderful orange-red in autumn.
▷ *Approx. height and spread after 10 years: 2.5 × 2m (8 × 6ft).*

Enkianthus campanulatus A subtle but very beautiful member of the same family as the brash rhododendrons and azaleas, with clusters of small bell-shaped flowers, creamy-yellow veined with red, so that they look peachy-pink from a distance. Its grey-green leaves turn vivid red in autumn.
▷ *Approx. height and spread after 10 years: 2.5 × 2m (8 × 6ft 6in).*

Fothergilla (major or monticola) These slow-growing shrubs have leaves not unlike the hazel's, which turn fiery shades of red, orange and gold in autumn. In spring, before the leaves appear, they carry small, fluffy white flowers. It prefers light shade but, to get the full benefit of the autumn colour, plant it where the sun strikes it in that season.
▷ *Approx. height and spread after 10 years: 2 × 2m (6ft 6in × 6ft 6in).*

Gaultheria (formerly Pernettya) mucronata) Although these dwarf evergreens are less well known than many other acid-lovers, they are well worth considering for a shady border. They have very small, glossy deep green leaves, masses of small white flowers and the most beautiful berries in autumn, ranging in colour from pearly white through various shades of pink to red and purple. To ensure a good crop of berries, plant them in groups of three or four, making sure you've got at least one male among them. The sex of a

Above: *There is no other plant with such a clear blue flower as that of the Himalayan popppy (Meconopsis betonicifolia). It is a perfect plant for a woodland garden, since, as well as a peaty soil, it also likes shade.*

Left: *A superb shrub for an acid soil in a woodland setting, Pieris 'Forest Flame' has young foliage of such a fiery red in early spring that it really lives up to its name. Clusters of small lily-of-the-valley like flowers appear at the same time.*

pernettya is not instantly obvious, expect perhaps to another pernettya, so ask at the garden centre for a guaranteed male form. Good varieties to look for include *P.m.* 'Alba' or 'Snow White' (white berries), 'Sea Shell' (pale shell-pink), 'Pink Pearl' (lilac-pink), 'Bell's Seedling' (dark red), 'Cherry Ripe' (bright red), 'Mulberry Wine' (magenta ageing to deep purple).

▷ *Approx. height and spread after 10 years: 80cm × 1.2m + (2ft 6in × 4ft +).*

Calico bush (*Kalmia latifolia*) This shrub is rather similar to the rhododendron in appearance, with large glossy green oval leaves, which will provide an ideal backdrop for the pretty clusters of rose-pink cup-shaped flowers that come out in the early summer. It will tolerate a little shade but for best results should be planted in a sunny spot.

▷ *Approx. height and spread after 10 years: 2 × 2m (6ft 6in × 6ft 6in).*

Leucothoë fontanesiana Although it has tassels of white pitcher-shaped flowers in spring, this is grown mainly for its evergreen foliage. *L.f.* 'Rainbow' is the best known, which has leathery dark green leaves that are splashed with pink when they're young, fading to cream.

▷ *Approx. height and spread after 10 years: 1.5 × 2m (5ft × 6ft 6in).*

Lithodora (formerly Lithospermum) diffusa A small evergreen carpeting shrub (ideal for tumbling over a wall) with flowers of the most beautiful vivid gentian blue between May and August. The best variety is *L.d.* 'Grace Ward' which grows more vigorously and has flowers of an even more intense blue, but it's not as widely available as *L.d.* 'Heavenly Blue', which itself is such a stunning plant that it is no real hardship! A light clipping-over after flowering will make it grow more densely.

▷ *Approx. height and spread after 10 years: 15 × 50cm (6 × 18in).*

Pieris These are perhaps the ideal evergreen shrubs for a very small garden because they really do earn their keep. In spring, tassels of small white flowers, which are bell-shaped rather like lily-of-the-valley, open at the same time as the new foliage is coming through. The crowns of new, slender, spear-shaped leaves start out an almost unbelievably vivid shade of scarlet, and slowly fade through pink, cream and pale green before acquiring their glossy summer mid-green. The clusters of small red buds, for next season's flowers which form in the autumn, add brightness during the winter months.

Look out for *Pieris formosa* 'Wakehurst', which has shorter, broader leaves than most but superb spring colour, *Pieris floribunda* 'Forest Flame', one of the hardiest varieties, with particularly bright new foliage, and *Pieris japonica* 'Variegata' whose leaves are variegated with creamy-white, flushed with pink, when they first open. It's slower growing than most and forms a smaller shrub, about two-thirds the average height and spread. There are many good new, very free-flowering hybrids, too, like 'Valley Valentine'.

▷ *Approx. height and spread after 5 years: 80cm × 1m (2.5 × 3ft). After 10 years: 1.5 × 2m (5 × 6ft).*

Rhododendrons These are without doubt among the most eye-catching of our spring-flowering shrubs and there are literally hundreds of different ones to choose from. Many of them, though, grow much too large for a small garden and, besides, have little more to offer in the way of interest once the large, brilliantly coloured flowers have faded. But there are some excellent dwarf rhododendrons worth considering for any border in dappled shade. Look out for 'Bluebird' with violet-blue flowers, 'Pink Drift' with lavender-pink flowers and aromatic, olive-green leaves, 'Scarlet Wonder' with trumpet-shaped, frilly red flowers, 'Moonstone' with rosy-crimson buds opening to a creamy pale primrose yellow, or the slightly more spreading *R. leucaspis* which has pale yellow flowers that fade to cream and last for weeks.

Also well worth considering is *R. yakushimanum* and its hybrids. *R. yakushimanum* itself is a stunner – not only does it have masses of rose-pink buds, opening to apple-blossom-pink flowers which slowly fade to white, but its foliage is striking too. Its long, narrow leathery leaves are silvery when they first appear, turning a really dark, glossy green on top, with woolly brown undersides. Its many hybrids – like 'Doc' (light pink fading to white), 'Grumpy' (pale yellow with a hint of pink, fading to white), 'Silver Sixpence' (creamy-white with pale lemon spots), and 'Surrey Heath' (rose-pink lightly tinged with orange) – have superb flowers in a range of striking colours, but none has the same beautiful foliage as the parent.

▷ *Approx. height and spread after 10 years: 80cm × 1m (2 × 3ft).*

Azaleas are members of the same family as rhododendrons. Some of the deciduous kinds have almost neon-bright flowers in shades of orange, yellow and pink, many of them scented, while the foliage has good autumn colour. Look for 'Koster's Brilliant Red' (vivid orange-red), 'Gibraltar' (dark red buds opening to flame-orange with orange flare), 'Coronation Lady' (salmon-pink with bright orange flare). There is a new range of hybrids coming on the market now, called 'Solent', which feature larger, scented flowers in a similar range of colours.

▷ *Average height and spread after 10 years: 1.5 × 1.5m (5 × 5ft).*

The evergreen azaleas make small rounded shrubs that are smothered in flowers in spring. Good varieties include 'Blue Danube' (blue-violet), 'Mother's Day' (semi-double, bright red), 'Blaauw's Pink' (salmon-pink), 'Hinomayo' (clear pink), and 'Palestrina' (pure white).
▷ *Approx. height and spread after 10 years: 80cm × 1m (2.5 × 3ft).*

Skimmia See page 33.

Zenobia pulverulenta An attractive slightly arching shrub which ought to be better known. It has glossy semi-evergreen leaves which turn red and gold in autumn and it carries sweet-scented bell-shaped white flowers, a bit like larger lily-of-the valley in early and midsummer.
▷ *Approx. height and spread after 10 years: 1 × 1m (3ft 3in × 3ft 3in).*

Perennials

There are only a few herbaceous plants which *must* have an acid soil to do well – most of those that dislike lime will grow happily in neutral to slightly acid soil.

Corydalis cashmiriana A beautiful little plant that likes woodland conditions – part shade and an acid soil. It has fresh green, fern-like leaves, masses of bright blue flowers in summer and was the 'in' plant among fashionable gardeners in 1993.
▷ *Height and spread: 10-25 × 10cm (4-10 × 4in).*

Gentian (Gentiana) Not all of this family with stunning vivid blue flowers need a moist acid soil to do well, but spreading *G. sino-ornata*, which is smothered in large flowers in late summer/early autumn, must have a lime-free soil.
▷ *Height and spread: 2.5-5 × 5-30cm (1-2 × 2-12in).*

Kirengeshoma palmata A stunning late-flowering plant for light shade, it has large, lobed bright green leaves on elegant dark stems and masses of creamy-yellow funnel-shaped flowers.
▷ *Height and spread: 1m × 60cm (3ft 3in × 2ft).*

Himalayan blue poppy (Meconopsis betonicifolia) This beautiful plant needs a cool, rich, acid soil if it is to do more than flower once

after several years and then die. Given the right conditions it produces flowers of a stunning rich sky-blue, with no hint of purple, in summer.
▷ *Height and spread: 90-120 × 45cm (3-4ft × 1ft 6in).*

False spikenard (Smilacina racemosa) Its foliage looks rather like that of Solomon's seal, but instead of dangling pears its flowers in late spring/early summer are spikes of creamy-white pompoms. It also has fleshy red fruits in late summer.
▷ *Height and spread: 75-90 × 45cm (2ft 6in-3ft × 18in).*

Wake-robin (Trillium) These are lovely woodland plants for rich, moist, acid or slightly acid but not heavy soil in part shade. Their botanical name comes from the fact that they have three of everything - three petals, three calyces and three leaves. The best are the wake-robin (*T. grandiflorum*) with pure white petals and the exquisite double form, *T.g.* 'Flore Pleno'. Since it takes some years to produce a decent sized plant, they are expensive.
▷ *Height and spread: 30-40 × 30cm (12-15 × 12in).*

Flame creeper (Tropaeolum speciosum) A stunning relative of the nasturtium, this climber has delicate, lobed leaves and masses of scarlet flowers. It's wonderful growing through a hedge or other shrubs, and grows like a weed where it's happy, and yet is impossible to get started in other seemingly similar situations. It likes its roots in shade and its head in sun.
▷ *Height: 1.5-3m (4-10ft).*

Bulbs

Erythronium See page 39.

Lilies Most lilies prefer rich, well-drained neutral to slightly acid soils, but some must have an acid soil to do well – mainly Japanese lilies, including the tall, late-summer flowering, very fragrant *L. speciosum*, both in its white and ruby-red forms, the golden-rayed lily of Japan (*L. auratum*), and oriental hybrids like the pure white 'Casa Blanca', and the spectacular 'Stargazer', the crimson petals of which are edged in white.
▷ *Height: 60cm-1.2m (2-4ft).*

ALKALINE SOIL

 The best advice to gardeners who have an alkaline soil is to concentrate on the doughnut, not on the hole – on the many beautiful plants that *will* thrive on this type of soil and not on those that won't. Do you really think that a rhododendron that has huge trusses of vivid purple flowers for a couple of weeks in late spring is essentially more beautiful than, say, *Clematis* 'Marie Boisselot', which has elegant large white flowers from May to September? Given that the human being is a perverse animal and usually wants what it can't have, many gardeners with limy soils will certainly hanker for a few acid-loving plants, and, of course, they can have them. One way would be to grow a few acid-lovers in special, lime-free compost in pots. Camellias are excellent in large tubs – some even seem to flower more prolifically in containers than they do in open ground – and so are some of the smaller rhododendrons, like 'Bluebird', 'Scarlet Wonder', 'Snow Lady' or *R. yakushimanum* and any of its many, and rapidly growing, number of hybrids.

If you want to grow more than just the odd specimen acid-lover, though, then a bit more effort is required. One thing you can't do is simply dig a hole, fill it with lime-free compost and plant acid-lovers in that because the limy water from the surrounding soil will simply drain into the hole, turn the compost alkaline very quickly and kill your plants.

What you can do, though, is build a raised bed, at least 30cm or so above the level of your soil, so that limy water can't drain up into it. Railway sleepers make a very effective and easily installed edging, or you could use log roll (lengths of split logs wired together), or, for something more permanent, you could use bricks.

Then you need to fill it with an acid soil. If yours is neutral or only slightly alkaline, you can mix your own soil with an acidifying soil improver like composted pine bark or cocoa shells. How much you'll need depends on how alkaline the soil is, so your best bet is to mix it in, then wait a month and test it again. If it's sufficiently acid, then you can put in the plants. If not, add some more soil improver and test it again a month later. It may seem a bit of a palaver, but look at it this way – even a few rhododendrons, azaleas, camellias, or pierises cost a lot of money, and if the soil isn't acid enough they will sicken and die.

Once the plants are in, spread a good layer of your chosen soil improver over the surface of the soil as a mulch. Since composted pine bark or cocoa shells will eventually break down in the soil and it will slowly become alkaline again, remember to top it up every year.

Even so, there is always a risk that acid-loving plants may begin to suffer as the soil turns slowly alkaline again – a yellowing of their leaves is the first sign that they are unable to take up the iron and magnesium they need from the soil – so it's worth treating them every spring with sequestered

The Californian tree poppy, Romneya coulteri, has large white flowers with golden centres in late summer. It needs a warm, sheltered spot and free-draining soil.

iron, watered on to the soil, or with sulphur chips sprinkled around the base of each shrub and carefully forked in to the top couple of inches of soil. Alkaline soils, provided they are deep and moisture-retentive, are very fertile soils and will grow a number of plants supremely well. Even some woodland plants that are usually thought of as needing acid, leafy soils, like wood anemones and many daphnes, will cope with some alkalinity as long as there is plenty of moisture always available in the soil.

The problem is that often they are shallow soils – over limestone or chalk, most commonly – where alkalinity is less of a problem than its poor, free-draining quality, and many plants listed as suitable for alkaline soils, like clematis or Michaelmas daisies which need plenty of moisture, won't thrive at all.

The reason they are usually very hungry soils, low in nutrients, isn't just because some vital trace elements are chemically locked up and unavailable to the plant. High alkalinity speeds up the bacteriological action that breaks down organic matter so that the nutrients produced in the process are released very quickly, and since the soil is also free-draining, they don't linger very long and so aren't available to the plant. And these soils are indeed very free-draining, very thirsty soils, and while digging in bulky organic matter helps make it more moisture-retentive, it is broken down more quickly than in other soils, and so the improvement it brings is more short-lived. And where the soil is shallow, too, over a solid layer of rock, it can be a case of feast then famine. After rain, the water may take a while to drain away – even forming puddles on the surface and water-logging the plants – but then the soil and

the upper layers of rock dry out, and any reserves of water lower down are available only to the plants with roots tough enough to force their way through the narrowest fissure to find it.

Soils are often limy because they are just a shallow layer overlaying chalk or limestone, both of which are of course alkaline. Gardening in 15 – or if you're lucky 30 – cm of soil over solid rock is clearly a challenge. While such soils are usually very light and easy to dig, apart from the odd chunks of chalk, you very soon reach bedrock, and something heftier than a spade – a pickaxe or a crowbar – is needed to make a planting hole for any reasonable-sized shrub or tree.

In this situation, the best thing to do is increase the depth of good soil as far as possible, by digging in as much bulky organic matter as you can and by mulching every year. Leaf mould is an excellent soil improver and mulch for chalky soils. Some gardeners recommend using it spring *and* autumn, but for most people this is a counsel of perfection because it takes a long time for leaves to rot down and those of us with small gardens have neither the necessary quantities of raw material nor the space needed to process it.

If you do have to make planting holes in the rock, then make them as large as you can manage and fill them with the best possible quality soil enriched with organic matter. You will probably need to feed the plants as well, though it would be a good idea to avoid alkaline fertilizers like bone-meal. Instead use something like sulphate of ammonia or, if you're an organic gardener, pelletted chicken manure which has a pH of 6. Although, in the longterm, the right plants should survive without regular watering, it makes sense to give them plenty of water in their first season, to get them off to a good start and enable them to fend for themselves.

PLANTS

In choosing the perfect plants for this situation, you have to bear in mind not only the alkalinity of the soil, but the fact that it may well be shallow and therefore poor and free-draining. Some plants can tolerate one or the other, but not both. The lovely Madonna lily (*Lilium candidum*) is one of the few lilies that can tolerate an alkaline soil, but it also needs a soil that is fertile and moist.

Trees need to be not only lime-tolerant but naturally fairly shallow-rooted, sending their roots out rather than straight down, otherwise they will not be firmly anchored in the soil and therefore likely to be blown over in a gale. Most shrubs and perennials that do well in hot, dry sites will also do well here, though a few, like broom (cytisus) and gorse (ulex) can cope with alkalinity or shallow dry soil, but not too well with both. In a sunny spot, rock plants will obviously do well because they have very shallow but wide-ranging roots adapted to finding whatever moisture and nutrients they can in the smallest fissures and crevices. Some annuals will do well, though usually they won't grow as large as they would in richer, deeper, moister soils. This can be a positive advantage with some really tough plants that are almost too invasive for better conditions, like the golden feverfew (*Tanacetum parthenium* 'Aureum'), the rampaging *Campanula portenschlagiana*, or the dead-nettle (*Lamium galeobdolon*), although even then, you'll need to keep an eye on them to make sure that they don't start smothering more refined plants in their vicinity.

Trees

Box elder (*Acer negundo*) A fast-growing deciduous tree for sun or part shade in fertile soil, with bright green leaves and clusters of inconspicuous, greenish-yellow flowers in late spring. More attractive are 'Variegatum' which has white-margined leaves and the newer 'Fla-mingo' whose young leaves are pink, initially, turning pink, cream and green. Since the young foliage is the most attractive, try growing them as shrubs and cutting them back each year.
▷ *Approx. height and spread after 20 years: 15 × 8m (46 × 25ft).*

Carpinus betulus See page 123.

Judas tree (*Cercis siliquastrum*) An attractive, spreading, bushy tree for fertile, well-drained soil in full sun. It has clusters of pea-like, bright pink flowers in mid-spring either just before or at the same time as the heart-shaped leaves appear. The flowers are followed by long purplish-red seed pods in late summer.
▷ *Approx. height and spread after 20 years: 10 × 8m (30 × 25ft).*

Crataegus oxyacantha* and *monogyna See page 90.
Holly (*Ilex aquifolium*) See page 31.
Laburnum See page 123.
Ornamental crab apple (*Malus*) See page 123.

Flowering cherry (*Prunus*) Many members of this accommodating family will grow happily on alkaline soils, provided they are rich and fertile, so dig in plenty of organic matter when you plant and mulch the tree afterwards with more of the same. See page 124.

Golden false acacia (*Robinia pseudoacacia* 'Frisia') See page 112.

Whitebeam (*Sorbus aria*) This very useful tree is tolerant of very alkaline conditions. If you can find it, *S.a.* 'Mitchellii' is the best form, with the largest leaves which are more silvery than the type and have a lot brighter autumn colour as well.

Rowan or Mountain ash (*Sorbus aucuparia*) Almost all the sorbuses are happy on limy soils, even relatively poor shallow ones, although *S. hupehensis* dislikes extreme alkalinity and *S.* 'Joseph Rock' needs a deep rich soil to do well. See page 91.

Conifers

Above: *The lovely flowering cherry,* Prunus *'Shogetsu', thrives on chalky soil.*

Right: Clematis, *'Marie Boisselot' will flower on and off all through the summer.*

Lawson cypress (*Chamaecyparis lawsoniana*)
This family of conifers provides some of the best conifers for small to average sized gardens. Some members of the family, like *C.l.* 'Green Pillar', do grow to 15m (50ft) or more so do make sure you know exactly which cultivar you are buying! Among the best are 'Ellwoodii' with steely blue-grey leaves, growing into a pyramid and reaching 3 × 1.5m (10 × 5ft), or 'Ellwood's Pillar' which is a smaller, narrower version of it; 'Minima' which forms a small round bush with light green foliage reaching only 1 × 1m (3 × 3ft); and 'Gnome' which is an even smaller bun-shaped bush and has

blue foliage, reaching no more than 50 × 50cm (20 × 20in).

Juniper As long as you can give them a place in full sun, many of these conifers will tolerate dry, sandy, alkaline soils very well indeed. Among the most useful upright, columnar varieties are *J. communis* 'Sentinel' (1.2m × 30cm/4 × 1ft) and the golden *J. communis* 'Golden Showers', the new growths of which arch gracefully, bringing to mind the firework 'golden rain'. There are also

many good varieties among the *Juniperus × media* group including 'Blue Gold', which has leaves variegated sky-blue and gold (1 × 1m/3 × 3ft). 'Plumosa Aurea' has wide-spreading branches, drooping at the tips, of feathery green-gold foliage that turns bronze in winter (1.3 × 1.3m/4 × 4ft). 'Pfitzeriana' is still sometimes sold as a dwarf conifer though it can reach 3 × 3-5m (10 × 10-15ft) with no difficulty. The golden form 'Pfitzeriana Aurea' is slightly slower-growing, but still large. Similar but much more compact is *I. × media* 'Gold Sovereign', reaching only approximately 60 × 90cm (2 × 3ft). Some of the more prostrate, mat-forming junipers like *J. horizontalis* will also do well in this type of soil. *J.h.* 'Douglasii' has blue foliage that turns purple in winter, 'Plumosa' has grey-green leaves, becoming purple in winter, while 'Emerald Spreader' has bright green foliage and doesn't reach more than about 10cm (4in) in height though it will spread to 1.5m (5ft) or more. *J. sabina* 'Tamariscifolia' isn't completely flat but it grows slowly into a low, elegant shrub with layered branches of feathery grey green foliage (30cm × 1.2m/1 × 4ft).

English yew (*Taxus baccata*) These extremely tough and accommodating conifers will put up with a number of problem places, including dry shade and also extremes of acidity and alkalinity. They have a reputation for being slow-growing, and while they are unlikely to give Leylandii a run for their money, they are nowhere near as slow as people think. They have the advantage over many other conifers in that they will regrow from old wood, so if you inherit an overgrown yew, or neglect one you've planted, you can cut it hard back. The golden form *T.b.* 'Aurea' forms a conical bush, while the very dark green and golden Irish yew (*T.b.* 'Fastigiata Robusta' and 'Standishii') both form narrow pillars up to 1.5m (5ft) tall.

White cedar (*Thuja occidentalis*) Another useful family of conifers for this situation, with some of the very best dwarf conifers among its members, like the stunning 'Rheingold' which is golden in summer and a coppery-gold in winter (1.2m × 90cm/4 × 3ft). Also very attractive are 'Danica', forming dwarf globes of dark green in summer, bronze-green in winter (40 × 50cm/16 × 20in), and

the tall *T.o.* 'Smaragd', which means 'emerald' and gives an indication of its colour (3m × 60cm/ 10 × 2ft).

Thuja orientalis Again this group contains some of the best dwarf conifers including *T.o.* 'Aurea Nana' which forms a small oval bush, with yellow-green foliage turning bronze in winter (60 × 60cm/2 × 2ft), and the less well known 'Rosedalis', another oval bush, the young foliage of which is tipped with creamy-yellow in spring, fading to green and then taking on a purplish tinge in winter (60 × 45cm/2ft × 1ft 6in).

Climbers

Clematis Most clematis prefer an alkaline soil, though it must be rich, fertile and moisture-retentive, with their heads in sun and their roots in shade, though some will grow in shade (see page 30). There are literally hundreds of different varieties to choose from – both large- and small-flowered, and in a wide range of colours. Good large-flowered varieties to look for include the mauve-pink free-flowering 'Comtesse de Bouchard', the pure white 'Marie Boisselot' and the lavender-blue 'Ascotensis'. Good small-flowered varieties of *C. alpina* and *C. macropetala* for instance, which have nodding blue, pink or white flowers in spring, are marvellous growing through evergreen shrubs like firethorn (*Pyracantha*). The late-flowering *C. viticella*, like the wine-red 'Madame Julia Correvon' or the double 'Purpurea Plena Elegans', is also good for growing through spring or early-summer flowering shrubs. Most varieties are either pruned back hard in winter to encourage better flowering or, in the case of *C. alpina*, are simply pruned to keep them within their allotted space. If you have a warm, sheltered wall, try the lovely evergreen *C. armandii*, with long slender glossy leaves and scented white flowers in late winter/early spring, or the fern-leafed clematis, *C. cirrhosa balearica* – also evergreen but with creamy, red-spotted bell-shaped flowers in winter and vigorous where it's happy.
▷ *Height: 2.5-7m (8-22ft).*

Chilean glory flower (*Eccremocarpus scaber*) Against a very sunny wall, and in any well-drained

soil, this exotic-looking climber with long, tubular orange-red flowers in summer will race away. It may get cut back by the frost but will usually produce new growth in the spring. In colder areas, protecting the base in winter will help.
▷ *Height: 2-3m (6-10ft).*

Ivies (*Hedera*) See page 30.

Common white jasmine (*Jasminum officinale*) This semi-evergreen or deciduous twining climber is a very untidy grower, but it's worth putting up with that for the abundance of very fragrant white flowers in summer and autumn. It needs full sun and fertile, well-drained soil.
▷ *Height and spread: 12 × 00m (40 × 00ft).*

Winter-flowering jasmine (*Jasminum nudiflorum*) One of the first shrubs to flower in winter (often before Christmas in sheltered gardens), it will thrive in almost any position except an east-facing spot where the early-morning sun can brown the golden-yellow flowers. Like its summer-flowering cousin, it is an untidy grower and will probably need tying.
▷ *Height and spread: 3 × 3m (10 × 10ft).*

Everlasting pea (*Lathyrus latifolius*) An old-fashioned cottage garden plant that thrives in fertile, well-drained soil in a sunny spot, with small pink-purple pea-flowers for weeks in summer/early autumn. There is also a stunning white form, *L.l.* 'Alba', that's well worth tracking down. Both are lovely winding through a picket fence or railings.
▷ *Height: 2m + (6ft +)*

Honeysuckle (*Lonicera*) Most of these twining climbers are happy on alkaline soils, provided they are fertile and moisture-retentive. See page 30.

Parthenocissus See page 30.

Roses The received wisdom is that roses won't grow in limy soils, but anyone who visited the Lime Kiln Rose Gardens in Suffolk in their prime knows that isn't necessarily the case. Admittedly the roses that grew to staggering sizes in that garden were not modern hybrid teas but a whole range of old roses, planted in large planting holes, filled with good rich soil and organic matter, and then basically left to get on with it. If you garden on an alkaline soil and must have roses, then be prepared to follow suit – dig large planting holes and fill them with the same sort of planting mixture. Mulching with something slightly acidic like composted pine bark or cocoa shells each year will help.

Star jasmine (*Trachelospermum jasminoides*) A very attractive evergreen climber for all but the coldest areas, it has masses of small, very fragrant white flowers in summer followed by attractive seed pods. 'Variegatum' has leaves variegated with cream and white. It is quite slow-growing so be prepared to be patient.
▷ *Height: 9m (28ft).*

Chinese wisteria (*Wisteria sinensis*) On a sunny wall, and in fertile, well-drained soil, this vigorous twining climber will grow up to 30m and more. It has long racemes of fragrant, lilac or pale violet flowers in early summer followed by velvety pods, while the white form 'Alba' has strongly scented white flowers. Some plants can be slow to start flowering, taking up to 5 years.
▷ *Height: 30m + (100ft +).*

Shrubs

Aucuba japonica See page 30.

Berberis Many of the berberis family will grow in these conditions. Among the evergreens, *B. darwinii* is a good choice or, better still, its offspring 'Stapehillensis' which flowers in autumn as well as in the spring (see page 40), while many of the deciduous varieties like *B. thunbergii* and its many hybrids will cope with alkalinity as long the soil isn't too dry. There are many good ones with brightly coloured foliage to choose from, like the wine-red *B.t.* 'Red Chief' or the older form 'Atropurpurea', the deep purple 'Helmond Pillar' and variegated pink and red varieties like 'Harlequin' or 'Rose Glow'. There is a golden form *B.t.* 'Aurea' with rounded golden leaves.
▷ *Approx. height and spread after 10 years: 60cm-2.5m × 60cm-2.5m × (2-8ft × 2-8ft).*

Brachyglottis (formerly *Senecio*) 'Sunshine' See page 52.

Buddleia davidii See page 52.

Buxus sempervirens See page 42.

Caragana arborescens See page 114.

Caryopteris See page 53.

Californian lilac (*Ceanothus impressus*) Although most ceanothus will grow well enough on deep, rich, moist, slightly alkaline soils, there aren't many that will cope with thin, chalky soils. This evergreen one, one of the hardiest, forms a spreading bush and is smothered in small clusters of deep blue flowers in mid-spring to early summer.
▷ *Approx. height and spread after 10 years: 1.6 × 3m (5 × 10ft).*

Ceratostigma wilemottianum See page 54.

Cistus See page 54.

Convolvulus cneorum See page 54.

Dogwood, Cornelian cherry (*Cornus mas*) A valuable large shrub for a garden that can give it the space it needs because it has small, star-shaped, yellow flowers on bare shoots in late winter and early spring, then edible, oblong, bright red fruits and good autumn colour. If you choose the smaller variegated form *C.m.* 'Variegata', then you get the added bonus of white and green variegated leaves all through the summer. Even smaller is 'Elegantissima' which also has variegated foliage, tinged pink when it's mature. It likes sun or semi-shade and does well on any soil.
▷ *Approx. height and spread after 10 years: 2-5 × 2-5m (6-15 × 6-15ft).*

Cotoneaster See page 42.

Deutzia This family of very free-flowering shrubs has members in a range of sizes, all of which will tolerate high alkalinity provided the soil is moisture-retentive. Among the best are the small *D. × rosea* 'Carminea' with deep carmine flowers with a paler shading, the medium-sized *D. × elegantissima* 'Rosealind' with deep carmine-pink flowers, and the large *D. longifolia* 'Veitchii' which has longer, paler green leaves than other deutzias and large clusters of single lilac-pink flowers.
▷ *Approx. height and spread after 10 years: 1-2.5 × 1-1.5 (3-8 × 3-5ft).*

Escallonia See page 114.

Euonymus See page 31.

Euphorbia See pages 43 and 58.

***Fremontodendron californicum* 'California Glory'** This is usually grown as a wall shrub, against a sheltered south-facing wall, and spectacular it is, too, reaching 3m (10ft) in height and spread within a few years. It has grey-green heart-shaped evergreen leaves with fuzzy brown undersides, and masses of large waxy-looking bright yellow flowers for months in summer. It must have a well-drained soil, and will tolerate high alkalinity. In a very sheltered garden it can be grown as a free-standing shrub. *F.c.* 'Pacific Sunset' is very similar but with deep orange flowers that fade to yellow.
▷ *Approx. height and spread after 10 years: 5 × 5m (16 × 16ft).*

Fuchsia Hardy fuchsias, which have much smaller, more subtle flowers than their much showier half-hardy relatives, are valuable shrubs for late summer colour and, in some cases, foliage colour too. They will grow happily in limy soils, provided they have enough moisture, and though they will usually be cut down by frost in winter, they will produce new growth in the spring. If the frost doesn't cut them hard back, then you must. Among the best are *F. magellanica* 'Alba' with very pale pink or blush-white flowers, the small 'Tom Thumb' with red and purple flowers and the lovely 'Versicolor' with deep crimson flowers and foliage that is a smoky blend of sage-green, cream and pink.
▷ *Approx. height and spread after 10 years: 30-90cm × 30cm-1m (1-3 × 1-3ft 3in).*

Hebe See page 114.

Helianthemum See page 55.

Hibiscus syriacus In a sunny spot and deep, rich but well-drained soil these shrubs are very valuable for late summer colour with their large hollyhock-like flowers. 'Diana' has pure white flowers, 'Blue Bird' has lilac-blue flowers with red centres, 'Red Heart' has large white flowers with conspicuous red centres, while probably the best known, 'Woodbridge', has carmine-pink flowers

Gypsophila 'Rosenschleier' – it means 'Veil of Roses' – and the startlingly bright Dianthus *'Princess Scarlet' both need a chalky, free-draining soil in a sunny spot to do well.*

with deeper-coloured centres. There is a newish, compact variety with large crimson-centred white flowers which has the rather unfortunate name of 'Monstrosus Dorothy Crane'.
▷ *Approx. height and spread after 10 years: 1.2-2.5m × 1-2m (4-8 × 3-6ft).*

St John's Wort or Rose of Sharon (*Hypericum calycinum*) See page 91.
Bachelor's Buttons (*Kerria japonica*) See page 32.

Beauty bush (*Kolkwitzia amabilis*) This shrub has lovely soft pink, bell-shaped flowers from late spring to midsummer, though a little patience is necessary as it produces them only on wood at

least three years old. It does best in full sun, although I have seen a large specimen trained very successfully against a north-facing wall. There's a variety called 'Pink Cloud' which has larger flowers.
▷ *Approx. height and spread after 10 years: 2.5 × 2.5m (8 × 8ft).*

Lavender (*Lavandula*) See page 55.
Ligustrum ovalifolium See page 42.
Lycium barbarum See page 115.
Mahonia aquifolium See page 32.
Jerusalem sage (*Phlomis fruticosa*) See page 55.
Flowering currant (*Ribes sanguineum*) See page 32.

Californian tree poppy (*Romneya coulteri*) This has large poppy-like white flowers in summer. It needs a warm, sunny spot.
▷ *Approx. height and spread after 10 years: 2 × 2m (6ft 6in ×6ft 6in).*

Rugosa rose (*Rosa rugosa*) See page 115.
Salvia See page 59.
Santolina See page 56.
Spartium junceum See page 56.
Spiraea japonica and ***Spiraea nipponica***
See page 92.
Thymus See page 62.
Viburnum opulus See page 34.
Vinca See page 34.
Weigela See page 129.
Yucca See page 57.

Perennials

Spiny bear's breeches (*Acanthus spinosus*)
See page 57.
Achillea filipendulina See page 57.
Lady's mantle (*Alchemilla mollis*) See page 34.

Alyssum montanum An evergreen, creeping rock plant for full sun and a well-drained soil, it has small, oval, hairy grey leaves and clusters of small, very fragrant soft yellow flowers in summer.
▷ *Height and spread: 15 × 15cm (6 × 6in).*

Pearl everlasting (*Anaphalis margaritacea* sometimes still sold as *A. yedoensis*) A very useful plant for dry soil, whether in sun or shade, which has silvery-grey leaves with white margins. It gets its common name from the many heads of small white flowers in late summer.
▷ *Height and spread: 60-75 × 60cm (2-2ft 6in × 2ft).*

Anemone × hybrida (Japanese anemone) See page 34.
Anthemis tinctoria 'E. C. Buxton'
See page 57.

Columbine or Granny's bonnets (*Aquilegia vulgaris*) These are the most delightful cottage garden plants with their attractive fern-like foliage and short-spurred flowers in shades of pink, crimson, purple and white, some single colours, some mixtures. They seed themselves freely so you always have plenty of young plants. You can buy named varieties, like 'Munstead White' or 'Crimson Star', but columbines are highly promiscuous so unless you keep them well segregated they will produce hybrids in all colours.
▷ *Height and spread: 1m × 50cm (3ft × 20in).*

Wall rock cress (*Arabis caucasica*) A very useful mat-forming evergreen for tricky situations like a dry bank, it has small white (or sometimes pink) fragrant flowers in late spring and summer. Good varieties include 'Plena' with double white flowers, 'Rosabella', with single deep pink flowers, and 'Variegata' with cream-splashed leaves and single, sometimes pink-tinged, white flowers.
▷ *Height and spread: 15 × 25cm (6 × 10in).*

Armeria See page 107.
Artemisia See page 57.
Aster See page 129.
Astilbe See page 74.

Aubrieta Dry stone walls and aubrieta seem made for each other! This attractive spring-flowering carpeter is at its best creeping or sprawling over a bank or wall. The most common type has large double, rich purple flowers, but there is a range of different colours available like the clear blue 'Triumphant', the pink 'Maurice Prichard' and the very attractive variegated *A. aurea* 'Variegata'.
▷ *Height and spread: 5-8 × 30cm (2-3 × 12in).*

Bellis perennis (Daisy) This pretty little perennial, with its pompom flowers in red, pink or white, grows in sun or semi-shade in fertile, but well-drained soil. The 'Carpet Series' has large flowers while 'Pomponette' has miniature double flowers.
▷ *Height and spread: 10-15 × 10-15cm (4-6 × 4-6in).*

Bergenia See page 34.
Campanula See page 107.
Centaurea montana See page 93.
Centranthus ruber See page 93.
Coreopsis See page 58.

Delphinium The most spectacular cottage garden plants if you can meet all their needs – an open sunny position that is also sheltered from the wind, and deep, rich, fertile but well-drained soil. If it's too heavy they will rot. The varieties to look for if you have an average to small sized garden are *belladonna* hybrids, like 'Lamartine' with purple-blue flowers, 'Wendy' with gentian-blue flowers and 'Blue Bees' with sky-blue flowers, and even smaller dwarf hybrids like 'Blue Fountains' and 'Blue Heaven'.
▷ *Height and spread: 1-1.5m × 60cm (3ft 6in-5 × 2ft).*

Dicentra See pages 35 and 42.

Burning bush (*Dictamnus albus*) This attractive plant has spikes of large white flowers with long, wispy stamens and aromatic leaves. Its common name comes from the fact that when the seed heads are ripening, the whole plant produces a vaporized oil which can be ignited with a match.
▷ *Height and spread: 90 × 60cm (3 × 2ft).*

Echinops See page 58.
Eryngium See page 58.
Euphorbia See page 58.
Geranium See page 43.

Avens (*Geum*) Another attractive plant for a sunny spot, with ferny, fresh green leaves and sprays of rounded, double flowers in summer. Among the best known are the brick-red 'Mrs Bradshaw' and the golden 'Lady Stratheden'.
▷ *Height and spread: 45-75 × 45cm (18-30 × 18in).*

Gypsophila paniculata and *repens* See page 59.
Helianthus See page 130.

Curry plant (*Helichrysum italicum*) If you like the smell of curry, this is a good plant for a sunny spot and a free-draining soil. Apart from its aromatic, silvery-grey leaves it has bobbly bright yellow flowers on long, upright white shoots during summer.
▷ *Height and spread: 60cm × 1m (2 × 3ft).*

Day lily (*Hemerocallis*) See page 75.

Sweet rocket (*Hesperis matronalis*) An old-fashioned plant with white or pale violet flowers which are wonderfully fragrant in the evening. An excellent plant to have near the patio.
▷ *Height and spread: 75 × 60cm (2ft 6in × 2ft).*

Hosta See page 35.
Iberis See page 59.
Kniphofia See page 116.

Edelweiss (*Leontopodium alpinum*) The key to success with this lovely alpine is grit – plenty dug into the soil, and spread as a mulch on top to keep the woolly leaves out of the wet, the one thing it cannot tolerate. In spring and early summer it has small, silvery-white flower heads, surrounded by petal-like, felted bracts in the shape of a star.
▷ *Height and spread: 15-20 × 15-20cm (6-8 × 6-8in).*

Limonium See page 116.
Honesty (*Lunaria rediviva*) See page 94.
Lychnis coronaria See page 59.
Catmint (*Nepeta* × *faassenii*) See page 50.

Peony (*Paeonia*) Undoubtedly they have the most exquisite flowers in spring, but in most cases their flowering season is too short, the space they occupy too large and their foliage too dull to make them good plants for small gardens. The exception is *P. mlokosewitschii* – known for understandable reasons, as 'mlok' or 'Molly the Witch' – which is attractive from the time its crimson shoots start pushing their way through the soil in late winter. They are followed by buds and leaves, at first tinged pinkish-bronze, then becoming a soft grey-green, and large, single pale lemon flowers with gold centres. In autumn, its seed pods split open to reveal rows of red and blue-black seeds. Like all peonies it likes sun but will cope with light shade, and dislikes being disturbed, so try and get it in the right place first time round! It takes some years for it to flower, which is why mature plants are expensive to buy, but it's worth splashing out. If you do have a bit more space, there are many excellent hybrids. Among the single-flowered varieties there's 'White Wings', the soft pink 'Mother of Pearl' and the scarlet 'Sunshine', while among the double-flowered varieties, 'Duchess de Nemours', which has fragrant flowers, white or just the palest creamy-yellow, the pale pink 'Sarah Bernhardt', and the wine-red, old cottage garden favourite *P. officinalis* 'Rubra Plena', are all first class, while among the anemone-flowered types 'Bowl of Beauty', which has clear pink petals and a creamy-yellow centre, is outstanding.
▷ *Height and spread: 60-90 × 60-90cm (2-3 × 2-3ft).*

Penstemon See page 59.
Knotweed (*Persicaria* – formerly *Polygonum*) See page 35.

Phlox paniculata A plant no self-respecting cottage garden would be without, for its long-

lasting, bright flowers in shades ranging from white through various pinks and mauves to scarlet and crimson. While they don't like wet soils, they suffer badly if it's too dry, so be prepared to water them in a long dry spell. Good, widely available varieties include the deep red 'Starfire', the violet-purple 'Border Gem', more salmon-orange than orange-orange 'Prince of Orange' and 'White Admiral'.
▷ *Height and spread: 90 × 50cm (3 × 1ft 6in).*

The dwarf phlox, *P. douglasii* and *P. subulata*, form low mats of green foliage and produce masses of flowers in early summer in the same range of colours as their larger relation, plus blue. Good varieties to look out for include the rose-pink *P.d.* 'Daniel's Cushion', 'Red Admiral' and 'May Snow', *P.s.* 'Oakington Blue', 'Temiskaming', a vivid rosy-red, and 'White Delight'.
▷ *Height and spread: 15 × 40cm (6 × 16in).*

Polygonatum See page 35.
Pulmonaria See page 37.

Pasque flower (*Pulsatilla vulgaris*) A very pretty plant for a rock garden, with feathery light green leaves, nodding cup-shaped flowers in shades of purple, red (*P.v.* 'Rubra'), pink (*P.v.* 'Barton's Pink') or white (*P.v.* 'Alba'), with bright yellow centres in spring. They don't like to be disturbed so do try and get them in the right place the first time around.
▷ *Height and spread: 15-23 × 15-23cm (6-9 × 6-9in).*

Primula This large and beautiful family includes members with a wide range of needs. Some prefer acid soils, but those listed below need a gritty alkaline soil, are happy in full sun or partial shade unless stated otherwise and flower in spring. *P. allionii* forms a tight cushion of oval green leaves, with tubular rose, white or mauve flowers. Height and spread: 8 × 8-15cm (3 × 3-6in). *P. auricula* has oval, soft, pale green to grey-green leaves with a white powdery bloom and large circular heads of flat yellow flowers. It prefers part shade.
▷ *Height and spread: 15-23 × 15cm (6-9 × 6in).*
▷ *P.* 'Linda Pope' has a similar bloom on its leaves, but the flowers are flat-faced and blue-mauve, and borne on short stalks. It's slightly smaller than *P. auricula. P. marginata* has similar leaves to 'Linda Pope' but funnel-shaped blue-lilac flowers.
▷ *Height and spread: 10-15 × 10-20cm (4-6 × 4-8in).*

Black-eyed susan (*Rudbeckia*) This family brings a warm glow to the late summer/early autumn border, with golden yellow or orange daisy flowers with prominent dark central cones. Look for *R. fulgida* (or *newmanii*) 'Deamii' or 'Goldsturm' or the much taller *R. laciniata* 'Goldquelle' which has finely divided foliage and double golden yellow flowers, like large French marigolds.
▷ *Height and spread: 80cm-2m × 40cm-1m (2ft 6in-6ft 6in × 16in-3ft 3in).*

Salvia nemorosa See page 59.
Bouncing bette (*Saponaria ocymoides*) See page 60.

Saxifrage (*Saxifraga*) Another huge family with members whose needs differ widely. There are quite a few which need an alkaline soil – indeed one group has its leaves naturally encrusted with lime. All those listed also need a sunny spot and very good drainage and they are evergreen. They all flower in early summer unless stated otherwise.
▷ *S. callosa* forms tight rosettes of long, stiff, lime-encrusted leaves above which it carries sprays of star-shaped white flowers with red-spotted petals, upright initially and then arching, in early summer.
▷ *Height and spread: 25 × 20cm (10 × 8in).*
▷ *S. cochlearis* forms rosettes of spoon-shaped green leaves with white encrusted edges and has rounded white flowers, often with red-spotted petals in early summer.
▷ *Height and spread: 20 × 25cm (8 × 10in).*
▷ *S. grisebachii* 'Wisley Variety' like *S. callosa* forms a rosette of long, narrow lime-encrusted leaves which throw up thick crosier-shaped stems, covered in pale pink to bright red hairs and dense clusters of dark red flowers.
▷ *Height and spread: 10 × 15cm (4 × 6in).*
▷ *S.* 'Tumbling Waters' is spectacular in flower, with its densely packed small white flowers looking just like a foaming waterfall tumbling over a rock. It too forms rosettes of lime-crusted leaves, which die off once they have flowered (which can take

This exquisite pale lemon flowered peony, P. mlokosewitschii is known, for obvious reasons, as 'mlok' or 'Molly-the-witch' for short. It also has curious red and black seed pods in autumn.

three to four years) but they produce offspring-small rosettes of leaves which will take over.
▷ *Height and spread: 60-20cm (2ft × 8in).*

Scabious (Scabiosa caucasica) These easy, clump-forming perennials are enjoying a great revival in popularity on account of the masses of flowers they bear throughout summer. 'Clive Greaves' has violet-blue flowers with a creamy pincushion centre, while 'Floral Queen' is similar but slightly larger and has frillier flowers. 'Miss Willmott' has creamy-white flower heads. Widely promoted in garden centres in recent years are 'Butterfly Blue' and 'Pink Mist', which are more compact plants, ideal for small gardens.
▷ *Height and spread: 30-60 × 30-60cm (1-2ft × 1ft 6in-2ft).*

Houseleek (Sempervivum) See page 107.

Sidalcea These are like miniature hollyhocks, with spires of small, flat-faced flowers in shades of pink and white. Good varieties include the shell-pink 'Loveliness', the clear pink 'Oberon' and the deep pink 'Puck'. *S. candida* is the white form.
▷ *Height and spread: 1-1.2 × 1m (3-4 × 3ft).*

Lamb's lugs (Stachys byzantina sometimes still sold as S. lanta or S. olympica) See page 62.

Tanacetum coccineum **(formerly known as *Chrysanthemum* or *Pyrethrum*)** These attractive plants have aromatic, feathery foliage and daisy-like flowers in a range of pink shades. 'Brenda'

has magenta-pink flower heads with yellow centres in late spring and early summer, while the no-nonsense 'Eileen May Robinson' has strong-stemmed pink flower heads with yellow centres in summer, and the flowers of 'Mrs James Kelway' start out a pinky-beige and age to pink.
▷ *Height and spread: 60 × 45cm + (24 × 18in +).*

Trollius See page 79.
Mullein (*Verbascum olympicum*) See page 62.
Greater and Lesser periwinkle (*Vinca major* and *minor*) See page 34.
Viola labradorica **'Purpurea'** See page 38.

Ferns

Although some ferns, like the male fern (*Dryopteris filix-mas*) and the common polypody (*Polypodium vulgare*) will cope with drier conditions than most ferns, it is still well worth preparing the soil with moisture-retentive organic matter when you plant them. Like most plants, they can cope much better with deprivation when they are established than they can when they have just been planted.

Maidenhair spleenwort (*Adiantum trichomanes*) See page 38.
Male fern (*Dryopteris filix-mas*) See page 38.
Hart's-tongue fern (*Phyllitis or Asplenium scolopendrium*) See page 38.
Common polypody (*Polypodium vulgare* 'Cornubiense') See page 38.
Soft shield fern (*Polystichum setiferum*) See page 39.

Annuals

Annuals, fortunately, are tolerant of a wide range of soil conditions, and all the best known and most widely grown varieties will grow well enough in an alkaline soil provided they have enough moisture and nutrients, which will mean adding plenty of organic matter and even a general fertilizer to very free-draining soil.

Where the soil is very poor and shallow, as well as alkaline, the choice is narrower. In these conditions some annuals won't grow as large as they would in more fertile soils, but should still flower freely enough to be well worth having.

Swan river daisy (*Brachyscome iberidifolia*) A bushy plant with very feathery bright green leaves and vivid blue daisy flowers with a bright yellow centre. You can buy mixed seed, with pink, mauve and white flowers as well, but it is not as striking as the plain blue.
▷ *Height and spread: 45 × 45cm (18 × 18in).*

Pot marigold (*Calendula officianalis*) See page 93.
Cornflower (*Centaurea cyanus*) See page 94.

Wallflower (*Cheiranthis cheiri*) As its name suggests, this old-fashioned biennial thrives in limy conditions. The perennial, mat-forming *C.* 'Moonlight', which doesn't reach much more than 5cm (2in) in height, has a succession of pale yellow flowers all through the summer, and does best in poor, free-draining soil.
▷ *Height and spread: 20-60cm × 20-40cm (8in-2ft × 8-16in).*

Star of the veldt (*Dimorphotheca aurantiaca* 'Glistening White') See page 63.
Viper's bugloss (*Echium vulgare*) See page 94.
Californian poppy (*Eschscholzia californica*) See page 63.

Toadflax (*Linaria maroccana*) 'Fairy Lights' is the best variety to grow here, with flowers like miniature snapdragons in a mixture of red, pink, purple, yellow and white.
▷ *Height and spread: 20 × 15cm (8 × 6in).*

Scarlet flax (*Linum grandiflorum*) See page 94.
Poached egg plant See page 94.
Alyssum (*Lobularia maritima*) See page 94.
Baby blue eyes (*Nemophila insignis*) See page 39.

Clary (*Salvia horminum*) With this annual member of the family the colour comes primarily not from the flowers proper but from the purple pink or white bracts that surround them. They dry well.
▷ *Height and spread: 45 × 20cm (18 × 8in).*

Nasturtiums (*Tropaeolum*) They really don't like good rich fertile soil – it makes them produce masses of leaves and fewer flowers. Good varieties for small gardens include 'Dwarf Jewel Mixed' which has semi-double flowers in several shades of yellow, orange and deep red, and 'Alaska' which has single flowers in red and orange, set off to perfection by marbled green and white foliage. If you prefer single colours, try 'Baby Salmon', which has dark foliage and salmon-pink flowers, or the somewhat more sophisticated 'Empress of India' which has spurred, velvety, deep crimson flowers and dark foliage.

▷ *Height and spread: 25-30 × 30cm (9-12 × 12in).*

Bulbs

Most bulbs, with the exception of a few acid-lovers like dog's-tooth violets (erythroniums) and some lilies, will grow in alkaline soils, again *provided* the soil is fertile and moisture-retentive. Some lilies, like the Madonna lily (*L. candidum*), *L. henryii*, the Trumpet Lily hybrids like 'African Queen' and 'Pink Pearl', actually prefer an alkaline soil, but it must be fertile, and moisture-retentive. Those listed below, almost all of which grow in poor, sunbaked soil on hillsides in their native habitat, will cope with poor, shallow alkaline soils in a sunny spot.

Ornamental onions (Alliums) A large family with a long flowering season, in a range of sizes from just a few centimetres tall to over 2m (6ft), and with flowers in a whole range of pinks, mauves and white, plus golden yellow. Among the smaller alliums, *A. ostrowskianum*, with its loosely packed rounded heads of bright carmine flowers in summer, and *A. moly*, which flowers about the same time but has bright golden flowers, are both excellent, as its *A. karataviense*, which has densely packed flower heads, like drumsticks, of whitish flowers tinged with mauvy-pink. The earlier-flowering *A. cowanii* with pure white flowers is lovely, as is *A. triquetrum*, which has loose heads of flowers like white bluebells. Among the taller varieties, look for *A. albopilosum* (or *christophii*) which has huge globular heads, the size of large grapefruit, made up of starry silver-mauve flowers that dry on the plant to a lovely subtle bleached straw colour, with small green seed pods in the centre of each star. Not surprisingly they are

much prized by flower arrangers. The tallest is *A. giganteum*, which can reach up to 2m (6ft) in height, with large round heads of purple flowers. Rather different in appearance is *A. siculum* (sometimes sold as *A. bulgaricum*, or now more correctly as *Nectaroscordum siculum* or *bulgaricum*), with heads of dangling bell-shaped flowers which are cream, marked with pink and tinged slightly with green.

▷ *Height and spread: 10cm-2m × 10-45cm (4in-6ft 6in × 4-18in).*

Anemone blanda See page 39.

Colchicum These look like large crocuses and flower in the autumn and so are often called, wrongly, 'autumn crocus'. Their flowers appear before the leaves – hence their other common name 'naked ladies' – and the foliage, which is large and floppy, sometimes doesn't appear till spring. It's important, therefore, to position it with care, ideally somewhere that the foliage isn't going to swamp smaller plants that emerge in spring, and where it is disguised by other plants. *C. speciosum* has lilac flowers, though there is a stunning white form, *C.s.* 'Alba'. *C.* 'Waterlily' has double flowers in a pinky-mauve colour.

▷ *Height and spread: 10-15 × 15cm (4-6 × 6in).*

Crocus See page 107.
Cyclamen hederifolium See page 39.

Fritillaries (Fritillaria) Some of the smaller ones like the snakeshead fritillary (*F. meleagris*) will cope in these conditions. The huge and flamboyant crown imperial (*F. imperialis*) with its heads of brick-red, orange or yellow bell-shaped flowers, also likes free-draining, alkaline soil, but it must have at least 15cm (6in) or better still 20cm (8in) of soil on top of the bulb otherwise it almost certainly won't flower in its second year. It's worth planting it on its side to stop water getting into the crown and rotting it.

▷ *Height and spread: 30cm-1.5m × 8-30cm (1-5ft × 3-12in).*

Narcissi The smaller varieties, like 'Tête à Tête' and 'Havera' that don't need to be planted as deep

as the larger ones, are a good choice here.
▷ *Height and spread: 20-30cm × 8cm (8-12in × 3in).*

Sternbergia lutea Another autumn-flowering bulb that looks like a crocus, but this time the dark green, crocus-like leaves appear at the same time as the flower, which is bright yellow.
▷ *Height and spread: 5-15 × 8-10cm (2-6 × 3-4in).*

Tulips Given that most of them originate from rocky, thin, alkaline soils on sun-baked hillsides, it's not surprising that most of them - particularly the small wild tulips and their hybrids - will thrive in these conditions. See page 63.

The Californian poppy, Eschscholzia californica.

INDEX

Figures in bold refer to pages with illustrations.

Abelia × *grandiflora* 126
Abies koreana 126
  A. picaea 86
Acaena 106
  A. inermis 106
Acanthus mollis 57, **116**
  A. spinosissimus 57
  A. spinosus 57, 150
Acer campestre 103, 111, 123
  A. japonicum 134
  A. negundo 103, 123, 143
  A. palmatum 134
  A. pseudoplatanus 90, 123
Achillea **45**, 57, 87, 90, 106
  A. filipendulina 57, 92, 150
  A. × *lewisii* 106
  A. millefolium 57
  A. ptarmica 57
aconites 26
Aconitum 34
Acorus 74
Adiantum 38
African lily 57
Agapanthus 57, 103
  A. campanulatus 57
air plants 8
Ajuga reptans 42, 87, 92
Alchemilla mollis 19, 34, 42, 150
alder 66–7
alder buckthorn 91
Algerian iris 59
Allium 63, 155
  A. triquetrum 39, 155

almond 124–5
Alpine phlox 107
alpines 8, 47–8, 87, 95, **96**, 98–9
Alstroemeria 63
alyssym 94
Alyssum montanum 150
  A. saxatile 57
Amelanchier lamarckii 72
Anaphalis margaritacea 150
  A. triplinervis **56**
Anemone **24**, 74
  A. blanda **36**, 39, 94, 155
  A. hupehensis 93
  A. × *hybrida* 34, 92–3, 129, 150
  A. japonica 34
  A. nemorosa 18, 27, 39, 43, 74
  Japanese 87, 92–3, 150
Anthemis tinctoria 57, 150
Anthyllis vulneraria 118
Aquilegia vulgaris 150
Arabis caucasica 150
  A. ferdinandi-coburgii 106
Arctostaphylos uva-ursi 104, 134
Armeria 107, 150
  A. caespitosa 107
  A. maritima 99, 111, 115
Artemisia 6, 7, 10, 46, 51, 57–8, **61**, 150
  A. lactiflora 58
  A. ludoviciana 58
  A. maritima 58
  A. schmidtiana 58
Arum italicum 39, 43, 81
arum lily 79, 103
Aruncus dioicus 71, 74

Arundinaria 79, 114
  A. japonica 91
  A. murielae 79
  A. nitida 79
  A. variegata 79
  A. viridistriata 79
Arundo donax 79
Asplenium 38, 71
  A. scolopendrium 154
Aster 150
  A. amellus 129–30
  A. × *frikartii* 130
  A. novae-angliae 130
  A. novi-belgii 130
Astilbe 7, **64**, 74–5, 150
Astilboides tabularis 70
astrantias **16**
Athyrium filix-femina 38
  A. nipponicum pictum 38
Aubretia 150
Aucuba 110, 126
  A. japonica **21**, 30–1, 40, 91, 147
Austrian pine 110
Avena 62
  A. sempervirens 93
avens 151
  water 75
azaleas 12, 134, 138–9

Baby blue eyes 39, 155
baby's breath 59
bachelor's buttons, 26, 32, 149
bamboo 23, 71, 79, 91, 114
barberry 40, 52
Ballota pseudodictamnus 58
bearberry 104, 134
bear's breeches 57
beauty bush 149

bell flower 107
Bellis perennis 150
Berberis 40, 87, 98, 105, 114, 126, 147
  B. darwinii 40, 114, 147
  B. julianae 91, 114
  B. stenophylla 40
  B. thunbergii 52, 114, 147
  B. wallichiana purpurea 89
Bergenia 19, 34, 42, 47, 130, 150
  B. cordifolia 34, 106
  B. crassifolia **101**
birch (*Betula*) 90, 98, 103, 123
  B. pendula 90, 123
bistort 117
black-eyed susan 152
Blechnum spicant 38
  B. tabulare 38
bleeding heart 18, 34
  Eastern 42
bluebells 18, 27, 43
blueberry 74
bog arum 74, 76–7
bog plants 8, 66–7
bouncing bette 60, 152
Bowles' golden grass 43, 80
box **20**, 42, **116**
box elder 143
Brachyglottis 46, 52, 67, 114, 148
Brachycombe iberidifolia 154
bramble, ornamental 27, 42
bridal wreath 127
Brompton stock 155
broom 54, 110, 143
  Mount Etna 52
  pineapple 50
  Spanish 51, 56, 115

Brunnera macrophylla 18, 106
Buddleia 105
  B. alternifolia 50, 53
  B. davidii 52, 148
  B. fallowiana 52
bugbane 75
bugle 42, 87, 92, 129
bugloss, Siberian 18, 106
burnet rose 111, 115
burning bush 151
busy lizzie 19, **21**, 23, 39
butterfly bush 52–3
Buxus sempervirens 42, 148

Cabbage palm 44, 54
Calendula 93–4
  C. officinalis 154
calico bush 134, 137
Californian fuchsia 62
Californian lilac 148
Californian poppy 44, 63, 94, 154, **156**
Californian tree poppy **141**, 150
Calla palustris 75
Calluna 91
  C. vulgaris 105, 134
Caltha palustris 75
Camussia leichtlinii 130
Camellia 12, 98, 131, **132**, 134, 135, 140
Campanula 107, 150
  C. cochleariifolia 107
  C. portenschlagiana 27, 107, 143
  C. poscharskyana **13**, 107
  C. rotundifolia 118
campion:
  double sea **117**
  rose 59
Campsis grandiflora 7
Canada hemlock 27
candytuft 59, 94
Caragana arborescens 114, 148
Carex 79
  C. morrowii 79
  C. stricta 79
Carpinus betulus 123, 143
Caryopteris **49**, 50–1, 148
  C. × clandonensis 53
  C. incana 53
catmint 59, 151
Ceanothus 102
  C. impressus 148
cedar, white 146
Centaurea 94
  C. cyanus 154
  C. montana 93, 150
  C. scabiosa 118
Centaurium erythraea 118
centaury, common 118

Centranthus ruber 87, 93, 150
Ceratostigma willmottianum 54, 102, 148
Cercidiphyllum japonicum 134
Cercis siliquastrum 143
Chaenomeles **124**, 126
  C. japonica 105
  C. speciosa 126
  C. × superba **124**, 126
Chamaecyparis lawsoniana 144
Cheiranthis cheiri 154
cherry: flowering 124–5, 143, **144**
  weeping 125–6
cherry laurel 42, 127
Chilean glory flower 102, 146–7
Chilean potato vine 101–2
Chionodoxa 94
Choisya ternata 86, 110
Christmas box 26, 32–3
Christmas rose 35, 106
Christmas tree 86
Chrysanthemum carinatum 94
Cimifuga 75
cinquefoil, shrubby 92
Cistus 44, 54, 102, 148
Clarkia 94
clary 154
Clematis 30, 71–2, 140, **145**, 146
  C. alpina 30, 72, 146
  C. armandii 146
  C. cirrhosa balearica 146
  C. flammula 72
  C. grandiflora 70
  C. macropetala 30, 146
  C. montana 30, 72
  C. m. rubens 30
  C. viticella 146
Clethra alnifolia 72, 134, 135
Cobaea scandens 7
Colchicum 155
  C. speciosum 43, 155
columbine 150
comfrey 37–8
Convolvulus cneorum 46, 51, 54, 148
coral flower 35
Cordyline 44
  C. australis 51, 54
Coreopsis 58, 150
  C. verticillata 58
cornelian cherry 148
cornflower 94, 154
Cornus 31, 126
  C. alba 73, 87, **105**
  C. canadensis 135
  C. kousa 135

C. mas 148
C. sanguinea 73, 110, 114
C. stolonifera 73, 105
Corsican pine 90, 104
Corydalis cashmiriana 139
Corylus avellana 90, 126
  C. maxima 90
Cotinus coggygria 105
Cotoneaster 11, 42, 87, 98, 105, 110, 126, 148
  C. dammeri 42, 91
  C. microphyllus 42, 91
  C. × suecicus 42
cotton lavender 46, 56
cowberry 33, 74
crabs, flowering 123, 143
cranesbill 26–7, 43, 106, 107
crassulas 47
Crataegus 103, 123
  C. monogyna 90, **104**, 111, 143
  C. oxyacantha 71, 143
Crocosmia 58, 130
Crocus 26, 27, 94, 107, 155
crown imperial 156
cup-and-saucer vine 7
Cupressus arizonica 103
currant, flowering 26, 32, 42, 127, 149
curry plant 151
Cyclamen:
  hardy 94
  C. hederifolium 18, 26, 39, 43, 155
Cynoglossum officinale 118
cypress, Lawson 144
Cytisus 50, 54, 143
  C. battandieri 50

Daffodils 27, 130
daisy bush 110, 115
Daphne 31
day lily 75, 151
dead-nettle 35, 43, 106, 130, 143
Delphinium 150
Deschampsia cespitosa 80
Deutzia 86, 106, 148
Dianthus **45**, 46, 52, 58, **149**
  D. allwoodii 58
  D. barbatus 94
  D. deltoides 58, 107
Dicentra 151
  D. eximia 42
  D. spectabilis 18, 34–5, 42
  D. s. alba 26, 35
Dictamnus albus 151
Digitalis 42
  D. ferruginea 43
  D. grandiflora 43
  D. × mertonensis 43
  D. purpurea 42

Dimorphoteca 63
  D. aurantiaca 154
dog's tooth violet 18, 26, 27, 39–40, 155
dogwood 11, 31, 73, 87, **105**, 110, 114, 148
  Chinese or Japanese 135
  creeping 135
double sea campion **117**
Dryopteris 27
  D. filix-mas 38, 154
Duke of Argyll's tea tree 115

Eccremocarpus scaber 102, 146–7
Echinops 151
  E. humilis 58
  E. ritro 46, 58
Echium vulgare 94, 118, 154
edelweiss 99, 151
eglantine 115
Elaeagnus 31, 98
  E. angustifolia 114
  E. commutata 106, 114
  E. × ebbingei 31, 91, 110, 114
  E. pungens 31
elder 74, 110
  box 143
  golden cut-leafed 12
elephant's ears 19, 34, 42, 106, 130
Endymion 18
Enkianthus campanulatus **133**, 135
Eranthis hyemalis 18, 39, 107, 130
Erica carnea 89, 91, 134–5
Eryngium **45**, 58, 115, 151
  E. giganteum 58
  E. maritimum 111
  E. oliverianum 58
  E. tripartitum 58
  E. varifolium 51, 58
Erythronium 139, 155
  E. dens-canis 18, 26, 27, 39
  E. revolutum 18
Escallonia 102, 110, 114, 148
Eschscholzia 44, 63, 94, 154, **156**
Euonymus 11, 87, 110, 148
  E. fortunei 26, 31, 87, 91, 98, 106, 114
  E. japonicus 87, 106, 114
Euphorbia 47, 58, 148, 151
  E. myrsinites 51, 58
  E. polychroma 58
  E. robbiae 26, 43
  E. wulfenii 58
evening primrose 59, 116–17
everlasting pea 147

False acacia 112, 143
false castor oil plant 19, 31
false spikenard 139
Fargesia nitida 71, 79
  F. spathacea 79
Fatsia japonica 19, **21**, 23, 31
ferns 6, **9**, 19–20, 27, 38, 66, 81, 154
fescue, blue 62, **88**, 93
Festuca glauca 62, **88**, 93
  F. punctoria 62
field maple 111, 123
Filipendula 75
firethorn 32, 115, 127
flame creeper 139
foamflower, 19, 106
Fothergilla 135
foxgloves 6, 42, 130
Fremontodendron californicum 148
fritillaries (*Fritillaria*) 155
  dwarf 94
  F. imperialis 156
  F. meleagris 156
Fuchsia 102, 148
  F. magellanica 102, 148

Galanthus nivalis 40, **41**, 81, 107
gardener's garters 70, 80
Garryea elliptica 31
Gaultheria mucronata 106, 135, 137
  G. shallon 42
Gazania 62
Genista aetnensis 52
  G. hispanica 51, 54
  G. lydia 54
gentian (*Gentiana*) 139
  G. sino-ornata 139
Geranium 106, 107, 151
  G. cinereum 107
  G. c. subcaulescens 107
  G. macrorrhizum 26–7, 43
  G. psilostemon **8**
  G. sanguineum lancastriense 107
geraniums 89–90, 106
germander 57
Geum 151
  G. rivale 75
Glaucium flavum 118
globe flower 79
globe thistle 46, 58
Glory-of-the-snow 94
Glyceria maxima 80
goat's beard 71, 74
golden cut-leafed elder 12
golden false acacia 143
golden feverfew 143
golden grass, Bowles' 43, 80
golden hop 72, 126
golden oats 93

golden privet 42
golden rod 154
gorse 92, 98, 106, 110, 115, **117**, 143
  Spanish 54
granny's bonnets 150
grape hyacinths 40, 107
Griselina littoralis 110
guelder rose 33, 42, 74, 92, 106, 110, 115, 128
Gunnera 66
  G. manicata 75
Gypsophila 59, **149**
  G. paniculata 151
  G. repens 59, 151

Halimium 54
  H. lasianthum 51
hard fern 38
harebell 118
hart's-tongue fern 38, 71, 154
hawthorn 71, 90, 98, **104**, 111, 123
hazel 90, 126
heathers 91, 105, 134–5
Hebe 44, 54–5, 101, 114, 148
Hedera 30, 104, 147
  H. colchica 30, 40, 104
  H. helix 19, 23, 40, 104
  H. hibernica 104
Helianthemum 50, **53**, 55, 148
Helianthus 130, 148
Helichrysum italicum 151
  H. petiolatum 44, 148
Helictotrichon sempervirens **61**, 62, 93
hellebore (*Helleborus*) **9**
  H. foetidus 43
  H. niger 35, 106
  H. orientalis 35
Hemerocallis 75–6, 130, 151
  H. flava 75
Hesperis matronalis 106
Heuchera sanguinea **16**, 35
Hibiscus syriacus 148–9
Himalayan balsam 81
Himalayan blue poppy **137**, 139
Hippophae 91
  H. rhamnoides 106, 110, 114
holly 31, **84**, 86, 87, 90, 98, 110, 126, 143
honesty 94, 151
honeysuckle 30, 147
  box-leafed 87–8, 92, 110
hornbeam 98, 123
Hosta 6, 8, **9**, **16**, 19, **21**, 23, 35, 65, 66, 76, **80**, 151
  H. fortunei 35, **37**
  H. sieboldiana 35
  H. s. elegans 70
hound's tongue 118

Houttuynia cordata 76
Humulus lupulus 72, 126
Hyacinthoides non-scriptus 18, 27, 43
Hydrangea 31
  climbing *see H. petiolaris*
  H. macrophylla 31
  H. paniculata 106
  H. petiolaris 7, 30, 40, 52, 70, 72, 104
  H. quercifolia 31
  H. villosa 31
Hypericum calycinum 91–2, 126, 149

Iberis 59
  I. saxatilis 59
  I. umbellata 94
ice plant 60
Ilex 31, 90, 98, 103
  I. aquifolium 143
  I. crenata 126
Impatiens 19, 39
  I. glandulifera 81
Iris 8, **64**, 65, 67, **69**, 76, **80**
  Algerian 59
  I. ensata 76
  I. foetidissima 43
  I. kaempferi 76
  I. laevigata 71, 76
  I. pseudacorus 71, 76
  I. reticulata 27
  I. sibirica 71, 76
  I. stylosa 59
  I. unguicularis 59
Irish ivy 19, 104
Irish yew 23, 146
ivy 19, **20**, 23, 30, 40, 104, 147

Jacob's ladder 130
Japanese anemone 87, 92–3, 150
Japanese banana plant **113**
Japanese crab 123
Japanese holly 126
Japanese maples 6, 12, 102, 134
Japanese painted fern 38
Japanese quince 105
japonica 126
jasmine (*Jasminum*) 147
Jerusalem sage 55, 149
Judas tree 143
juniper (*Juniperus*) 110, 144–6
  J. communis 104, 144
  J. horizontalis 104, 146
  J. × media 104, 146
  J. sabina 146

Kalmia latifolia 134, 137
Katsura tree 134

Kerria 126
  Kerria japonica 24, 26, 32, **33**, 106, 149
kidney vetch 118
kingcup 75
Kirengeshoma palmata 139
knapweed, greater 118
Kniphofia 103, **116**, 151
knotweed 35, 78, 106, 117, 152
kolkwitzia amabilis 149
Korean fir 126

Laburnum 104, 123, 143
lady fern 38
lady's mantle, 19, 34, 42, 150
lamb's lugs 46, 62, 117, 154
Lamium galeobdolon 143
  L. maculatum 27, 35, **37**, 43, 106, 130
Lathyrus latifolius 147
laurel:
  cherry 42, 127
  spotted 30–1, 91, 126
Lavatera trimensis 94
lavender (*Lavandula*) 46, 47, 51, 149
  L. angustifolia alba 55
  L. spica 55
  L. stoechas 51, 55
Lawson cypress 144
lemon balm 87
lemon verbena 46
Lenten rose 35
Leontopodium alpinum 99, 151
Leucanthemum vulgare 118
Leucojum vernum and aestivum 81
Leucothoë fontanesiana 138
Leycesteria formosa 26, 32
Ligularia 9, 66, **69**, 70, 76
  L. clivorum 76
  L. stenocephala 76
Ligustrum ovalifolium 42, 114, 149
lilac 128
lily 23, 139
  African 57
  arum 79, 103
  day 75, 151
  L. auratum 139
  L. candidum 143, 155
  L. henryii 155
  L. martagon **16**
  L. speciosum 139
Lilyturf 27, 43
Madonna 143, 155
Peruvian 63
plantain 35, 76
trumpet 155
Turk's cap **16**
Limnanthes douglasii 94, 155

Limonium 151
  L. latifolium 116
  L. vulgara 111
Linaria maroccana 154
  L. vulgaris 118
Linum grandiflorum 94, 155
Lippia citriodora 46
Liriope muscari 24, 27, 43
Lithodora diffusa 138
Livingstone daisies 47, 62
Lobelia 65, **69**, , 76
  L. cardinalis 70
Lobularia maritima 94, 155
Lonicera 30, 147
  L. americana 30
  L. japonica 30
  L. nitida 87–8, 92, 110
loosestrife 77
Lunaria 94
  L. rediviva 151
lungwort 27, 37, 43, 106
Luzula maxima 80
Lychnis coronaria **45**, 59, 151
Lycium barbarum 115, 149
Lysichiton 6, 66, 76–7
Lysimachia 77–8
  L. chlethroides 78, 130
  L. nummularia 77–8, 130
  L. punctata 77, 130

Macleya cordata 26
Madonna lily 143, 155
Magnolia 127
  M. × *soulangeana* **125**, 127
Mahonia aquifolium 32, 42,
  106, 149
  M. japonica 32
maiden pinks 107
maidenhair fern, hardy 38
maidenhair fern, spleenwort
  154
male fern 38, 154
mallow 94
Malus 123, 143
maple 98, 103, 111, 123
  Japanese 6, 12, 102, 134
Marsh marigold 75
marigold:
  pot 93, 154
Matteuccia struthiopteris 38,
  66, 71, 81
Matthiola incana 155
meadow saffron 43
meadowsweet 75
Meconopsis betonicifolia **137**,
  139
Mesembryanthemum 44, 47,
  62–3
Mexican orange-blossom 86,
  110
Michaelmas daisies 129–30
Milium effusum 43, 80
Mimulus 39, **64**, 78, 81

Miscanthus 80, **93**
  M. sinensis 80, 93
mock orange 86, 106, 127
Molinia caerulea 80
monkey flower 39, 81
monkey musk 78
monkshood 34
mosses 7
Mount Etna broom 52
mountain ash 11, 71, 86, 91,
  104, **108**, 126, 143
mountain cornflower 93
mountain pine 86, 87, **88**, 89,
  90–1, 104
mullein 62, 154
Musa basjoo **113**
Muscari 107
  M. armediacum 40
  M. botryoides 40
Myosotis palustris 78

Narcissus 26, 107, 130, 155
  N. lobularis 27
nasturtiums 63, 154
Nectaroscordum siculum 155
Nemophila insignis 39, 155
  N. maculata 39
Nepeta × *faassenii* 59, **61**, 151
  N. mussinii 59
Nerine bowdenii 63
New Zealand burr 106
New Zealand flax 55
nutmeg, flowering 26, 32
Nyssa sinensis 134
  N. sylvatica 134

Oat grass, blue 93
Oenothera biennis 116–17
  O. missouriensis 59
Olearia × *haastii* 115
  O. macrodonta 110, 115
Oleaster 114
onions, ornamental 63, 155
Onoclea sensibilis 81
Oregon grape 32, 42
Ornithogalum nutans 27
osier, common 112
Osmunda regalis 66, 81
Osteospermum **49**, 51, 52, 59
  O. ecklonii prostrata 59
ostrich plume fern 38, 81
ox-eye chamomile 57
ox-eye daisy 118

Pachysandra terminalis 32,
  106
Parthenocissus 30, 40, 147
  P. henryana 30
  P. tricuspidata **101**, 104
pasque flower 152
passionflower 52, 102
pea tree 114, 148
pear, weeping willow-leafed
  125–6

pearl everlasting 150
pelargoniums 47
Penstemon 59, 152
peony (*Paeonia*) 151
  P. mlokosewitschii 151, **153**
  P. officinalis 151
periwinkle 34, 42, 129, 154
Pernettya 86, 106, 135, 137
Perovskia 55
  P. atriplicifolia **61**
Persicaria 35, 78, 130, 152
  P. affinis 35, 106
  P. bistorta 117
Peruvian lilies 63
Phalaris arundinacea picta
  70, 80–1
Philadelphus 86, 106, **121**,
  127
Phlomis fruticosa 55, 149
  P. italica 55
Phlox 106
  P. douglasii 152
  P. paniculata 152
  P. subulata 107, 152
Phormium 117
  P. cookianum 55
  P. tenax 55
Phyllitis 38
  P. scolopendrium 71, 154
Physocarpus opulifolius 73
piceas 110
pickerel weed 78
Pieris 12, 131, 136, 138
  P. floribunda 106, 138
  P. formosa 138
  P. japonica 138
piggy-back plant 19, 43
pineapple broom 50
pinks 46, 58, 107
Pinus mugo 86, **88**, 90–1, 104
  P. nigra 104
  P. nigra maritima 90, 104,
  110
  P. sylvestris 104
Pittosporum 44, 101
plantain lillies 35, 76
Pleioblastus 79
plumbago, hardy 54, 102
poached egg plant 94, 155
Polemonium caeruleum 130
  P. foliosissimum 130
Polygonatum 18, 35, 152
Polygonum see Persicaria
Polypodium vulgare 38, 154
Polystichum setiferum 39, 154
Pontaderia cordata 78
poppy:
  Californian 44, 63, 94, 154,
  156
  Himalayan blue **137**, 139
  plume 26
  yellow horned 118
Portulaca 63

pot marigold 93, 154
Potentilla 86, 87, **88**
  P. fruticosa 92, 106
primrose 18, 106
Primula 6, 8, 35, 152
  candelabra, 6, 65, 78
  P. allionii 152
  P. auricula 152
  P. beesiana 78
  P. bulleyana 78
  P. chungensis 78
  P. denticulata 78
  P. florindae 78
  P. helodoxa 78
  P. japonica 78
  P. marginata 152
  P. pulverulenta 78
  P. vulgaris 78, 106
privet 114
  golden 42
Prunus 124–5, 143, **144**
  P. laurocerasus 42, 127
  P. sargentii 124
  P. subhirtella 124–5
  P. × *yedoensis* 125
Pseudosasa japonica 91
  P. viridistriata 79
Pulmonaria 26, 37, 43, 152
  P. officinalis 37, 106
  P. saccharata 27, 37, **41**, 106
Pulsatilla vulgaris 152
Pyracantha 32, 92, 127, 146
Pyrus salicifolia 125–6

Quickthorn 90, 111

Ranunculus 106
raoulia 99
red hot poker 103, **116**
Rhamnus frangula 91
Rheum 66
  R. palmatum 78
Rhododendron 6, 12, 14, **85**,
  131, 134, 138, 140
  R. leucaspis 138
  R. ponticum 106
  R. yakushimanum 106, 138,
  140
Ribes 127
  R. sanguineum 26, 32, 42,
  149
Robinia pseudoacacia 86,
  103, 112, 143
rock roses 50, 54, 55, 102
Rodgersia 6, 65, 66, **69**, 78–
  9, 130
  R. aesculifolia 70, 78
  R. podophylla 78
  R. tabularis 70, 79
Romneya coulteri **141**, 150
Rosa glauca 111
  R. moyesii 111
  R. pimpinellifolia 111, 115

Rodgersia—contd
  R. p. harisonii 115
  R. rubiginosa 111, 115
  R. rugosa 111, 115, 150
rose campion 59
rose of Sharon 91–2, 126, 149
rosemary 6, 10, 46, 47, 55–6
roses 127, 147
  climbing 23
  salt-resistant 110–11
rowan *see* mountain ash
royal fern 81
Rubus 32
  R. calycinoides 32, 42
  R. tricolor 27, 32
Rudbeckia **128**, 152
rue 46
Russian sage 55

Sage 10, 46, **56**, 59–60, 101, 149
  Jerusalem 55, 149
  Russian 55
St John's wort 91–2, 126, 149
Salix 73, 92, 106, 127
  S. alba 73, 126
  S. × boydii 73
  S. eleagnos 71, 73, 92
  S. exigua 70, **72**, 73, 92
  S. hastata 73
  S. helvetica 73
  S. lanata 73
  S. melanostachys 73
  S. purpurea 73
  S. repens argentea 73
  S. rosmarinifolia 71, 73, 92
  S. viminalis 112
salt tree 114
Salvia 51, 52, 150
  S. guaranitica 51, 60
  S. horminum 155
  S. nemorosa 60, 152
  S. officinalis 59–60, 101
  S. patens 51, 60
  S. × superba 60
  S. × uliginosa 60
Sambucus 74
  S. niger 74, 150
  S. racemosa 12, 74, 150
Santolina 150
  S. chamaecyparissus 46, 56
  S. incana **56**
  S. neapolitana 56
  S. virens 26, 56
Saponaria ocymoides 60, 152
Sarcococca humilis 26, 32–3
saxifrage (*Saxifraga*) 152–3
scabious (*Scabiosa caucasica*) **61**, 153
scarlet flax 94, 154
Scotch rose 111, 115
Scots pine 104
sea buckthorn 110, 114

sea campion, double **117**
sea holly 58, 111, 116
sea lavender 111, 116
sea thrift 115
sea wormwood 118
seaweed 14–15
sedge 79
Sedum 47, 52, 99, 107
  S. acre 107
  S. spathulifolium 107
  S. spectabile **49**, 51, 60, 87
Sempervivum 47, 99, 107, 153
Senecio see Brachyglottis
sensitive fern 81
shuttlecock fern 38, 71, 81
Siberian bugloss 18, 106
Sidalcea 153–4
Silene maritima 117
Sinarundinaria 79
Skimmia 33, 127, 139
  S. japonica 33
Smilacina racemosa 37, 79, 139
smoke tree 105
snakeshead fritilleries 156
snowberry 33, 74, 106, 115, 128
snowdrops 26, 40, **41**, 81, 94, 107
snowy mespilus 72
soft shield fern 39, 154
Solanum crispum 102
Solidago 154
Solomon's seal 18, 35
Sorbus aria 104, 110, 126, 143
  S. aucuparia 71, 86, 91, 104, **108**, 126, 143
  S. × hostii 112
  S. hupehensis 143
Spanish broom 51, 56, 115
Spanish gorse 54
Spartium 56–7
  S. junceum 115, 150
spindle 31, 91
spiny bear's breeches 150
Spiraea 92, 106
  blue 53
  S. arguta 127
  S. × bumalda 92
  S. japonica 150
  S. nipponica 150
spring snowflake 81
spurge 26, 43, 47, 58
Stachys byzantina **56**, 62, 117, 154
  S. lanata **45**, 46, 62, 117, 154
  S. olympica 62, 117, 154
star jasmine 147
star of Bethlehem 27
star of the veldt 63, 154
Sternbergia lutea 156

stinking hellebore 43
stinking iris 43
Stipa gigantea 62, 93
stonecrops 47, 99
strawberry tree 91
summer snowflake 81
sunflower 130
swan river daisy 154
sweet briar 115
sweet flag 74
sweet pepper bush 72, 134, 135
sweet rocket 106, 151
sweet william 94
sycamore 90
Symphoricarpos 33, 74, 115, 128, 150
  S. albus 106
  S. × doorenbosii 74
Symphytum 37–8
Syringa 128

Tamarisk (*Tamarix*) 106, **112**
  T. gallica 115
Tanacetum coccineum 154
  T. parthenium 143
  T. vulgare 118
tansy 118
Taxus baccata 27, 104, 126, 146
Teucrium 44
  T. fruticans 57
thrift 107
Thuja occidentalis 104, 146
  T. orientalis 146
  T. plicata 91, 126
thyme (*Thymus*) 6, 46, **56**, 62, 118, 150
  T. praecox 118
  T. serpyllum 62
  T. vulgaris 62
Tiarella cordifolia 19, 38, 106
  T. wherryi 106
toadflax 118, 154
Tolmiea menziesii 19, 43
Trachelospermum jasminoides 147
Trillium 79, 139
  T. grandiflorum 38, 139
Trollius **64**, **77**, 154
  T. × cultorum 79
  T. europaeus 79
Tropaeolum 63, 154–5
  T. speciosum 139
trumpet lilies 155
trumpet vine 7
Tsuga canadensis 27
tufted hair grass 80
tulips 63, 107, 156
turf lily 27, 43
Turk's cap lilies **16**
Typha minor 79

Ulex 98, 115, 143
  U. europaeus 92

Vaccinium corymbosum 74
  V. vitis-idaea 33, 74
valerian, red 87, 93
Verbascum 62
  V. olympicum 62, 154
Veronica:
  shrubby 114
Viburnum 11, 33–4, 91, 128–9
  V. davidii 33
  V. farreri 67–8
  V. lantana 106, 115
  V. opulus 34, 42, 74, 89, 92, 106, 110, 128, 150
  V. plicatum **129**
  V. rhytidophyllum 34, 91, 98
  V. tinus 128, 150
Vinca major 154
  V. minor 34, 42, 129, 150, 154
vines 7, 126
Viola labradorica 38, 43, 80, 154
viper's bugloss 94, 118, 154
Virginia creeper 23, 30, 40, 104
Vitis coignetiae 126

Wake-robin 38, 139
Waldsteinia ternata 43
wall rock cress 150
wallflower 154
water avens 75
water forget-me-not 78
wayfaring tree 106, 115
Weigela 129, 150
  W. florida 129
white cedar 146
whitebeam 104, 112, 126
willows 67, 70, 72, 73, 106, 112, 126, 127
winter aconite 18, 39, 107
wintergreen 31, 137
Wisteria sinensis 147
wood anemone 18, 39, 43
woodrush 80

Yarrow 57, 87, 92, 106
yew 27, 104, 126, 146
  Irish 23, 146
Yucca 44, 57, **113**, 150
  Y. filamentosa 51, 57, 115
  Y. flaccida 115
  Y. gloriosa 57

Zantedeschia **80**
  Z. aethiopica 79, 103
Zauschneria californica 62
  Z. c. cana (microphylla) 62
Zenobia pulverulenta 139